HIGH HOLY DAY WORSHIP

WILSHIRE BOULEVARD TEMPLE

From *Book of Customs,* Klau Library, Cincinnati
Amsterdam 1723, "Blowing the Shofar"
From the Collection of the Hebrew Union College
Skirball Museum

CONTENTS

THIS
HIGH HOLY DAY
PRAYERBOOK

Prayer is our opportunity to stand in the presence of God, to struggle with the meaning of our lives, our disappointments and hopes. In prayer, we express our gratefulness for the wonder of existence; we weigh our deeds against God's will for justice and mercy, truth and love.

The High Holy Day season of Jewish tradition is devoted to *heshbon ha-nefesh,* to the art of "self-judgment." The wisdom of Judaism teaches that "No person lives without sinning" *(Ecclesiastes 7:20).* All make mistakes, encounter failures and must seek *teshuvah,* "repentance." High Holy Day prayer opens the gates to God's presence reminding that God requires and welcomes our repentance, and urges us to answer the question, "Where are you?"

The High Holy Day *Machzor,* or "prayerbook," has evolved over centuries. It embodies the distilled genius of the Jewish spirit, the artistry of poets and prophets, moralists and dreamers. In each generation, pious Jews have added their yearnings, doubts and agonies to its pages and have expanded the engagement of the Jewish people with God.

Early Reform Jews understood that it is the duty of each generation to adapt the values and visions of Jewish faith to its particular time and place. The long history of prayerbook reform is a testimony to the continuing evolution and creativity of the Jewish people.

This High Holy Day prayerbook continues the tradition of Reform Jewish creativity here at Wilshire Boulevard Temple. Like its companion, *Shabbat Worship,* the language, transliterations, art and commentary are meant to enrich and involve the worshiper in the sacred meanings of prayer. This volume also includes services for the Home, meditations for the Ten Days of Repentance between Rosh Hashanah and Yom Kippur, prayers for visiting the graves of loved ones, and an Album to be used for recording important personal and family events. It is hoped that this *Machzor* will not only become a treasured companion for prayer, but a precious heirloom passed on from generation to generation.

I am grateful for the support of our Temple's President, Lionel Bell and our Board of Trustees, and for the critical responses and suggestions of our Wilshire Boulevard Temple Worship Committee: Rochelle Ginsburg, Chair; Joseph Weisman, Vice-Chair; Brenda Levin-Abel, Nancy M. Berman, Marjorie Blatt, Harry Golden, Sandra Harris, Anthony Hatch, Mark Loeterman, Sandra Mosk, George Nagler, Burt Pressman, Linda Roberts, Mark Tarica, D.D.S., and Marco Weiss. Special thanks, as well, to Rabbis Shelton J. Donnell, Steven Zane Leder and Alfred Wolf, and to Steve Breuer, Charles Feldman, Esther Lewis, Nan McCullough, Barbara Kessler, Judith A. Stearns and Beverly Berman for all their assistance and wise comments.

The photography of ritual art objects from our Wilshire Boulevard Temple Belousoff collection was done by Robert Kositchek, Jr. We express appreciation to the Hebrew Union College Skirball Museum for illustrations from its collection.

We are grateful for the generosity of Ted Mann for making possible the publication of this High Holy Day Prayerbook, and to Henry Jaffe for his underwriting its significant phases of development.

Permission was granted by the Central Conference of American Rabbis for use of some versions of prayers from *The Union Prayer Book for Jewish Worship II, Newly Revised,* New York, 1945; from *Gates of Prayer, The New Union Prayerbook,* New York, 1975; and from *Gates of Repentance, The New Union Prayerbook for the Days of Awe,* New York, 1978.

Centuries ago, the Psalmist declared, "Sing a new song to God." *(98:1)* May this new *Machzor* carry our prayers to the gates of heaven. *Avinu malkeinu,* may we be inscribed in the Book of Life for blessings.

Rabbi Harvey J. Fields
13 Sivan, 5750—June 6, 1990

SELICHOT SERVICE

Havdalah Spice Box
Austrian
1860

Havdalah means "separation" or "distinction." The ritual of distinguishing between the Sabbath and the other days of the week is of Talmudic origin and is attributed to the leaders of the Great Assembly (*Berachot 33a*). The introductory verses are from *Isaiah 12:2-3; Psalms 3:9, 46:12, 84:13, 20:10; Esther 8:16;* and *Psalms 116:13.*

Just as the Sabbath and festivals are welcomed with the lighting of candles and the sharing of wine and bread, so are they concluded by drinking wine, smelling sweet spices and extinguishing a burning braided candle. Wine symbolizes pleasure, the spices are for the wisdom and renewal acquired through Sabbath study, and the woven candle reminds us that life is a tightly textured pattern of sacred moments bound with ordinary experiences. The *Havdalah* ceremony of Selichot distinguishes between the year that is past and our hopes for the future.

Reader

In these moments, as day gives way to night, we separate between the Sabbath and the week to come, and we prepare to separate between one year and the next.

This is a time for making separations and distinctions. Havdalah reminds us that life is a full cup. It overflows with opportunities we seize, with joys we share, with sorrows we endure, with successes that swell us with pride, and with disappointments which wound us with pain.

Grateful for all the distinctions, for life itself, for this past year and all the bounty of our years, we lift this cup, this spice box, this braided candle, and praise God with words of our tradition.

Cantor

הִנֵּה אֵל יְשׁוּעָתִי, אֶבְטַח וְלֹא אֶפְחָד.
כִּי עָזִּי וְזִמְרָת יָהּ יְיָ, וַיְהִי־לִי לִישׁוּעָה.

Behold, God is my Deliverer; in God I trust, I am not afraid. For the Lord is my strength and my stronghold, the Source of my deliverance.

וּשְׁאַבְתֶּם מַיִם בְּשָׂשׂוֹן מִמַּעַיְנֵי הַיְשׁוּעָה.
לַיְיָ הַיְשׁוּעָה, עַל־עַמְּךָ בִרְכָתֶךָ, סֶּלָה.

With joy shall we draw water from the wells of salvation. The Lord brings deliverance, a blessing to the people.

All sing

לַיְּהוּדִים הָיְתָה אוֹרָה וְשִׂמְחָה, וְשָׂשׂוֹן וִיקָר;

La-ye-hu-dim ha-ye-ta o-rah ve-si-me-chah, ve-sa-son vi-kar. (2)

Give us light and joy, gladness and honor, as in the happiest days of Israel's past.

Cantor

כֵּן תִּהְיֶה לָּנוּ.   כּוֹס יְשׁוּעוֹת אֶשָּׂא, וּבְשֵׁם יְיָ אֶקְרָא.

Then we will lift up the cup to rejoice in Your saving power and call out Your name in praise.

THE WINE

Wine gladdens the heart. May the New Year be a sweet one for us and for our loved ones. May it bring new joys and the promise of new blessings.

All sing

בָּרוּךְ אַתָּה, יְיָ אֱלֹהֵינוּ, מֶלֶךְ הָעוֹלָם, בּוֹרֵא פְּרִי הַגָּפֶן.

Ba-ruch a-ta, A-do-nai E-lo-hei-nu, me-lech ha-o-lam, bo-rei pe-ri ha-ga-fen.

Blessed is the Lord our God, Ruler of the universe, Creator of the fruit of the vine.

THE SPICES

Reader

The spices in this castle of silver celebrate the diverse wonders of human existence. We are crowned with awareness, the gift of amazement, the endowment of awe. We are born to build out of the gift of our years towers of hope and castles of caring for one another.

All sing

בָּרוּךְ אַתָּה, יְיָ אֱלֹהֵינוּ, מֶלֶךְ הָעוֹלָם, בּוֹרֵא מִינֵי בְשָׂמִים.

Ba-ruch a-ta, A-do-nai E-lo-hei-nu, me-lech ha-o-lam, bo-rei mi-nei ve-sa-mim.

Blessed is the Lord our God, Ruler of the universe, Creator of all the spices.

THE CANDLE

Reader

In the bright light of this twisted candle, we sense the warmth and power of faith: a faith that binds us together as a covenant community, a faith that teaches us to cherish wisdom against the darkness of ignorance, a faith that mandates us to weave out of our years deeds of justice, mercy and peace.

All sing

בָּרוּךְ אַתָּה, יְיָ אֱלֹהֵינוּ, מֶלֶךְ הָעוֹלָם, בּוֹרֵא מְאוֹרֵי הָאֵשׁ.

Ba-ruch a-ta, A-do-nai E-lo-hei-nu, me-lech ha-o-lam, bo-rei me-o-rei ha-eish.

Blessed is the Lord our God, Ruler of the universe, Creator of the light of fire.

SEPARATIONS

Reader

We extinguish the light now in the sweet overflow of wine. May God, who separates Sabbath from weekday and year from year, bless us with power to distinguish holy from profane, truth from falsehood, the pursuit of love from selfishness.

בָּרוּךְ אַתָּה, יְיָ אֱלֹהֵינוּ, מֶלֶךְ הָעוֹלָם, הַמַּבְדִּיל בֵּין קֹדֶשׁ לְחוֹל, בֵּין אוֹר לְחֹשֶׁךְ, בֵּין יוֹם הַשְּׁבִיעִי לְשֵׁשֶׁת יְמֵי הַמַּעֲשֶׂה.

Blessed is the Lord our God, Ruler of the universe, who separates sacred from profane, light from darkness, the seventh day of rest from the six days of labor.

בָּרוּךְ אַתָּה, יְיָ, הַמַּבְדִּיל בֵּין קֹדֶשׁ לְחוֹל.

Blessed is the Lord, who separates the sacred from the profane.

The song *Ei-li-ya-hu ha-na-vi,* "Elijah the prophet," may have originated as early as the eleventh century. The words of the song are based on the prophecy found in *Malachi 3:23-24.*

THE CANDLE IS EXTINGUISHED

All sing

Ha-mav-dil, bein ko-desh, bein ko-desh
le-chol, cha-to-tei-nu Hu yim-chol,
zar-ei-nu ve-chas-pei-nu yar-beh ka-chol,
ve-cha-ko-cha-vim ba-lai-la
Sha-vu-a tov...

הַמַּבְדִּיל בֵּין קֹדֶשׁ לְחוֹל,
חַטֹּאתֵינוּ הוּא יִמְחֹל,
זַרְעֵנוּ וְכַסְפֵּנוּ יַרְבֶּה כַּחוֹל,
וְכַכּוֹכָבִים בַּלָּיְלָה.
שָׁבוּעַ טוֹב . . .

May God, who separates between sacred and profane, remove all wrongdoing from us. May our descendants and riches be as numerous as the sands of the sea and stars of the heavens. May this be a good week.

THERE WILL COME A TIME

Reader

There will come a time when greed will be transformed into generosity. There will come a time when fear will give way to faith. There will come a time when war will be no more and peace will prevail. That is the time Elijah will bring. And we shall bring Elijah with our hopes, our mitzvah-deeds and our song.

All sing

Ei-li-ya-hu ha-na-vi,
Ei-li-ya-hu ha-tish-bi;
Ei-li-ya-hu, Ei-li-ya-hu,
Ei-li-ya-hu ha-gil-a-di.

Bi-me-hei-ra ve-ya-mei-nu,
ya-vo ei-lei-nu; im ma-shi-ach
ben Da-vid, im ma-shi-ach ben
David.
Ei-li-ya-hu...

אֵלִיָּהוּ הַנָּבִיא, אֵלִיָּהוּ
הַתִּשְׁבִּי; אֵלִיָּהוּ, אֵלִיָּהוּ,
אֵלִיָּהוּ הַגִּלְעָדִי.
בִּמְהֵרָה בְיָמֵינוּ, יָבֹא
אֵלֵינוּ; עִם מָשִׁיחַ בֶּן
דָּוִד, עִם מָשִׁיחַ בֶּן
דָּוִד. אֵלִיָּהוּ . . . .

Reader

These Selichot moments are meant to prepare us for the Days of Awe. *Selichot* means "forgiveness," "reconciliation," finding the pulse beat of truth in the flesh of our existence. Selichot brings us to self-judgment, to the sacred season of repentance.

Now is the time for turning. The leaves are beginning to turn from green to red and orange. Summer's harvests are finished. The old year is fading.

But for us, turning does not come easily. It takes an act of will for us to make a turn. It means breaking with old habits. It means admitting that we have been wrong, and this is never easy. It means losing face; it means starting all over again, and this is always painful. It means saying, "I am sorry." It means recognizing that we have the ability to change, that we are not trapped forever in yesterday's ways.

Congregation

Lord, help us to turn from callousness to sensitivity, from hostility to love, from pettiness to purpose, from envy to contentment, from carelessness to discipline, from fear to faith. Turn us and bring us back toward You. Hear our prayer.

"Now is the time…" is adapted from Rabbi Jack Riemer in *New Prayers for the High Holy Days, 1971.*

Responsively

שְׁמַע קוֹלֵנוּ, פְּתַח לָנוּ שְׁעָרֶיךָ!

Hear our prayer. Open the gates; listen to our plea for a world drenched with Your nurture of mercy.

Hear our prayer, though we regret so many of the words which fly like arrows from our lips and wound those we love.

Hear our prayer. Forgive us all the opportunities for joy we have wasted.

Hear our prayer. Pardon our indifference to the pain of others and our apathy instead of anger in the face of injustice.

Hear our prayer. Turn our lofty meditations into mandates for generosity and for healing the bruised and battered about us.

Hear our prayer. Do not allow us to speak pious words and then abandon them in the sanctuary.

Hear our prayer. Uplift us to the beauty of holiness. Remind us that holiness resides in what we do with the sacred energies of our lives.

Hear our prayer. As the flower bends toward the warmth of sun, pull us toward You. Charge us with Your radiance that we may sweeten all life with Your blessings.

God of the beginning, God of the end, God of all creatures, Lord of all generations, with love You guide the world; with love You walk hand in hand with all
the living.

You created us in Your image, capable of love and justice, that, in creation's long
unfolding, we might be Your partners. You endowed us with freedom. We must
not enslave others. You gave us judgment; we must not dictate the choices
of others.

You set before us many paths to tread, that we might search and find the way that
is true for us. We thank You for Your gift of choice. Without it, where would our
greatness lie? Where our triumphs and where our failures? Created in Your
image, we are called upon to choose.

Let our reflections help us to bring into our lives the harmony we seek and the
love we would share.

There are moments when we hear the call of our higher selves, the call that links
us to the divine. Then we know how blessed we are with life and love. May this
be such a moment, a time of deeper attachments to the godlike in us and in our
world, for which we give thanks and praise.

Responsively

סַרְנוּ מִמִּצְוֹתֶיךָ וּמִמִּשְׁפָּטֶיךָ הַטּוֹבִים וְלֹא שָׁוָה לָנוּ.
וְאַתָּה צַדִּיק עַל כָּל־הַבָּא עָלֵינוּ, כִּי אֱמֶת עָשִׂיתָ
וַאֲנַחְנוּ הִרְשָׁעְנוּ.

We have neglected Your commandments, and it has brought us no benefit. We have spurned Your summons for generosity and goodness, for justice and understanding, and have not profited.

What shall we say before You? What excuses shall we utter? For You know all the secrets of our hearts. Nothing is hidden from You.

So let us judge ourselves honestly. Help us to search our souls. Expose us to our failings. Lift the veil from our wrongdoing. Conceal no vanity or selfishness from our confession.

Pardon our transgressions, for our sins are an alphabet of woe.

On the edge of the New Year, grant us atonement for all the sins we have sinned against You.

"We have neglected Your commandments..." reflects the view that failure to live by the ritual and ethical obligations of Jewish tradition wastes human potentials and distances us from a life of "benefit," purpose and fulfillment, according to the counsel of Job's friends (*33:27*).

Responsively, Reader, then Congregation

עַל חֵטְא שֶׁחָטָאנוּ לְפָנֶיךָ בְּאֹנֶס וּבְרָצוֹן,

Al cheit she-cha-ta-nu...For **Acts** of wrongdoing committed under stress or by choice, forgive us.

עַל חֵטְא שֶׁחָטָאנוּ לְפָנֶיךָ בִּבְלִי דָעַת.

Al cheit she-cha-ta-nu...For **Blunders** committed unintentionally, forgive us.

עַל חֵטְא שֶׁחָטָאנוּ לְפָנֶיךָ בְּגִלּוּי עֲרָיוֹת,

Al cheit she-cha-ta-nu...For **Glibly** excusing immorality out of self-interest, forgive us.

עַל חֵטְא שֶׁחָטָאנוּ לְפָנֶיךָ בְּדַעַת וּבְמִרְמָה.

Al cheit she-cha-ta-nu...For **Deceiving** others and ourselves, forgive us.

עַל חֵטְא שֶׁחָטָאנוּ לְפָנֶיךָ בְּהַרְהוֹר הַלֵּב,

Al cheit she-cha-ta-nu...For **Harnessing** our hearts to selfish thoughts, forgive us.

עַל חֵטְא שֶׁחָטָאנוּ לְפָנֶיךָ בִּוְעִידַת זְנוּת.

Al cheit she-cha-ta-nu...For **Vainly** seeking out flattery and not the truth, forgive us.

עַל חַטְא שֶׁחָטָאנוּ לְפָנֶיךָ בְּזָדוֹן וּבִשְׁגָגָה:

Al cheit she-cha-ta-nu...For **Zealously** defending our stubbornness and errors, forgive us.

עַל חֵטְא שֶׁחָטָאנוּ לְפָנֶיךָ בְּחִלּוּל הַשֵׁם.

Al cheit she-cha-ta-nu…For **Choosing** to profane God's name by dealing unfairly with others, forgive us.

עַל חֵטְא שֶׁחָטָאנוּ לְפָנֶיךָ בְּטֻמְאַת שְׂפָתָיִם,

Al cheit she-cha-ta-nu…For **Trading** hurtful rumors and gossip, forgive us.

עַל חֵטְא שֶׁחָטָאנוּ לְפָנֶיךָ בְּיוֹדְעִים וּבְלֹא יוֹדְעִים.

Al cheit she-cha-ta-nu…For **Yielding** to wrongdoing wittingly and unwittingly, forgive us.

All sing

Ve-al ku-lam, E-lo-ah se-li-chot,
se-lach la-nu, me-chal la-nu,
ka-per la-nu!

וְעַל כֻּלָּם, אֱלוֹהַּ
סְלִיחוֹת, סְלַח לָנוּ,
מְחַל לָנוּ, כַּפֶּר-לָנוּ!

For all these sins, O God of mercy, forgive us, pardon us, grant us atonement!

Al Cheit, "For the sin…," forms the central prayer of the Yom Kippur confession. It was originally composed as an alphabetical acrostic with six verses by Saadia Gaon (892-942 C.E., Babylonia). Later it was doubled in length by Amram Gaon (b. 875 C.E., Babylonia), author of the first prayer book in Jewish tradition. Moses Maimonides (1135-1204) enlarged it to twenty-two verses, one for each letter of the alphabet, and it was later doubled in length.

Reader

Lord, we are not so arrogant as to pretend that the trial of our lives does not reveal our flaws. We know ourselves, in this moment of prayer, to have failed the ones we love and the stranger, again and again. We know how often we did not bring to the surface of our lives the hidden goodness within. Where we have achieved, O Lord, we are grateful; where we have failed, we ask forgiveness. Remember how exposed we are to the chances and terrors of life. Often we are afraid. We sometimes choose to fail. So we pray: Turn our thoughts from the hurt to its remedy. Free us of the torments of guilt.

Congregation

Forgiven, O Lord, we shall then forgive others; failing, we shall learn to understand failure; renewed and encouraged, we shall strive to be like those who came before us; human. Sinners sometimes, yet a blessing.

MUSICAL INTERLUDE
AND MEDITATION

"Lord, we are not..." was written by Rabbi Norman Hirsch.

Reader

On this Selichot evening, let us remember the earth's oppressed. For unless we speak out for justice, we condone with our silence the torture of the weak, the suffering of the innocent, and indifference to those imprisoned without cause.

Congregation

Let us never forget those who suffer in fear and loneliness, for we were strangers in the land of Egypt.

Reader

Let us never forget those whose rights are trampled or those imprisoned without just cause or those brutalized behind closed doors, for we know the anguish of their hearts. We were transported, alone and forsaken, to Auschwitz, Treblinka and Bergen-Belsen.

Congregation

Let us remember, O God, the wisdom by which You would have us live. "Be faithful, be true, pursue justice, love one another as you love yourselves."

Reader

But the world is dark. It is cold with fear and rage.

Congregation

The hammer of chaos beats loudly within us: How can we endure?

Reader

מִמַּעֲמַקִּים קְרָאתִיךָ, יְיָ. אֲדֹנָי, שִׁמְעָה בְקוֹלִי.

Out of the depths do we call to You, O Lord. Lord, hearken to us.

Congregation

For the sin of silence,
For the sin of indifference,
For the secret complicity of the neutral,
For the closing of borders,
For the washing of hands,
For the crime of indifference,
For the sin of silence,
For the closing of borders,
For all that was done,
For all that was not done,
Let there be no forgetfulness before the Throne of Glory;

Let there be remembrance within the human heart;
And let there at last be forgiveness
When Your children, O God,
Are free and at peace.

Reader

Our God and God of our ancestors, may You rule in glory over all the earth, and let Your grandeur be acclaimed throughout the world. Reveal the splendor of Your majesty to all who dwell on earth, that all your works may know You as their Maker, and all the living acknowledge You as their Creator. Then all who breathe shall say: "The Lord God of Israel's dominion extends to all creation."

"For the sin of silence..." is adapted from *Gates of Prayer,* the *New Reform Prayer Book, p. 408.*

Cantor

שְׁמַע קוֹלֵנוּ, יְיָ אֱלֹהֵינוּ, חוּס וְרַחֵם עָלֵינוּ, וְקַבֵּל
בְּרַחֲמִים וּבְרָצוֹן אֶת־תְּפִלָּתֵנוּ. הֲשִׁיבֵנוּ יְיָ אֵלֶיךָ
וְנָשׁוּבָה, חַדֵּשׁ יָמֵינוּ כְּקֶדֶם.

Hear our voice, O Lord our God; have compassion upon us, and with that compassion accept our prayer. Help us to return to You, O Lord; then truly shall we return. Renew our days as in the past.

WHITE SYMBOLIZES...

Congregation rises as ark is opened

Reader

On this Selichot evening as we prepare ourselves for the Days of Awe to come, we also prepare this sacred place of worship.

We dress these holy scrolls of Torah in the white celebration covers of our tradition. White symbolizes the cleansing of our spirits at this High Holy Day season. White is for the purity of our aspirations. White is for the wisdom Torah embodies. White is for the heat of our renewed commitments as we prepare for the New Year.

Congregation

אָבִינוּ מַלְכֵּנוּ, שְׁמַע קוֹלֵנוּ.

Avinu Malkeinu, she-ma ko-lei-nu.
Avinu Malkeinu, hear our prayer.

אָבִינוּ מַלְכֵּנוּ, חָטָאנוּ לְפָנֶיךָ.

Avinu Malkeinu, cha-ta-nu le-fa-ne-cha.
Avinu Malkeinu, we have sinned against You.

אָבִינוּ מַלְכֵּנוּ, חֲמוֹל עָלֵינוּ וְעַל עוֹלָלֵינוּ וְטַפֵּנוּ.

Avinu Malkeinu, cha-mol a-lei-nu ve-al o-la-leinu ve-ta-pei-nu.
Avinu Malkeinu, have mercy upon us and upon our children.

אָבִינוּ מַלְכֵּנוּ, כַּלֵּה דֶבֶר וְחֶרֶב וְרָעָב מֵעָלֵינוּ.

Avinu Malkeinu, ka-lei de-ver, ve-che-rev, ve-ra-av mei-a-leinu.
Avinu Malkeinu, rid us of pestilence, war and famine.

אָבִינוּ מַלְכֵּנוּ, כַּלֵּה כָל־צַר וּמַשְׂטִין מֵעָלֵינוּ.

Avinu Malkeinu, ka-lei kol tsar u-mas-tin mei-a-lei-nu.
Avinu Malkeinu, rid us of all hatred and oppression.

אָבִינוּ מַלְכֵּנוּ, כָּתְבֵנוּ בְּסֵפֶר חַיִּים טוֹבִים.

Avinu Malkeinu, kot-vei-nu be-sei-fer cha-yim to-vim.
Avinu Malkeinu, inscribe us for blessing in the Book of Life.

Avinu Malkeinu..., "Our Father, our King...," is attributed to Rabbi Akiba (2nd century C.E.), whose first version contained twenty-two verses, one for each letter of the Hebrew alphabet. In the 14th century, the prayer was expanded to forty-four verses. Traditionally, the prayer is recited throughout the High Holy Day period from Rosh Hashanah to Yom Kippur *(Taanit 25b)*.

אָבִינוּ מַלְכֵּנוּ, מַלֵּא יָדֵינוּ מִבִּרְכוֹתֶיךָ.

Avinu Malkeinu, ma-lei ya-dei-nu mi-bir-cho-te-cha.
Avinu Malkeinu, fill our hands with Your blessings.

אָבִינוּ מַלְכֵּנוּ, כָּתְבֵנוּ בְּסֵפֶר סְלִיחָה וּמְחִילָה.

Avinu Malkeinu, kot-vei-nu be-sei-fer se-li-cha u-me-chi-lah.
Avinu Malkeinu, inscribe us for blessing in the Book of Forgiveness.

אָבִינוּ מַלְכֵּנוּ, חָנֵּנוּ וַעֲנֵנוּ, כִּי אֵין בָּנוּ מַעֲשִׂים,
עֲשֵׂה עִמָּנוּ צְדָקָה וָחֶסֶד וְהוֹשִׁיעֵנוּ.

Avinu Malkeinu, cho-nei-nu va-a-nei-nu, ki ein ba-nu ma-a-sim,
a-sei i-ma-nu tse-da-kah va-che-sed, ve-ho-shi-ei-nu.
Avinu Malkeinu, be gracious and answer us. Treat us generously and
with kindness, and help us.

All sing

Avinu Malkeinu,
cho-nei-nu va-a-nei-nu (2)
ki ein ba-nu ma-a-sim.

A-sei i-ma-nu tse-da-kah va-che-sed (2)
ve-ho-shi-ei-nu.

Avinu Malkeinu,
cho-nei-nu va-a-nei-nu (2)
ki ein ba-nu ma-a-sim.

אָבִינוּ מַלְכֵּנוּ, חָנֵּנוּ וַעֲנֵנוּ,
כִּי אֵין בָּנוּ מַעֲשִׂים, עֲשֵׂה
עִמָּנוּ צְדָקָה וָחֶסֶד וְהוֹשִׁיעֵנוּ.

Shofar
From Wilshire Boulevard Temple
Collection

The *shofar,* "ram's horn," may not be artificially constructed or decorated. It must be used in its natural form and given sound only by the human breath. It is meant to stir all who hear it with the message that God does not want charming or clever artifice, but human deeds of caring, justice, generosity and love.

Reader

This is Your glory: You are slow to anger, ready to forgive. Lord, it is not the death of sinners You seek, but that they should turn from their ways and live.

Until the last day You wait for them, welcome them as soon as they turn to You.

So let us hear the ancient summons to the New Year, to its prayer and opportunities for renewal.

SHOFAR SOUNDS

Tekiah Shevarim-Teruah	תקיעה שברים־תרועה
Tekiah	תקיעה
Tekiah Shevarim Tekiah	תקיעה שברים תקיעה
Tekiah Teruah Tekiah	תקיעה תרועה תקיעה

BENEDICTION

Reader

And now, as we prepare for a New Year, we pray for
The spirit of wisdom and understanding.
The spirit of insight and courage.
The spirit of knowledge and reverence.
The spirit of justice and peace.

ROSH HASHANAH EVENING
HOME SERVICE

(Set table festively with flowers, candles for lighting, wine for Kiddush, a special holiday challah, sliced apples and a dish of honey. Members of family may wish to prepare special readings. These may take the place of any of those suggested below.)

LIGHTING OF HOLIDAY
(AND SHABBAT) CANDLES

(Light Candles)

Reader

With these lights
We welcome **(Shabbat and)** Rosh Hashanah.
In their glow of contrasting colors
We discern
The light and dark of our days;
We recall
All the disappointments and joys
We have shared,
All the hopes and intentions
We now nurture
For the New Year.

בָּרוּךְ אַתָּה, יְיָ אֱלֹהֵינוּ, מֶלֶךְ הָעוֹלָם, אֲשֶׁר קִדְּשָׁנוּ
בְּמִצְוֹתָיו וְצִוָּנוּ לְהַדְלִיק נֵר שֶׁל (שַׁבָּת וְשֶׁל) יוֹם טוֹב.

Ba-ruch a-ta, A-do-nai E-lo-hei-nu, me-lech ha-o-lam, a-sher
ki-de-sha-nu be-mits-vo-tav ve-tsi-va-nu le-had-lik neir
shel **(Shabbat ve-shel)** Yom Tov.

Be praised, O Lord our God, Ruler of the Universe, who has enabled us to attain holiness through the religious duty of kindling the **(Shabbat and)** festival lights.

Of Rosh Hashanah the Torah tells us:

The Lord spoke to Moses, saying: Speak to the Israelite people and tell them:

In the seventh month, on the first day of the month, you shall observe a complete rest, a sacred occasion commemorated with loud blasts. You shall not work at your occupations, and you shall bring an offering by fire to the Lord.

"A complete rest" means: Not even a thought or a word about your daily work.

"A sacred occasion" means: Celebrate with extraordinary sharing and love.

"Commemorated with loud blasts" means: Be silent so that the Shofar sounds startle you.

"You shall not work at your occupations" means: You shall work at self-scrutiny and honesty.

"You shall bring an offering by fire to the Lord" means: Only hearts and minds illuminated by repentance, prayer and generosity are acceptable.

"Of Rosh Hashanah..." is from *Leviticus 23:33-36.*

(Leader, holding cup of wine, says following prayer, then all join together in singing Kiddush.)

We praise You, O God, and give thanks for the year that is gone; for life, health and strength; for home, love and friendship; and for the happiness of our successes. May the sweetness of this wine symbolize our joy and hopes as we enter the New Year.

(If Rosh Hashanah occurs on Shabbat, continue with following prayer.)

Va-ye-hi e-rev, va-ye-hi vo-ker,
yom ha-shi-shi. Va-ye-chu-lu
   ha-sha-ma-yim ve-ha-a-rets
ve-chol tse-va-am, va-ye-chal E-lo-him
   ba-yom
ha-she-vi-i me-lach-to a-sher a-sa;
va-yish-bot ba-yom ha-she-vi-i mi-kol
me-lach-to a-sher a-sa. Va-ye-va-rech
E-lo-him et yom ha-she-vi-i
   va-ye-ka-deish
o-to, ki vo sha-vat mi-kol me-lach-to
a-sher ba-ra E-lo-him la-a-sot.

וַיְהִי עֶרֶב, וַיְהִי בֹקֶר,
יוֹם הַשִּׁשִּׁי. וַיְכֻלּוּ הַשָּׁמַיִם וְהָאָרֶץ
וְכָל צְבָאָם, וַיְכַל אֱלֹהִים בַּיּוֹם
הַשְּׁבִיעִי מְלַאכְתּוֹ אֲשֶׁר עָשָׂה;
וַיִּשְׁבֹּת בַּיּוֹם הַשְּׁבִיעִי מִכָּל
מְלַאכְתּוֹ אֲשֶׁר עָשָׂה. וַיְבָרֶךְ
אֱלֹהִים אֶת־יוֹם הַשְּׁבִיעִי וַיְקַדֵּשׁ
אֹתוֹ, כִּי בוֹ שָׁבַת מִכָּל־מְלַאכְתּוֹ
אֲשֶׁר בָּרָא אֱלֹהִים לַעֲשׂוֹת.

(If Rosh Hashanah occurs on weekday, continue here.)

Ba-ruch a-ta, A-do-nai E-lo-hei-nu,
me-lech ha-o-lam,
bo-rei pe-ri ha-ga-fen.

בָּרוּךְ אַתָּה, יְיָ אֱלֹהֵינוּ,
מֶלֶךְ הָעוֹלָם,
בּוֹרֵא פְּרִי הַגָּפֶן.

Ba-ruch a-ta, A-do-nai E-lo-hei-nu,
me-lech ha-o-lam, a-sher
ba-char ba-nu mi-kol am,
ve-ro-me-ma-nu mi-kol la-shon,
ve-ki-de-sha-nu be-mits-vo-tav.

בָּרוּךְ אַתָּה, יְיָ אֱלֹהֵינוּ,
מֶלֶךְ הָעוֹלָם, אֲשֶׁר
בָּחַר בָּנוּ מִכָּל־עָם,
וְרוֹמְמָנוּ מִכָּל־לָשׁוֹן,
וְקִדְּשָׁנוּ בְּמִצְוֹתָיו.

Va-ti-ten la-nu, A-do-nai E-lo-hei-nu,
be-a-ha-va et yom
(ha-sha-bat ha-zeh, ve-et yom)
ha-zi-ka-ron ha-zeh, yom te-ru-a,
mik-ra ko-desh, zei-cher li-tsi-at
Mits-ra-yim

Ki va-nu va-char-ta ve-o-ta-nu ki-dash-ta
mi-kol ha-a-mim, u-de-va-re-cha e-met
ve-ka-yam la-ad.

Ba-ruch a-ta, A-do-nai me-lech al
kol ha-a-rets, me-ka-deish
(ha-sha-bat ve-) Yis-ra-eil ve-yom
    ha-zi-ka-ron

Ba-ruch a-ta, A-do-nai
E-lo-hei-nu, me-lech ha-o-lam,
she-he-che-ya-nu ve-ki-ye-ma-nu
ve-hi-gi-a-nu la-ze-man ha-zeh.

וַתִּתֶּן־לָנוּ, יְיָ אֱלֹהֵינוּ,
בְּאַהֲבָה אֶת־יוֹם
(הַשַּׁבָּת הַזֶּה, וְאֶת־יוֹם)
הַזִּכָּרוֹן הַזֶּה, יוֹם תְּרוּעָה,
מִקְרָא קֹדֶשׁ, זֵכֶר לִיצִיאַת
מִצְרָיִם.

כִּי־בָנוּ בָחַרְתָּ וְאוֹתָנוּ קִדַּשְׁתָּ
מִכָּל־הָעַמִּים, וּדְבָרְךָ אֱמֶת
וְקַיָּם לָעַד.

בָּרוּךְ אַתָּה, יְיָ, מֶלֶךְ עַל
כָּל־הָאָרֶץ, מְקַדֵּשׁ
(הַשַּׁבָּת וְ)יִשְׂרָאֵל וְיוֹם הַזִּכָּרוֹן.

בָּרוּךְ אַתָּה, יְיָ
אֱלֹהֵינוּ, מֶלֶךְ הָעוֹלָם,
שֶׁהֶחֱיָנוּ וְקִיְּמָנוּ
וְהִגִּיעָנוּ לַזְּמַן הַזֶּה.

KIDDUSH TRANSLATION

*(Recited on **Sabbath** only)*
(The heaven and earth were finished, and all their array. And on the seventh day God finished the work of creation and rested. And God blessed the seventh day and declared it holy because on it God ceased from all the work of creation.)

Be praised, O Lord our God, Ruler of the universe, who creates the fruit of the vine. Be praised, O Lord our God, Ruler of the Universe, who has chosen us from among all peoples, exalted and sanctified us with mitzvot, and given us, in love, **(this Sabbath and)** this day of memorial, a day for blowing the horn, holy moments recalling our Exodus from Egypt. For You have chosen and distinguished us from all peoples, and Your word of truth stands forever. Be praised, Ruler of the world, who sanctifies **(the Sabbath and)** Israel and this memorial day. Be praised, O God, who has kept us in life, sustained us, and enabled us to reach this joyful festival.

Challah Cover
Germany 19th c.
John R. Forsman, Photographer
From the Collection of the Hebrew Union College
Skirball Museum

Tradition suggests a round challah, reminding us of the cycle of life, and the dipping of apples in honey as an expression of the hope that as the wheel of our lives turns, it will be blessed with sweet fulfillments.

Everyone

בָּרוּךְ אַתָּה, יְיָ אֱלֹהֵינוּ, מֶלֶךְ הָעוֹלָם, הַמּוֹצִיא לֶחֶם מִן הָאָרֶץ.

Ba-ruch a-ta, A-do-nai E-lo-hei-nu, me-lech ha-o-lam, ha-mo-tzi le-chem min ha-a-retz.

Be praised, O Lord our God, Ruler of the Universe, through whose wondrous power food is provided for our sustenance.

(Dip apples in honey and say)

בָּרוּךְ אַתָּה, יְיָ אֱלֹהֵינוּ, מֶלֶךְ הָעוֹלָם, בּוֹרֵא פְּרִי הָעֵץ.

Ba-ruch a-ta, A-do-nai E-lo-hei-nu, me-lech ha-o-lam, bo-rei pe-ri ha-eitz.

Be praised, O Lord our God, Ruler of the Universe, Creator of the fruit of the tree.

יְהִי רָצוֹן מִלְפָנֶיךָ, יְיָ אֱלֹהֵינוּ וֵאלֹהֵי אֲבוֹתֵינוּ, שֶׁתְּחַדֵּשׁ עָלֵינוּ שָׁנָה טוֹבָה וּמְתוּקָה.

Ye-hi ra-tzon mil-fa-ne-cha, A-do-nai Elo-hei-nu vei-lo-hei a-vo-tei-nu, she-te-cha-desh a-lei-nu Sha-nah Tovah u-me-tu-kah.

Lord our God and God of our people, may the New Year be sweet and good for all of us.

ROSH HASHANAH
EVENING SERVICE

Sabbath Lamp
Germany Frankfurt late 17th c. silver
John R. Forsman, Photographer
From the Collection of the Hebrew Union College
Skirball Museum

The *Yamim No-ra-im,* "Days of Awe," are an invitation to *heshbon ha-nefesh,* "taking stock of one's soul." "We confess our failure to span the gap between conscience and conduct, between the standards we profess and the actions we perform. We remember what we should have done and did not do. This chasm between *believing* and *living* may or may not always be surmountable, but the refusal to try to span it is *sin* and the will to bridge it, at least to narrow it, is *atonement* and *redemption.*" During these High Holy Days Jewish tradition emphasizes *teshuvah,* "repentance," as the way in which we turn from the wrong path to the right one, from sin to *at-one-ment* with humanity and with God. (Adapted from Israel Knox in *The Rosh Hashanah Anthology* by Philip Goodman, pp. 153-156.)

A Silent Prayer

In the twilight of the vanishing year, I lift my heart to You, O God.

I give thanks for all the blessings which fill my life with joy, for the love of family and support of friends, for the comfort others have given me in difficult moments, and for the privilege of life that You have granted me.

Now the time of repentance and renewal has come. These Days of Awe provide me with moments to meditate on the meaning of my life, on the worth of my deeds, and upon the regrets that mock my noblest intentions. No human being lives without failures. No year passes without its disappointments, its sorrows, its sins.

On this eve of the New Year, awaken me to the wisdom of my faith and people. Let these sacred days remind me that life is Your precious gift and that You have called me to Your service. You have made me in Your image, a fragile soul empowered with goodness and truth, justice and love.

So turn me to You now. Open the gates of the New Year, and grant to me, to my loved ones, my people, and all peoples, life and health, contentment and peace.

Mizrach 39.17 Phillip Cohn U.S., 1861
(An art piece hung on Eastern wall facing Jerusalem)
Marvin Rand, Photographer
From the Collection of the Hebrew Union College
Skirball Museum

"In the seventh month…" from *Leviticus 23:23-24* is the commandment to observe Rosh Hashanah. We follow the ancient tradition of announcing each new month, greeting it with a procession of celebration and words of the *Hallel* prayer as sung in the ancient Jerusalem Temple. "Open the gates…" is from *Psalms 118:19-24*.

OPEN UNTO US THE GATES

Reader

בַּחֹֽדֶשׁ הַשְּׁבִיעִי, בְּאֶחָד לַחֹֽדֶשׁ, יִהְיֶה
לָכֶם שַׁבָּתוֹן, זִכְרוֹן תְּרוּעָה, מִקְרָא־קֹֽדֶשׁ.
כָּל־מְלֶאכֶת עֲבוֹדָה לֹא תַעֲשׂוּ.

In the seventh month, on the first day of the month, there shall be a sacred assembly, a day of no work, a day commemorated with the sound of the horn.

All rise as Torah scrolls are carried into the sanctuary. Those who have difficulty standing may remain seated during this part of the service.

Choir

פִּתְחוּ־לִי שַׁעֲרֵי־צֶֽדֶק; אָבֹא־בָם, אוֹדֶה יָהּ.
זֶה־הַשַּֽׁעַר לַיָי, צַדִּיקִים יָבֹֽאוּ בוֹ.
אוֹדְךָ כִּי עֲנִיתָֽנִי, וַתְּהִי־לִי לִישׁוּעָה.
אֶֽבֶן מָאֲסוּ הַבּוֹנִים, הָיְתָה לְרֹאשׁ פִּנָּה.
מֵאֵת יְיָ הָֽיְתָה זֹּאת; הִיא נִפְלָאת בְּעֵינֵֽינוּ.
זֶה־הַיּוֹם עָשָׂה יְיָ, נָגִֽילָה וְנִשְׂמְחָה בוֹ.

Open the gates of righteousness that I may enter them and praise the Lord. This is the gateway to God; the righteous shall enter it. I praise You, for You have answered me and have become my help. The stone which the builders rejected has become the chief cornerstone. This is God's doing; it is marvelous in our sight. This is the day that the Lord has made; let us exalt and rejoice in it.

All rise as ark is opened

Reader

אֲדֹנָי, מָעוֹן אַתָּה הָיִיתָ לָּנוּ בְּדֹר וָדֹר. בְּטֶרֶם הָרִים
יֻלָּדוּ, וַתְּחוֹלֵל אֶרֶץ וְתֵבֵל, וּמֵעוֹלָם עַד־עוֹלָם אַתָּה
אֵל.

On this evening of the New Year we come before You, O God, our dwelling place in all generations. Reverently, we bear these Torah scrolls. Within their flaming letters is the proud legacy of our people, Your sacred covenant with us. You have summoned us to this place. We gather all the fragments of our lives and bring them before You. Mend our shattered hopes. Repair our disappointments. Strengthen us for honest self-scrutiny, that out of our prayers we may grow in wisdom and be worthy of our faith.

Congregation

Let the New Year begin and end with Your abundant blessings.

A-do-nai ma-on…is from *Psalms 90:1* and is translated: "O Lord, You have been our dwelling place in all generations. Before the mountains came into being, before You brought forth the earth and the world, from eternity to eternity You are God."

Reader

יְהִי רָצוֹן מִלְּפָנֶיךָ, יְיָ אֱלֹהֵינוּ וֵאלֹהֵי אֲבוֹתֵינוּ,
שֶׁתְּחַדֵּשׁ עָלֵינוּ וְעַל־כָּל־בֵּית יִשְׂרָאֵל אֶת־הַשָּׁנָה
הַזֹּאת, שְׁנַת חֲמֵשֶׁת אֲלָפִים וּשְׁבַע מֵאוֹת וְ.... ,,
לְחַיִּים וּלְשָׁלוֹם, לְשָׂשׂוֹן וּלְשִׂמְחָה, לִישׁוּעָה
וּלְנֶחָמָה, וְנֹאמַר: אָמֵן.

May it be Your will, O Lord our God, and God of our people, that the New Year Five Thousand Seven Hundred and .... bring to us and to the people of Israel life and peace, joy and contentment, redemption and comfort.

Congregation

Amen.

Torah scrolls are returned to the ark

Choir

תִּקְעוּ בַחֹדֶשׁ שׁוֹפָר, בַּכֶּסֶה לְיוֹם חַגֵּנוּ.
כִּי חֹק לְיִשְׂרָאֵל הוּא, מִשְׁפָּט לֵאלֹהֵי יַעֲקֹב.

Sound the Shofar at the new moon, at the turning of the year, at the time of our celebration. For this is a statute binding on Israel, a law of the God of Jacob.

"May it be Your will..." is taken from the blessing of the New Month first mentioned in the Talmud *(Berachot 16b)*. The order of the Hebrew lunar calendar is Nisan, Iyar, Sivan, Tamuz, Av, Elul, Tishre, Cheshvan, Kislev, Tevet, Shevat and Adar. Rosh Hashanah is celebrated on the first day of Tishre, precisely in the middle of the year. That may explain why the Zodiac sign for Tishre is balances and why the theme of Rosh Hashanah is judgment and self-scrutiny. "Sound the Shofar..." is from *Psalms 81:4-5.*

Havdalah Spice Box
Eastern Europe
Late 19th c.

The *Shema and its Blessings* make up the second section of the service. Following the themes of *Genesis* and *Exodus,* these prayers praise God as "Creator," "Lover of Israel," "Giver of Torah," and Source of Israel's "liberation from Egypt." The formula of the *Barechu* comes from *Nehemiah 9:5.* The *Ma-ariv Aravim* or "Evening" prayer corresponds to the *Yotzer Or* prayer of the morning, and both were written during the Talmudic period.

THE SHEMA AND ITS BLESSINGS
BARECHU—BE PRAISED...

All sing

Ba-re-chu et A-do-nai ha-me-vo-rach.

בָּרְכוּ אֶת־יְיָ הַמְבֹרָךְ!

Ba-ruch A-do-nai ha-me-vo-rach
le-o-lam va-ed.

בָּרוּךְ יְיָ הַמְבֹרָךְ לְעוֹלָם וָעֶד!

Be praised, O God, to whom our praise is due.
Praised be the Lord, to whom our praise is due, now and forever.

MA-ARIV ARAVIM—CREATOR OF EVENING

Reader

בָּרוּךְ אַתָּה, יְיָ אֱלֹהֵינוּ, מֶלֶךְ הָעוֹלָם, אֲשֶׁר בִּדְבָרוֹ
מַעֲרִיב עֲרָבִים. בְּחָכְמָה פּוֹתֵחַ שְׁעָרִים, וּבִתְבוּנָה
מְשַׁנֶּה עִתִּים, וּמַחֲלִיף אֶת־הַזְּמַנִּים, וּמְסַדֵּר אֶת־
הַכּוֹכָבִים בְּמִשְׁמְרוֹתֵיהֶם בָּרָקִיעַ כִּרְצוֹנוֹ. בּוֹרֵא יוֹם
וָלָיְלָה, גּוֹלֵל אוֹר מִפְּנֵי חֹשֶׁךְ וְחֹשֶׁךְ מִפְּנֵי אוֹר,
וּמַעֲבִיר יוֹם וּמֵבִיא לָיְלָה, וּמַבְדִּיל בֵּין יוֹם וּבֵין
לָיְלָה, יְיָ צְבָאוֹת שְׁמוֹ. אֵל חַי וְקַיָּם, תָּמִיד יִמְלֹךְ
עָלֵינוּ, לְעוֹלָם וָעֶד. בָּרוּךְ אַתָּה, יְיָ, הַמַּעֲרִיב עֲרָבִים.

Congregation

Be praised, O God, by whose will the shadows of evening fall and the gates of
morning are opened. Creator of heaven and earth, we praise You for the day and
its work and for the night and its rest.

Havdalah Spice Box
Near East
19th c.

It was the prophet Jeremiah who fashioned the phrase "eternal love" in connection with God's relationship to the people of Israel. He wrote: "God was revealed to me of old. Eternal love I conceived for you then..." *(Jeremiah 31:3).* Like the *Ahavah Rabbah* of the morning worship, the *Ahavat Olam* prayer was written by the rabbis during the time of the Jerusalem Temple. It expresses God's love for Israel and Israel's devotion to God through carrying out *mitzvot,* the ethical and ritual commandments of Jewish tradition.

Reader

אַהֲבַת עוֹלָם בֵּית יִשְׂרָאֵל עַמְּךָ אָהַבְתָּ: תּוֹרָה
וּמִצְוֹת, חֻקִּים וּמִשְׁפָּטִים אוֹתָנוּ לִמַּדְתָּ.

With eternal love You have sustained our people.

Congregation

Your commandments give meaning to our lives and length to our days. Let Your
love never depart from our hearts.

Reader

בָּרוּךְ אַתָּה, יְיָ, אוֹהֵב עַמּוֹ יִשְׂרָאֵל.

Be praised, O God, Source of love, the One and Eternal of time and space.

All sing

She-ma Yis-ra-eil: A-do-nai   שְׁמַע יִשְׂרָאֵל: יְיָ אֱלֹהֵינוּ, יְיָ אֶחָד!
E-lo-hei-nu, A-do-nai E-chad.

Ba-ruch sheim ke-vod   בָּרוּךְ שֵׁם כְּבוֹד מַלְכוּתוֹ לְעוֹלָם וָעֶד!
mal-chu-to le-o-lam va-ed.

Hear, O Israel: the Lord is our God, the Lord is One: Blessed is God's glorious
Power forever and ever.

Ark is closed; all are seated

Mezuzah Case
37.36 Moshe Zabari U.S. 1974
Marvin Rand, Photographer
From the Collection of the Hebrew Union College
Skirball Museum

The words "You shall love..." are from *Deuteronomy 6:4-9*. Together with *Deuteronomy 11:13-21* and *Numbers 15:37-41,* they form the traditional sections of the Shema as found in the *mezuzah* placed on the doorpost, and in the *tefilin,* or "phylacteries" worn on the hand and between the eyes during morning worship.

The words of the *Mi cha-mo-cha* (p. 50) are from the poem of liberation found in *Exodus 15:11.* The poem recalls the joy of the people after they had crossed the Red Sea to freedom. Liberation from oppression is a central theme of Jewish tradition.

VE-A-HAV-TA—YOU SHALL LOVE

Ve-a-hav-ta eit A-do-nai E-lo-he-cha,
be-chol le-va-ve-cha, u-ve-chol
naf-she-cha, u-ve-chol me-o-de-cha.
Ve-ha-yu ha-de-va-rim ha-ei-leh, a-sher
a-no-chi me-tsa-ve-cha ha-yom, al
le-va-ve-cha. Ve-shi-nan-tam le-va-ne-cha,
ve-di-bar-ta bam be-shiv-te-cha
be-vei-te-cha u-ve-lech-te-cha va-de-rech
u-ve-shoch-be-cha u-ve-ku-me-cha.
U-ke-shar-tam le-ot al ya-de-cha, ve-ha-yu
le-to-ta-fot bein ei-ne-cha, U-che-tav-tam
al me-zu-zot bei-te-cha u-vish-a-re-cha.

וְאָהַבְתָּ אֵת יְיָ אֱלֹהֶיךָ בְּכָל־
לְבָבְךָ וּבְכָל־נַפְשְׁךָ וּבְכָל־
מְאֹדֶךָ. וְהָיוּ הַדְּבָרִים הָאֵלֶּה, אֲשֶׁר אָנֹכִי
מְצַוְּךָ הַיּוֹם, עַל־לְבָבֶךָ. וְשִׁנַּנְתָּם
לְבָנֶיךָ, וְדִבַּרְתָּ בָּם בְּשִׁבְתְּךָ
בְּבֵיתֶךָ, וּבְלֶכְתְּךָ בַדֶּרֶךְ,
וּבְשָׁכְבְּךָ וּבְקוּמֶךָ. וּקְשַׁרְתָּם לְאוֹת
עַל־יָדֶךָ, וְהָיוּ לְטֹטָפֹת בֵּין עֵינֶיךָ.
וּכְתַבְתָּם עַל־מְזֻזוֹת בֵּיתֶךָ,
וּבִשְׁעָרֶיךָ.

Le-ma-an tiz-ke-ru, va-a-si-tem et kol
mits-vo-tai, vi-hi-yi-tem ke-do-shim
lei-lo-hei-chem. A-ni A-do-nai
E-lo-hei-chem: a-sher ho-tsei-ti e-te-chem
mei-e-rets Mits-ra-yim, li-hi-yot la-chem
lei-lo-him. A-ni A-do-nai E-lo-hei-chem.

לְמַעַן תִּזְכְּרוּ וַעֲשִׂיתֶם אֶת־כָּל־
מִצְוֹתָי, וִהְיִיתֶם קְדֹשִׁים
לֵאלֹהֵיכֶם. אֲנִי יְיָ אֱלֹהֵיכֶם, אֲשֶׁר
הוֹצֵאתִי אֶתְכֶם מֵאֶרֶץ מִצְרַיִם
לִהְיוֹת לָכֶם לֵאלֹהִים. אֲנִי יְיָ
אֱלֹהֵיכֶם.

You shall love the Lord your God with all your heart, with all your soul, and with all your might. And these words which I command you this day shall be upon your heart. You shall teach them diligently to your children and shall speak of them when you sit in your house, when you walk by the way, when you lie down, and when you rise up. You shall bind them for a sign upon your hand, and they shall be for frontlets between your eyes. You shall write them upon the doorposts of your house and upon your gates, that you may remember and do all my commandments and be holy unto your God.

Reader

We hold all of this to be true: the Lord is our God, and we are Israel, devoted to God's service. We were redeemed from Egypt to liberate the oppressed and to bring hope to those who wait in darkness.

Congregation

When our people stood at the shore of freedom's sea, they proclaimed their faith, as we do now, with a song of praise.

All sing

Mi cha-mo-cha ba-ei-lim, A-do-nai?
Mi ka-mo-cha, ne-dar ba-ko-desh,
no-ra te-hi-lot o-sei fe-leh?

מִי־כָמֹכָה בָּאֵלִם, יְיָ?
מִי כָּמֹכָה, נֶאְדָּר בַּקֹּדֶשׁ,
נוֹרָא תְהִלֹּת, עֹשֵׂה פֶלֶא?

Who is like You, Eternal One, among the gods that are worshiped? Who is like You, majestic in holiness, awesome in splendor, doing wonders?

Cantor

מַלְכוּתְךָ רָאוּ בָנֶיךָ, בּוֹקֵעַ יָם לִפְנֵי מֹשֶׁה; "זֶה אֵלִי!" עָנוּ וְאָמְרוּ:

Your redeemed people sang of Your power as the sea opened before Moses: "This is my God! God will reign forever and ever."

All sing

"A-do-nai yim-loch le-o-lam va-ed."

"יְיָ יִמְלֹךְ לְעֹלָם וָעֶד!"

Reader

וְנֶאֱמַר: "כִּי־פָדָה יְיָ אֶת יַעֲקֹב, וּגְאָלוֹ מִיַּד חָזָק מִמֶּנּוּ." בָּרוּךְ אַתָּה, יְיָ, גָּאַל יִשְׂרָאֵל.

O God, as You have redeemed Israel from powers of oppression, liberate all who are persecuted. Be praised, Redeemer of Israel.

HASH-KI-VEI-NU—OUR PRAYER AT EVENING

Reader

הַשְׁכִּיבֵנוּ, יְיָ אֱלֹהֵינוּ, לְשָׁלוֹם, וְהַעֲמִידֵנוּ, מַלְכֵּנוּ, לְחַיִּים.
וּפְרוֹשׁ עָלֵינוּ סֻכַּת שְׁלוֹמֶךָ.

This has been our evening prayer for centuries. Assaulted by persecution and slaughter, our people resisted despair and lifted their voices in praise. Our night and morning prayers for a world without enemies, without hunger, poverty, suffering and fear, have foundered against the resistance of selfishness and cynicism, and yet we pray. With hearts trembling, we dare to yearn for peace.

Congregation

For our evening prayer is a triumph over darkness and disappointment. Our prayer is a song of hope and attachment to You, O God.

Reader

בָּרוּךְ אַתָּה, יְיָ, הַפּוֹרֵשׂ סֻכַּת שָׁלוֹם עָלֵינוּ, וְעַל-כָּל-עַמּוֹ
יִשְׂרָאֵל וְעַל יְרוּשָׁלָיִם.

Be praised, O God, who spreads over us a shelter of peace, whispering that one day all the dark forces of evil will be defeated and peace will prevail for us, for the people of Israel, for all peoples, and over Jerusalem.

(On Sabbath continue with *Ve-sha-me-ru, p. 52*)

The *Hash-ki-vei-nu* prayer is mentioned in the Mishnah where it is described by the rabbis as the second benediction following the evening recitation of the *Shema*. Written during the time of the Temple, it was also used at the end of the service as a concluding prayer. In its original it contains the words: "Remove also Satan from before us and behind us." In early Jewish tradition the figure of "Satan" was the embodiment of all evil. The night prayer was a hope for protection from all dangers—a yearning for the defeat of Satan and the triumph of righteousness, loving kindness and peace.

All sing

Ve-sha-me-ru ve-nei Yis-ra-eil et
    ha-sha-bat,
la-a-sot et ha-sha-bat le-do-ro-tam, be-rit
o-lam. Bei-ni u-vein be-nei Yis-ra-eil ot
hi le-o-lam. Ki shei-shet ya-mim a-sa
A-do-nai
et-ha-sha-ma-yim ve-et ha-a-rets
    u-va-yom
ha-she-vi-i sha-vat va-yi-na-fash.

וְשָׁמְרוּ בְנֵי־יִשְׂרָאֵל אֶת־הַשַּׁבָּת,
לַעֲשׂוֹת אֶת־הַשַּׁבָּת לְדֹרֹתָם
בְּרִית עוֹלָם. בֵּינִי וּבֵין בְּנֵי
יִשְׂרָאֵל אוֹת הִיא לְעֹלָם, כִּי
שֵׁשֶׁת יָמִים עָשָׂה יְיָ אֶת־הַשָּׁמַיִם
וְאֶת־הָאָרֶץ, וּבַיּוֹם הַשְּׁבִיעִי
שָׁבַת וַיִּנָּפַשׁ.

The people of Israel shall keep the Sabbath, observing the Sabbath in every generation as a covenant for all time. It is a sign forever between Me and the people of Israel, for in six days the Eternal God made heaven and earth, and on the seventh day God rested from all the work of creation.

Ve-sha-me-ru…from *Exodus 31:16-17* contains the commandment to observe the Sabbath as a symbol of God's *brit,* or "covenant," with the Jewish people.

All rise as ark is opened.

A Silent Meditation for the Amidah

Prayer enlarges our awareness, extends and enriches our perceptions. To pray is to be seized with surprise, to encounter a tide of amazement. Prayer opens us to the power of creativity and love that flows through all existence. We are taught: "Know before whom you stand."

Reader

אֲדֹנָי, שְׂפָתַי תִּפְתָּח, וּפִי יַגִּיד תְּהִלָּתֶךָ.

Eternal God, open our lips, that our mouths may declare Your glory.

(Amidah continues on p. 55)

Amidah means "standing" and is the third section of the service. On the weekday this section, also known as *Tefilah,* "the Prayer," contains nineteen prayers. On the Sabbath and Holy Days the first three and last three prayers of this section are retained, and a special "Sanctification of the Day" is added. According to tradition, the *Amidah* was written by the rabbis of the Great Assembly and made an official part of Jewish worship by Rabban Gamliel, head of the Yavneh Academy in about 100 C.E.

From Book of Customs, Klau Library Cincinnati
Amsterdam 1723, "Rabbi Teaching"
From the Collection of the Hebrew Union College
Skirball Museum

The *Avot* prayer celebrates the passing of Jewish tradition from generation to generation, and the affirmation that the God of Abraham, Isaac and Jacob continues to inspire devotion today. The *zoch-rei-nu,* or "Remember us," with its reference to meriting judgment and inscription in the "Book of Life," was interpolated into the *Avot* prayer on Rosh Hashanah and Yom Kippur sometime during the 8th or 9th centuries, C.E.

Cantor

Ba-ruch a-ta, A-do-nai, E-lo-hei-nu
vei-lo-hei a-vo-tei-nu, E-lo-hei Av-ra-ham,
E-lo-hei Yits-chak, vei-lo-hei Ya-a-kov:
ha-eil ha-ga-dol, ha-gi-bor ve-ha-no-ra, Eil
el-yon, go-meil cha-sa-dim to-vim,
ve-ko-nei ha-kol, ve-zo-cheir cha-se-dei
a-vot, u-mei-vi ge-u-lah li-ve-nei
ve-nei-hem le-man-an she-mo, be-a-ha-va.

בָּרוּךְ אַתָּה, יְיָ אֱלֹהֵינוּ
וֵאלֹהֵי אֲבוֹתֵינוּ, אֱלֹהֵי
אַבְרָהָם, אֱלֹהֵי יִצְחָק
וֵאלֹהֵי יַעֲקֹב: הָאֵל הַגָּדוֹל,
הַגִּבּוֹר וְהַנּוֹרָא, אֵל עֶלְיוֹן,
גּוֹמֵל חֲסָדִים טוֹבִים וְקוֹנֵה
הַכֹּל, וְזוֹכֵר חַסְדֵי אָבוֹת,
וּמֵבִיא גְאֻלָּה לִבְנֵי בְנֵיהֶם
לְמַעַן שְׁמוֹ בְּאַהֲבָה.

All sing

Zoch-rei-nu le-cha-yim, me-lech
cha-feitz ba-cha-yim, ve-cho-te-vei-nu
be-sei-fer ha-cha-yim, le-ma-a-ne-cha
Elo-him cha-yim.

זָכְרֵנוּ לַחַיִּים, מֶלֶךְ חָפֵץ
בַּחַיִּים, וְכָתְבֵנוּ בְּסֵפֶר
הַחַיִּים, לְמַעַנְךָ אֱלֹהִים
חַיִּים.

Cantor

Me-lech o-zeir u-mo-shi-a u-ma-gein.
Ba-ruch a-ta A-do-nai, ma-gein
Av-ra-ham.

מֶלֶךְ עוֹזֵר וּמוֹשִׁיעַ וּמָגֵן.
בָּרוּךְ אַתָּה יְיָ, מָגֵן
אַבְרָהָם.

Responsively

Source of all being, we turn to You as did our fathers and mothers in ancient days.

They knew You in their hearts; they sought You in their lives.

On the eve of this New Year, we embrace their quest for lives dedicated to acts of caring and love.

O God of life, may we merit inscription in Your Book of Life.

Havdalah Spice Box
Russian
20th c.

The *Gevurot* prayer celebrates God's creative and renewing Power at work in all nature, and the human responsibility to embody and express that Power for creativity, healing, liberation and hope. Even in death, God's Power for life sustains the memory and contributions of loved ones in the minds and hearts of succeeding generations. "You are holy..." is from the third prayer of the *Amidah* and emphasizes that holiness is achieved through our deeds.

Reader

אַתָּה גִבּוֹר לְעוֹלָם, אֲדֹנָי, מְחַיֵּה הַכֹּל אַתָּה, רַב
לְהוֹשִׁיעַ.

מְכַלְכֵּל חַיִּים בְּחֶסֶד, מְחַיֵּה הַכֹּל בְּרַחֲמִים רַבִּים.
סוֹמֵךְ נוֹפְלִים, וְרוֹפֵא חוֹלִים, וּמַתִּיר אֲסוּרִים,
וּמְקַיֵּם אֱמוּנָתוֹ לִישֵׁנֵי עָפָר.

מִי כָמְוֹךָ, בַּעַל גְּבוּרוֹת, וּמִי דּוֹמֶה לָּךְ, מֶלֶךְ מֵמִית
וּמְחַיֶּה וּמַצְמִיחַ יְשׁוּעָה? מִי כָמְוֹךָ אַב הָרַחֲמִים,
זוֹכֵר יְצוּרָיו לְחַיִּים בְּרַחֲמִים? וְנֶאֱמָן אַתָּה לְהַחֲיוֹת
הַכֹּל. בָּרוּךְ אַתָּה, יְיָ, מְחַיֵּה הַכֹּל.

Congregation

God of eternal might, through us send help to the fallen, healing to the sick, freedom to the captive; confirm Your faithfulness to those who sleep in the dust. For
You are mindful in mercy of all Your creatures. We praise You, the Source of life.

YOU ARE HOLY

Reader

אַתָּה קָדוֹשׁ וְשִׁמְךָ קָדוֹשׁ, וּקְדוֹשִׁים בְּכָל-יוֹם
יְהַלְלְוּךָ סֶּלָה.

Congregation

You are holy beyond compare, and we seek You each day by uplifting our lives
with deeds of holiness.

Ark is closed; all are seated

Havdalah Spice Box
American
20th c.

U-ve-chein..., "Now, O God...," is ascribed to Rabbi Yochanan ben Nuri (2nd Century C.E.) and was written during the Hadrianic persecutions when the brutality of Rome threatened to destroy the Jewish people and its faith. The prayer is divided into three sections and expresses the hope for a time when fear will be replaced by tranquility, hatred by trust, and arrogance by mutual and moral responsibility.

U-VE-CHEIN—MAY REVERENCE RULE US

Reader

וּבְכֵן תֵּן פַּחְדְּךָ, יְיָ אֱלֹהֵינוּ, עַל כָּל־מַעֲשֶׂיךָ,

וּבְכֵן תֵּן כָּבוֹד, יְיָ לְעַמֶּךָ, תְּהִלָּה לִירֵאֶיךָ וְתִקְוָה
לְדוֹרְשֶׁיךָ,

וּבְכֵן צַדִּיקִים יִרְאוּ וְיִשְׂמָחוּ...וְתִמְלֹךְ אַתָּה, יְיָ,
לְבַדֶּךָ עַל כָּל־מַעֲשֶׂיךָ, כַּכָּתוּב בְּדִבְרֵי קָדְשֶׁךָ: יִמְלֹךְ
יְיָ לְעוֹלָם, אֱלֹהַיִךְ צִיּוֹן, לְדֹר וָדֹר. הַלְלוּיָהּ!

Responsively

O Lord, our God, may reverence for all creation fill our hearts. Inspire with courage those who seek a time when violence and injustice will be no more.

May we be counted among them.

Strengthen the resolve of those who work for the time when wickedness will vanish like smoke and the rule of arrogance and tyranny will be banished from earth.

May we be counted among them.

Let the day come soon when all humanity will be gathered under a banner of peace and exalt You with deeds of righteousness and words of love on their lips.

May we be counted among them.

Cantor and Choir

קָדוֹשׁ אַתָּה וְנוֹרָא שְׁמֶךָ, וְאֵין אֱלוֹהַּ מִבַּלְעָדֶיךָ, כַּכָּתוּב:

וַיִּגְבַּהּ יְיָ צְבָאוֹת בַּמִּשְׁפָּט, וְהָאֵל הַקָּדוֹשׁ נִקְדַּשׁ בִּצְדָקָה.

בָּרוּךְ אַתָּה, יְיָ, הַמֶּלֶךְ הַקָּדוֹשׁ.

You are holy; awe inspiring is Your name. There is no God but You. As the prophet taught, "The Lord of hosts is exalted by justice; the God of holiness is sanctified by righteousness. Be praised, O God of holiness.

Kadosh a-ta, "You are holy...," was composed by the rabbis of the Mishnah *(Rosh Hashanah 2:1)* for High Holy Day and Festival worship. It echoes the highest aspiration of Jewish ethics, which is the imitation of God's holiness through acts of justice, compassion and love. This theme, known as *kiddush ha-Shem,* "the sanctification of God's Name," also forms the central core of the Yom Kippur afternoon Torah portion, which begins with the commandment, "You shall be holy, for I, the Lord your God, am holy" *(Leviticus 19:2).* "The Lord of hosts..." is from *Isaiah 5:16.* "You have chosen our people..." is the fourth, or middle prayer of the *Amidah* and was composed by the ancient rabbis *(Yoma 87b).* It speaks of God's "choice" of the Jewish people for fulfilling the commandments of Torah and thereby bringing justice and mercy into the world.

KEDUSHAT HA-YOM—SANCTIFICATION OF THE DAY

Reader

אַתָּה בְחַרְתָּנוּ מִכָּל־הָעַמִּים, אָהַבְתָּ אוֹתָנוּ וְרָצִיתָ
בָּנוּ, וְרוֹמַמְתָּנוּ מִכָּל־הַלְּשׁוֹנוֹת וְקִדַּשְׁתָּנוּ בְּמִצְוֹתֶיךָ,
וְקֵרַבְתָּנוּ מַלְכֵּנוּ לַעֲבוֹדָתֶךָ, וְשִׁמְךָ הַגָּדוֹל וְהַקָּדוֹשׁ
עָלֵינוּ קָרָאתָ.

You have chosen our people and entrusted us with commandments of compassion, goodness, truth and peace. On this Day of Remembrance, open our
eyes to the nobility of life and its sacred opportunities for service. Renew us
with ambitions beyond ourselves. When wrongs and injustices sadden our
hearts, strengthen us with hope against despair. Let no trial, however severe,
embitter our souls and shake our trust in You. May the wisdom of Torah
brighten our eyes and its light purify our hearts. Lead us to repair our troubled
world with Your healing rule of truth sealed in love.

Congregation

Be praised, O God, who rules over all the earth, and who sanctifies **(the
Sabbath),** the people of Israel, and this Day of Remembrance.

Cantor

Ba-ruch a-ta, A-do-nai…   בָּרוּךְ אַתָּה, יְיָ,

All sing

Me-lech al kol ha-aretz, me-ka-desh   מֶלֶךְ עַל כָּל־הָאָרֶץ,
(ha-Sha-bat v…) Yis-ra-el…   מְקַדֵּשׁ (הַשַּׁבָּת וְ) יִשְׂרָאֵל

Cantor

ve-Yom ha-Zi-ka-ron.   וְיוֹם הַזִּכָּרוֹן.

61

Reader

רְצֵה, יְיָ אֱלֹהֵינוּ, בְּעַמְּךָ יִשְׂרָאֵל, וּתְפִלָּתָם בְּאַהֲבָה תְקַבֵּל,
וּתְהִי לְרָצוֹן תָּמִיד עֲבוֹדַת יִשְׂרָאֵל עַמֶּךָ.

בָּרוּךְ אַתָּה, יְיָ, שֶׁאוֹתְךָ לְבַדְּךָ בְּיִרְאָה נַעֲבוֹד.

Look with favor, O God, upon us, and may our worship and deeds be acceptable to You. Be praised, O God, whom alone we serve in reverence.

HODA-AH—WE GIVE THANKS

Congregation

מוֹדִים אֲנַחְנוּ לָךְ, שָׁאַתָּה הוּא יְיָ אֱלֹהֵינוּ וֵאלֹהֵי אֲבוֹתֵינוּ
לְעוֹלָם וָעֶד. צוּר חַיֵּינוּ, מָגֵן יִשְׁעֵנוּ, אַתָּה הוּא לְדוֹר וָדוֹר.
נוֹדֶה לְךָ וּנְסַפֵּר תְּהִלָּתֶךָ, עַל־חַיֵּינוּ הַמְּסוּרִים בְּיָדֶךָ, וְעַל־
נִשְׁמוֹתֵינוּ הַפְּקוּדוֹת לָךְ, וְעַל־נִסֶּיךָ שֶׁבְּכָל־יוֹם עִמָּנוּ, וְעַל־
נִפְלְאוֹתֶיךָ וְטוֹבוֹתֶיךָ שֶׁבְּכָל־עֵת, עֶרֶב וָבֹקֶר וְצָהֳרָיִם. הַטּוֹב
כִּי לֹא־כָלוּ רַחֲמֶיךָ, וְהַמְרַחֵם: כִּי־לֹא תַמּוּ חֲסָדֶיךָ, מֵעוֹלָם
קִוִּינוּ לָךְ.

We gratefully acknowledge, O Lord our God, that You are our Creator and Preserver, the Rock of our lives and our protecting Shield. We give thanks to You for our lives, which are in Your hand, for our souls which are in Your keeping, for Your wondrous providence and Your continuous goodness, which You bestow upon us day by day. Truly, Your mercies never fail, and Your loving kindness never ceases. Therefore do we put our trust in You. Be praised, O God, to whom our thanks are due.

The traditional *Avodah* prayer referred to the sacrifices offered at the Jerusalem Temple. Our rendition emphasizes the Jewish view that reverence for God consists of both prayer and deeds. The theme of *Hoda-ah,* "thanksgiving," is one of the oldest in the history of prayer, and this rendition may have been recited in the Jerusalem Temple before it became a part of the synagogue service.

Reader

שָׁלוֹם רָב עַל־יִשְׂרָאֵל עַמְּךָ וְעַל־כָּל־הָעַמִּים תָּשִׂים לְעוֹלָם,
כִּי אַתָּה הוּא מֶלֶךְ אָדוֹן לְכָל־הַשָּׁלוֹם. וְטוֹב בְּעֵינֶיךָ לְבָרֵךְ
אֶת־עַמְּךָ יִשְׂרָאֵל וְאֶת־כָּל־הָעַמִּים בְּכָל־עֵת וּבְכָל־שָׁעָה
בִּשְׁלוֹמֶךָ.

Bless us, all Israel Your people, and all humanity with peace and goodness, mercy and compassion. Bless us with the light of Torah, for You have given us a heritage of love and commandments for kindness, charity and peace.

Cantor and Choir

בְּסֵפֶר חַיִּים בְּרָכָה וְשָׁלוֹם וּפַרְנָסָה טוֹבָה נִזָּכֵר
וְנִכָּתֵב לְפָנֶיךָ, אֲנַחְנוּ וְכָל־עַמְּךָ בֵּית יִשְׂרָאֵל, לְחַיִּים
טוֹבִים וּלְשָׁלוֹם. בָּרוּךְ אַתָּה, יְיָ, עוֹשֵׂה הַשָּׁלוֹם.

Reader

May our deeds be worthy before You, and may we, and all Israel, be inscribed in the Book of Life for blessing, sustenance and peace. Be praised, O God, Source of peace.

Silent Prayer

The final prayer of the *Amidah* is the *Birkat Shalom*, or "blessing for peace." This is the evening version of the prayer as developed by the rabbis for the early synagogue in the 2nd century B.C.E. The inclusion of the words "may we, and all Israel, be inscribed in the Book of Life..." is unique to Rosh Hashanah and Yom Kippur when the theme of God's judgment is paramount and when consideration of how much or how little one has done to advance the cause of peace is all-important.

Mizrach 39.5
(An art piece hung on Eastern wall facing Jerusalem)
Europe 19th c.
John Forsman, Photographer
From the Collection of the Hebrew Union College
Skirball Museum

"Let my heart be open…" is based on a poem by Hillel Bavli (1892-1961). "May the words…" is taken from *Psalms 19.*

MEDITATION FOR THE TURNING OF THE YEAR

At this turning of the year,

    Let my heart be open
    To every broken spirit,
    To those who try my patience,
    To those I have wronged and hurt,
    To those groping and lonely in the shadows.

    Let my senses be open
    To bearers of wisdom and new light,
    Awakening me to behold anew
    This green, flowering world,
    That I may grasp the secret
    Of blossoming into blessing,
    Turning frustration into forgiveness,
    And forgiveness into love
    Without expectation of reward.

    Essence of my life,
    Urge me to honesty,
    Judge me in mercy,
    Bend me into giving.
    Guide me in this turning of the year.

All sing

יִהְיוּ לְרָצוֹן אִמְרֵי־פִי וְהֶגְיוֹן לִבִּי לְפָנֶיךָ, יְיָ, צוּרִי וְגוֹאֲלִי.

Yi-he-yu le-ra-tzon im-rei fi, ve-heg-yon li-bi le-fa-ne-cha, A-do-nai, tzu-ri ve-go-a-li.

May the words of my mouth and the meditations of my heart be acceptable to You, my Rock and my Redeemer.

All rise; ark is opened

Congregation

אָבִינוּ מַלְכֵּנוּ, שְׁמַע קוֹלֵנוּ.

Avinu Malkeinu, she-ma ko-lei-nu.
Avinu Malkeinu, hear our prayer.

אָבִינוּ מַלְכֵּנוּ, חָטָאנוּ לְפָנֶיךָ.

Avinu Malkeinu, cha-ta-nu le-fa-ne-cha.
Avinu Malkeinu, we have sinned against You.

אָבִינוּ מַלְכֵּנוּ, חֲמוֹל עָלֵינוּ וְעַל עוֹלָלֵינוּ וְטַפֵּנוּ.

Avinu Malkeinu, cha-mol a-lei-nu ve-al o-la-lei-nu ve-ta-pei-nu.
Avinu Malkeinu, have mercy upon us and upon our children.

אָבִינוּ מַלְכֵּנוּ, כַּלֵּה דֶּבֶר וְחֶרֶב וְרָעָב מֵעָלֵינוּ.

Avinu Malkeinu, ka-lei de-ver, ve-che-rev, ve-ra-av mei-a-lei-nu.
Avinu Malkeinu, rid us of pestilence, war and famine.

אָבִינוּ מַלְכֵּנוּ, כַּלֵּה כָּל־צַר וּמַשְׂטִין מֵעָלֵינוּ.

Avinu Malkeinu, ka-lei kol tsar u-mas-tin mei-a-lei-nu.
Avinu Malkeinu, rid us of all hatred and oppression.

אָבִינוּ מַלְכֵּנוּ, כָּתְבֵנוּ בְּסֵפֶר חַיִּים טוֹבִים.

Avinu Malkeinu, kot-vei-nu be-sei-fer cha-yim to-vim.
Avinu Malkeinu, inscribe us for blessing in the Book of Life.

Avinu Malkeinu..., "Our Father, our King...," is attributed to Rabbi Akiba (2nd century C.E.), whose first version contained twenty-two verses, one for each letter of the Hebrew alphabet. In the 14th century, the prayer was expanded to forty-four verses. Traditionally, the prayer is recited throughout the High Holy Day period from Rosh Hashanah to Yom Kippur *(Taanit 25b)*.

אָבִינוּ מַלְכֵּנוּ, מַלֵּא יָדֵינוּ מִבִּרְכוֹתֶיךָ.

Avinu Malkeinu, ma-lei ya-dei-nu mi-bir-cho-te-cha.
Avinu Malkeinu, fill our hands with Your blessings.

אָבִינוּ מַלְכֵּנוּ, כָּתְבֵנוּ בְּסֵפֶר סְלִיחָה וּמְחִילָה.

Avinu Malkeinu, kot-vei-nu be-sei-fer se-li-cha u-me-chi-lah.
Avinu Malkeinu, inscribe us for blessing in the Book of forgiveness.

אָבִינוּ מַלְכֵּנוּ, חָנֵּנוּ וַעֲנֵנוּ, כִּי אֵין בָּנוּ מַעֲשִׂים,
עֲשֵׂה עִמָּנוּ צְדָקָה וָחֶסֶד וְהוֹשִׁיעֵנוּ.

Avinu Malkeinu, cho-nei-nu va-a-nei-nu, ki ein ba-nu ma-a-sim, a-sei i-ma-nu
tse-da-kah va-che-sed, ve-ho-shi-ei-nu.
Avinu Malkeinu, be gracious and answer us. Treat us generously and with
kindness, and help us.

All sing

Avinu Malkeinu,
cho-nei-nu va-a-nei-nu (2)
ki ein ba-nu ma-a-sim.

A-sei i-ma-nu tse-da-kah va-che-sed (2)
ve-ho-shi-ei-nu.

Avinu Malkeinu,
cho-nei-nu va-a-nei-nu (2)
ki ein ba-nu ma-a-sim.

אָבִינוּ מַלְכֵּנוּ, חָנֵּנוּ וַעֲנֵנוּ,
כִּי אֵין בָּנוּ מַעֲשִׂים, עֲשֵׂה
עִמָּנוּ צְדָקָה וָחֶסֶד וְהוֹשִׁיעֵנוּ.

All are seated

ROSH HASHANAH EVENING SERMON

All rise, ark is opened

All sing

A-lei-nu le-sha-bei-ach la-a-don
ha-kol,
la-teit ge-du-lah le-yo-tseir
be-rei-sheet,
she-lo a-sa-nu ke-go-yei
ha-a-ra-tsot,
ve-lo sa-ma-nu ke-mish-pe-chot
ha-a-da-mah,
she-lo sam chel-kei-nu ka-hem,
ve-go-ra-lei-nu ke-chol ha-mo-nam.

עָלֵינוּ לְשַׁבֵּחַ לַאֲדוֹן הַכֹּל,
לָתֵת גְּדֻלָּה לְיוֹצֵר בְּרֵאשִׁית,
שֶׁלֹּא עָשָׂנוּ כְּגוֹיֵי הָאֲרָצוֹת,

וְלֹא שָׂמָנוּ כְּמִשְׁפְּחוֹת הָאֲדָמָה;
שֶׁלֹּא שָׂם חֶלְקֵנוּ כָּהֶם,
וְגֹרָלֵנוּ כְּכָל־הֲמוֹנָם.

Let us adore the ever-living God, rendering praise to the Creator of all, who chose us from all peoples, singling us out for sacred service, assigning us to a unique destiny.

Va-a-nach-nu ko-re-im u-mish-ta-cha-vim
u-mo-dim
lif-nei me-lech ma-le-chei
ha-me-la-chim, ha-ka-dosh ba-ruch Hu.

וַאֲנַחְנוּ כּוֹרְעִים וּמִשְׁתַּחֲוִים וּמוֹדִים
לִפְנֵי מֶלֶךְ מַלְכֵי הַמְּלָכִים,
הַקָּדוֹשׁ בָּרוּךְ הוּא.

We bow the head in reverence and worship the God of all, the Holy One, whom we praise.

Some scholars believe that the *Aleinu* prayer was composed during Maccabean times as a form of protest against idolatry, the worship of images and objects as gods. It was later placed within the Rosh Hashanah liturgy by the Babylonian sage Rav (d.247 C.E.); in the 13th century it was made the concluding section of the daily and Sabbath liturgy because it expressed the hope for the Messianic day of peace when God, alone, will be worshiped in all the earth.

MBS *MBS*

Congregation

Eternal God, we face tomorrow with hope made stronger by the vision of Your rule: a world where poverty and war are banished, where injustice and hate are no more. Teach us to share the pain of others, to heed Your call for justice, to pursue the blessing of peace. Help us, O God, to gain victory over evil and to bring nearer the day when all the world shall be one.

Cantor

Ve-ne-e-mar: "Ve-ha-ya A-do-nai le-me-lech al kol ha-a-rets...

וְנֶאֱמַר: "וְהָיָה יְיָ לְמֶלֶךְ עַל כָּל־הָאָרֶץ.

All sing

ba-yom ha-hu yi-he-yeh A-do-nai e-chad u-she-mo e-chad."

בַּיּוֹם הַהוּא יִהְיֶה יְיָ אֶחָד וּשְׁמוֹ אֶחָד."

And it has been said: "God shall reign over all the earth; on that day the Eternal shall be One, and God's name shall be One."

This second section of the *Aleinu* prayer is based on *Deuteronomy 4:39:* "Know therefore this day and keep in mind that the Lord alone is God in heaven above and on earth below, there is no other" and *Exodus 15:18:* "God will reign..." and *Zechariah 14:19:* "God shall reign over all the earth...."

Kaddish is the profound praise of the living,
Praise for the generous gift of life;

Praise for the presence of loved ones,
  bonds of friendship,
  the link of memory;

Praise for the toil and searching,
  dedication and vision,
  ennobling aspirations;

Praise for the precious moorings of faith,
  for courageous souls,
  for prophets, psalmists, and sages;

Praise for those who walked before us,
  the sufferers in the valley of shadows,
  the steadfast in the furnace of hate.

Kaddish is praise for the God of our people,
  the Source of all growth and goodness,
  the Promise on which we build tomorrow.

All rise

Yit-ga-dal ve-yit-ka-dash she-mei ra-ba
be-al-ma di-ve-ra chi-re-u-tei, ve-yam-lich
mal-chu-tei
be-cha-yei-chon u-ve-yo-mei-chon
u-ve-cha-yei de-chol beit Yis-ra-eil,
ba-a-ga-la u-vi-ze-man ka-riv, ve-i-me-ru:
a-mein.

יִתְגַּדַּל וְיִתְקַדַּשׁ שְׁמֵהּ רַבָּא
בְּעָלְמָא דִי־בְרָא כִרְעוּתֵהּ,
וְיַמְלִיךְ מַלְכוּתֵהּ בְּחַיֵּיכֹון
וּבְיֹומֵיכֹון וּבְחַיֵּי דְכָל־בֵּית
יִשְׂרָאֵל, בַּעֲגָלָא וּבִזְמַן קָרִיב,
וְאִמְרוּ: אָמֵן.

Ye-hei she-mei ra-ba me-va-rach le-a-lam
u-le-al-mei al-ma-ya.

יְהֵא שְׁמֵהּ רַבָּא מְבָרַךְ לְעָלַם
וּלְעָלְמֵי עָלְמַיָּא.

Yit-ba-rach ve-yish-ta-bach, ve-yit-pa-ar
ve-yit-ro-mam ve-yit-na-sei,
ve-yit-ha-dar ve-yit-a-leh ve-yit-ha-lal
she-mei de-ku-de-sha, be-rich hu,
le-ei-la min kol bi-re-cha-ta ve-shi-ra-ta
tush-be-cha-ta ve-ne-che-ma-ta,
da-a mi-ran be-al-ma,
ve-i-me-ru: a-mein.

יִתְבָּרַךְ וְיִשְׁתַּבַּח, וְיִתְפָּאַר
וְיִתְרֹומַם וְיִתְנַשֵּׂא, וְיִתְהַדַּר
וְיִתְעַלֶּה וְיִתְהַלָּל שְׁמֵהּ
דְּקוּדְשָׁא, בְּרִיךְ הוּא, לְעֵלָּא
מִן־כָּל־בִּרְכָתָא וְשִׁירָתָא,
תֻּשְׁבְּחָתָא וְנֶחֱמָתָא דַּאֲמִירָן
בְּעָלְמָא, וְאִמְרוּ: אָמֵן.

Ye-hei she-la-ma ra-ba
min she-ma-ya ve-cha-yim
a-lei-nu ve-al kol Yis-ra-eil
ve-i-me-ru: a-mein.

יְהֵא שְׁלָמָא רַבָּא מִן־שְׁמַיָּא
וְחַיִּים עָלֵינוּ וְעַל־כָּל־יִשְׂרָאֵל,
וְאִמְרוּ: אָמֵן.

O-seh sha-lom bi-me-ro-mav, hu ya-a-seh
sha-lom a-lei-nu
ve-al kol Yis-ra-eil
ve-i-me-ru: a-mein.

עֹשֶׂה שָׁלֹום בִּמְרֹומָיו, הוּא
יַעֲשֶׂה שָׁלֹום עָלֵינוּ וְעַל־
כָּל־יִשְׂרָאֵל
וְאִמְרוּ: אָמֵן.

Havdalah Spice Box
Eastern Europe
19th c.

The *Kaddish* prayer may be derived from *Psalms 113:2,* or from *Daniel 2:20.* The prayer was composed in Aramaic, the vernacular spoken by Jews from the Babylonian exile (586 B.C.E.) to the 5th century C.E. Over the centuries, five variations of the *Kaddish* have evolved: The *chatzi Kaddish,* or "half Kaddish," used at the conclusion of each section of worship; the *Kaddish shalem,* or "complete Kaddish," recited after the Amidah; the *Kaddish yatom,* or "mourners Kaddish," used in this service on p. 71; the *Kaddish derabanan,* or Rabbis' Kaddish," said after the study of Torah, and the *Kaddish lehitchadeta,* or "funeral Kaddish," recited by the mourner at the grave just after burial. In essence, the *Kaddish* is a poem of praise to God.

May God's great name be magnified and made holy in the world created according to Divine will. May God soon establish a reign of justice and peace during our life and days, and during the lifetime of the whole house of Israel. And let us say, Amen.

May God's great name be blessed now and forever.

May the name of the Holy One be blessed, praised, glorified, exalted, extolled, honored, magnified, and celebrated, even though God is above and beyond all the blessings, songs, praises and consolations that are spoken in the world. And let us say, Amen.

May there be great peace from heaven and life for us and all Israel. And let us say, Amen.

May the One who makes peace in the heavens make peace for us and for all Israel. And let us say, Amen

ROSH HASHANAH MORNING SERVICE

Mizrach 39.23
(An art piece hung on Eastern wall facing Jerusalem)
North Africa 19th c.
Marvin Rand, Photographer
From the Collection of the Hebrew Union College
Skirball Museum

The *Pesukei de-zimra,* or "Songs and Prayers of Praise," form the first section of the service. They are meant to prepare one for prayer, to awaken a sense of awe and wonder, of gratefulness and thanksgiving for the gifts of life. *"How lovely are your tents..."* is drawn from *Numbers 24:5* and *Psalms 5:8, 26:8,* and *69:14.*

Congregation and Choir

Ma to-vu o-ha-le-cha, Ya-a-kov,
mish-ke-no-te-cha, Yis-ra-eil.
Va-ani, be-rov chas-de-cha , a-vo vei-te-cha.
Esh-ta-cha-ve el hei-chal ko-de-she-cha
be-yir-ah-te-cha.
A-do-nai, ah-hav-ti me-on bei-te-cha,
u-me-kom mish-kan ke-vo-de-cha, va-a-ni
esh-ta-cha-ve ve-ech-ra-ah, ev-re-cha lif-nei
A-do-nai o-si, v-a-ni te-fi-la-ti le-cha,
A-do-nai, eit ra-tzon. E-lo-him, be-rov
chas-de-cha, a-nei-ni be-emet yish-e-cha.

מַה־טֹּבוּ אֹהָלֶיךָ, יַעֲקֹב,
מִשְׁכְּנֹתֶיךָ, יִשְׂרָאֵל!
וַאֲנִי, בְּרֹב חַסְדְּךָ אָבֹא בֵיתֶךָ,
אֶשְׁתַּחֲוֶה אֶל־הֵיכַל קָדְשְׁךָ
בְּיִרְאָתֶךָ.
יְיָ, אָהַבְתִּי מְעוֹן בֵּיתֶךָ,
וּמְקוֹם מִשְׁכַּן כְּבוֹדֶךָ.
וַאֲנִי אֶשְׁתַּחֲוֶה וְאֶכְרָעָה,
אֶבְרְכָה לִפְנֵי־יְיָ עֹשִׂי.
וַאֲנִי תְפִלָּתִי לְךָ, יְיָ, עֵת רָצוֹן.
אֱלֹהִים, בְּרָב־חַסְדֶּךָ,
עֲנֵנִי בֶּאֱמֶת יִשְׁעֶךָ.

How lovely are your tents, O Jacob, your dwelling-places, O Israel!

In Your abundant loving kindness, O God, let me enter Your house reverently to worship in Your holy temple.

Lord, I love Your house, the place where Your glory dwells. There I would worship with humility; I would seek blessing in the presence of God, my Maker.

To You, then, O Eternal One, does my prayer go forth. May this be a time of joy and favor. In Your great love, O God, answer me with Your saving truth.

Responsively

נִשְׁמַת כָּל־חַי תְּבָרֵךְ אֶת־שְׁמְךָ, יְיָ אֱלֹהֵינוּ, וְרוּחַ כָּל־
בָּשָׂר תְּפָאֵר וּתְרוֹמֵם זִכְרְךָ, מַלְכֵּנוּ, תָּמִיד.

Let every living soul praise Your name, O God, and proclaim Your majesty forever.

Be praised, O God, whose wondrous power creates all beginnings.

Be praised, O God, whose love embraces all creatures.

Be praised, O God, who nurtures the fallen with hope and rescues the oppressed.

Be praised, O God, who makes firm the steps of those who toil for justice and pursue peace.

Be praised, O God, who gathers our people Israel together on this Rosh Hashanah day.

בָּרוּךְ אַתָּה, יְיָ, הַבּוֹחֵר בְּשִׁירֵי זִמְרָה, מֶלֶךְ אֵל חַי הָעוֹלָמִים.

Be praised, O God, who delights in our prayer and song, the One and eternal life of the universe who summons us to serve.

"Every living soul..." was designated by Rabbi Yochanan (3rd century) as *Birkat Ha-shir*, "The Blessing of the Song," and is not only recited as part of the Sabbath and festival services but is also included in the Pesach Haggadah. "Be praised..." are blessings written in Persia during the 5th and 6th centuries C.E.

All rise and sing

Ba-re-chu et A-do-nai ha-me-vo-rach.

בָּרְכוּ אֶת־יְיָ הַמְבֹרָךְ!

Ba-ruch A-do-nai ha-me-vo-rach
le-o-lam va-ed.

בָּרוּךְ יְיָ הַמְבֹרָךְ לְעוֹלָם וָעֶד!

Be praised, O God, to whom our praise is due.
Praised be the Lord, to whom our praise is due, now and forever.

YOTZER OR—CREATOR OF LIGHT

Reader

בָּרוּךְ אַתָּה, יְיָ אֱלֹהֵינוּ, מֶלֶךְ הָעוֹלָם, יוֹצֵר אוֹר וּבוֹרֵא
חֹשֶׁךְ, עֹשֶׂה שָׁלוֹם וּבוֹרֵא אֶת־הַכֹּל. הַמֵּאִיר לָאָרֶץ וְלַדָּרִים
עָלֶיהָ בְּרַחֲמִים, וּבְטוּבוֹ מְחַדֵּשׁ בְּכָל־יוֹם תָּמִיד מַעֲשֵׂה
בְרֵאשִׁית. בָּרוּךְ אַתָּה, יְיָ, יוֹצֵר הַמְּאוֹרוֹת.

Congregation

Heaven and earth are the work of Your hands. You form light and darkness, renewing daily the wonder of creation. The mysteries of life and death, of growth and decay reveal Your creative power. O God, the whole universe is Your dwelling-place, a hymn to Your glory.

———————————————

"The Shema and its Blessings" make up the second section of the service. Following the themes of *Genesis* and *Exodus,* these prayers praise God as "Creator," "Lover of Israel," "Giver of Torah," and Source of Israel's "liberation" from Egypt. The formula for the *Barechu* comes from *Nehemiah 9:5.* The *Yotzer Or* is partially based on *Isaiah 45:7* and may have been used as a part of the Jerusalem Temple liturgy. Its counterpart in the evening worship service is the *Ma-ariv Aravim,* or evening prayer.

Havdalah Spice Box
Eastern Europe
Early 19th c.

The *Ahavah Rabah* prayer was a part of the Temple service. Like its counterpart, the *Ahavat Olam* of the evening service, its themes of God's love for Israel and the Jewish people's devotion to God culminate in the *Shema,* which is taken from *Deuteronomy 6:4* and represents Israel's pledge of faith at Mt. Sinai just after hearing the Ten Commandments. In reciting the *Shema,* a Jew stands, once again, at Sinai.

Reader

Great has been Your love for us. Our people put their trust in You, and You taught them laws for life. Be gracious also to us. Enlighten us with the wisdom of Torah. Inspire us to carry out Your will with deeds of mercy, justice and love. Lead us to lives enriched by faithfulness to Your teachings.

Congregation

You have sanctified us for Your service. You have drawn us to You in love. You have summoned us to proclaim Your unity.

Reader

בָּרוּךְ אַתָּה, יְיָ, הַבּוֹחֵר בְּעַמּוֹ יִשְׂרָאֵל בְּאַהֲבָה.

Be praised, O God, who in love has chosen our people Israel to serve You.

All sing

She-ma Yis-ra-eil: A-do-nai
E-lo-hei-nu, A-do-nai E-chad.

שְׁמַע יִשְׂרָאֵל: יְיָ אֱלֹהֵינוּ, יְיָ אֶחָד!

Ba-ruch sheim ke-vod
mal-chu-to le-o-lam va-ed.

בָּרוּךְ שֵׁם כְּבוֹד מַלְכוּתוֹ לְעוֹלָם וָעֶד!

Hear, O Israel: the Lord is our God, the Lord is One!
Blessed is God's glorious power forever and ever.

All are seated

Congregation

Ve-a-hav-ta eit A-do-nai E-lo-he-cha,
be-chol le-va-ve-cha, u-ve-chol
naf-she-cha, u-ve-chol me-o-de-cha.
Ve-ha-yu ha-de-va-rim ha-ei-leh, a-sher
a-no-chi me-tsa-ve-cha ha-yom, al
le-va-ve-cha. Ve-shi-nan-tam le-va-ne-cha,
ve-di-bar-ta bam be-shiv-te-cha
be-vei-te-cha u-ve-lech-te-cha va-de-rech
u-ve-shoch-be-cha u-ve-ku-me-cha.
U-ke-shar-tam le-ot al ya-de-cha, ve-ha-yu
le-to-ta-fot bein ei-ne-cha, U-che-tav-tam
al me-zu-zot bei-te-cha u-vish-a-re-cha.

Le-ma-an tiz-ke-ru, va-a-si-tem et kol
mits-vo-tai, vi-hi-yi-tem ke-do-shim
lei-lo-hei-chem. A-ni A-do-nai
E-lo-hei-chem: a-sher ho-tsei-ti e-te-chem
mei-e-rets Mits-ra-yim, li-hi-yot la-chem
lei-lo-him. A-ni A-do-nai E-lo-hei-chem.

וְאָהַבְתָּ אֵת יְיָ אֱלֹהֶיךָ בְּכָל־
לְבָבְךָ וּבְכָל־נַפְשְׁךָ וּבְכָל־
מְאֹדֶךָ.
וְהָיוּ הַדְּבָרִים הָאֵלֶּה, אֲשֶׁר אָנֹכִי
מְצַוְּךָ הַיּוֹם, עַל־לְבָבֶךָ. וְשִׁנַּנְתָּם
לְבָנֶיךָ, וְדִבַּרְתָּ בָּם בְּשִׁבְתְּךָ
בְּבֵיתֶךָ, וּבְלֶכְתְּךָ בַדֶּרֶךְ,
וּבְשָׁכְבְּךָ וּבְקוּמֶךָ. וּקְשַׁרְתָּם לְאוֹת
עַל־יָדֶךָ, וְהָיוּ לְטֹטָפֹת בֵּין עֵינֶיךָ.
וּכְתַבְתָּם עַל־מְזֻזוֹת בֵּיתֶךָ,
וּבִשְׁעָרֶיךָ.

לְמַעַן תִּזְכְּרוּ וַעֲשִׂיתֶם אֶת־כָּל־
מִצְוֹתָי, וִהְיִיתֶם קְדשִׁים
לֵאלֹהֵיכֶם. אֲנִי יְיָ אֱלֹהֵיכֶם, אֲשֶׁר
הוֹצֵאתִי אֶתְכֶם מֵאֶרֶץ מִצְרַיִם
לִהְיוֹת לָכֶם לֵאלֹהִים. אֲנִי יְיָ
אֱלֹהֵיכֶם.

You shall love the Lord your God with all your heart, with all your soul, and with all your might. And these words which I command you this day shall be upon your heart. You shall teach them diligently to your children and shall speak of them when you sit in your house, when you walk by the way, when you lie down, and when you rise up. You shall bind them for a sign upon your hand, and they shall be for frontlets between your eyes. You shall write them upon the doorposts of your house and upon your gates, that you may remember and do all my commandments and be holy unto your God.

(For comment, see p. 48)

Responsively

אֱמֶת וְיַצִּיב וְנָכוֹן וְקַיָּם וְיָשָׁר וְנֶאֱמָן וְטוֹב וְיָפֶה הַדָּבָר הַזֶּה.

True and enduring is Your saving power, O God.

> You have sustained our people in times of trouble, and have been our refuge in all generations.

As You saved Israel from Egyptian bondage, send help to all who are broken and oppressed.

> As You lifted us out of suffering, send us to heal the hurt of others.

May Your law of love transform our words and deeds for goodness.

> O God, we glorify You now as did our people in ancient days.

All sing

Mi cha-mo-cha ba-ei-lim, A-do-nai?
Mi ka-mo-cha, ne-dar ba-ko-desh,
no-ra te-hi-lot, o-sei fe-leh?

מִי־כָמֹכָה בָּאֵלִם, יְיָ?
מִי כָּמֹכָה, נֶאְדָּר בַּקֹּדֶשׁ,
נוֹרָא תְהִלֹּת, עֹשֵׂה פֶלֶא?

Who is like You, Eternal One, among the gods that are worshiped? Who is like You, majestic in holiness, awesome in splendor, doing wonders?

Cantor

שִׁירָה חֲדָשָׁה שִׁבְּחוּ גְאוּלִים לְשִׁמְךָ עַל־שְׂפַת הַיָּם; יַחַד כֻּלָּם
הוֹדוּ וְהִמְלִיכוּ וְאָמְרוּ:

Those who were redeemed sang a new song to Your name. At the shore of the Sea, saved from destruction, they proclaimed Your sovereign power: "God will reign forever and ever."

All sing

"A-do-nai yim-loch le-o-lam va-ed."

"יְיָ יִמְלֹךְ לְעֹלָם וָעֶד!"

(For comment, see p. 48)

83

Reader

צוּר יִשְׂרָאֵל, קוּמָה בְּעֶזְרַת יִשְׂרָאֵל, וּפְדֵה כִנְאֻמֶךָ יְהוּדָה וְיִשְׂרָאֵל. גֹּאֲלֵנוּ יְיָ צְבָאוֹת שְׁמוֹ, קְדוֹשׁ יִשְׂרָאֵל. בָּרוּךְ אַתָּה, יְיָ, גָּאַל יִשְׂרָאֵל.

O Rock of Israel, redeem those who are oppressed and liberate those who are persecuted. Be praised, O God, Redeemer of Israel.

THE AMIDAH

All rise as ark is opened

A Silent Meditation for the Amidah

Pray as if everything depended on God, and act as if everything depended on you.

To pray is to take notice of the wonder, to regain a sense of the mystery that animates all beings, the divine margin in all attainments. Prayer is our humble answer to the inconceivable surprise of living.

Reader

אֲדֹנָי, שְׂפָתַי תִּפְתָּח, וּפִי יַגִּיד תְּהִלָּתֶךָ

Eternal God, open our lips that our mouths may declare Your glory.

(For comment, see pp. 53, 54)

Cantor

Ba-ruch a-ta, A-do-nai, E-lo-hei-nu
vei-lo-hei a-vo-tei-nu, E-lo-hei Av-ra-ham,
E-lo-hei Yits-chak, vei-lo-hei Ya-a-kov:
ha-eil ha-ga-dol, ha-gi-bor ve-ha-no-ra, Eil
el-yon, go-meil cha-sa-dim to-vim,
ve-ko-nei ha-kol, ve-zo-cheir cha-se-dei
a-vot, u-mei-vi ge-u-lah li-ve-nei
ve-nei-hem le-man-an she-mo, be-a-ha-va.

All sing

Zoch-rei-nu le-cha-yim, me-lech
cha-feitz ba-cha-yim, ve-cho-te-vei-nu
be-sei-fer ha-cha-yim, le-ma-a-ne-cha
Elo-him cha-yim.

Cantor

Me-lech o-zeir u-mo-shi-a u-ma-gein.
Ba-ruch a-ta A-do-nai, ma-gein
Av-ra-ham.

בָּרוּךְ אַתָּה, יְיָ אֱלֹהֵינוּ
וֵאלֹהֵי אֲבוֹתֵינוּ, אֱלֹהֵי
אַבְרָהָם, אֱלֹהֵי יִצְחָק,
וֵאלֹהֵי יַעֲקֹב: הָאֵל הַגָּדוֹל,
הַגִּבּוֹר וְהַנּוֹרָא, אֵל עֶלְיוֹן,
גּוֹמֵל חֲסָדִים טוֹבִים,
וְקוֹנֵה הַכֹּל, וְזוֹכֵר חַסְדֵי
אָבוֹת, וּמֵבִיא גְאֻלָּה לִבְנֵי
בְנֵיהֶם, לְמַעַן שְׁמוֹ, בְּאַהֲבָה.

זָכְרֵנוּ לְחַיִּים, מֶלֶךְ חָפֵץ
בַּחַיִּים, וְכָתְבֵנוּ בְּסֵפֶר הַחַיִּים,
לְמַעַנְךָ אֱלֹהִים חַיִּים.

מֶלֶךְ עוֹזֵר וּמוֹשִׁיעַ וּמָגֵן.
בָּרוּךְ אַתָּה, יְיָ, מָגֵן אַבְרָהָם.

Responsively

You are our God, even as You were the God of Abraham, Isaac and Jacob, the God of Sarah, Rebekah, Leah and Rachel.

Their faith was strong that all humanity would one day be redeemed from injustice, fear and pain.

As we remember their vision, remember us with the blessings of life.

O God of life, may we merit inscription in Your Book of Life.

Havdalah Spice Box
Undetermined origin
Mid-19th c.

Prayer is not an escape from duty. It is not a substitute for the deed. Prayer seeks the power to do wisely, to act generously, to live helpfully. It helps to reinforce the act rather than to replace it. . . . Our prayers are answered, not when we are given what we ask, but when we are challenged to be what we can be *(Rabbi Morris Adler, 1906-1966).*

Reader

אַתָּה גִבּוֹר לְעוֹלָם, אֲדֹנָי, מְחַיֵּה הַכֹּל אַתָּה, רַב
לְהוֹשִׁיעַ.
מְכַלְכֵּל חַיִּים בְּחֶסֶד, מְחַיֵּה הַכֹּל בְּרַחֲמִים רַבִּים.
סוֹמֵךְ נוֹפְלִים, וְרוֹפֵא חוֹלִים, וּמַתִּיר אֲסוּרִים,
וּמְקַיֵּם אֱמוּנָתוֹ לִישֵׁנֵי עָפָר.
מִי כָמוֹךָ, בַּעַל גְּבוּרוֹת, וּמִי דוֹמֶה לָּךְ, מֶלֶךְ מֵמִית
וּמְחַיֵּה וּמַצְמִיחַ יְשׁוּעָה? מִי כָמוֹךָ אַב הָרַחֲמִים,
זוֹכֵר יְצוּרָיו לְחַיִּים בְּרַחֲמִים? וְנֶאֱמָן אַתָּה לְהַחֲיוֹת
הַכֹּל. בָּרוּךְ אַתָּה, יְיָ, מְחַיֵּה הַכֹּל.

O God, the power of Your spirit sustains all creation. When we open our hearts to You, we are filled with the strength to bear the afflictions of our kind and to refuse them victory.

Congregation

May we be among those who lift up the fallen, who set free the captive, who bring healing to the sick and help to those in need. And when we must walk in the valley of the shadows, may Your light and love dispel our terror of the darkness. Be praised, O God, for the gift of life.

All are seated; ark is closed

(For comment, see p. 56)

Havdalah Spice Box
Austrian
19th c.

U-ne-ta-ne to-kef, "We proclaim...," conveys the spiritual drama of the ten-day period from Rosh Hashanah to Yom Kippur as a time for the judgment of each person's moral integrity and deeds. Each passes before God. Each is judged. Yet from Rosh Hashanah to Yom Kippur, each person can repent, find forgiveness, and embrace life with new opportunities for generosity, goodness, justice and love. This prayer, attributed to Kalonymos ben Meshullam of Mayence, Germany (1100 C.E.), recalls the emphasis of Jewish theology that "the moral quality of our life is determined by the extent to which we believe that the seal of our own hand is set to the record of our deeds" (Max Arzt, *Justice and Mercy, p. 169).*

Cantor and Choir

וּנְתַנֶּה תְּקֶף קְדֻשַׁת הַיּוֹם כִּי הוּא נוֹרָא וְאָים. וּבוֹ
תִנָּשֵׂא מַלְכוּתֶךָ וְיִכּוֹן בְּחֶסֶד כִּסְאֶךָ וְתֵשֵׁב עָלָיו
בֶּאֱמֶת.

Reader

We proclaim the sacred power of this day, for it is awesome and full of dread. Today, O God, Your rule is exalted. Your glory is celebrated. You are our Judge, our Conscience. You know our dreams and disappointments. We are an open book before You.

Congregation

You remember all that we have forgotten, and today You measure our deeds as the unique signature of our lives.

Choir

וּבְשׁוֹפָר גָּדוֹל יִתָּקַע, וְקוֹל דְּמָמָה דַקָּה יִשָּׁמַע,
וּמַלְאָכִים יֵחָפֵזוּן וְחִיל וּרְעָדָה יֹאחֵזוּן וְיֹאמְרוּ: הִנֵּה
יוֹם הַדִּין.

Reader

The great Shofar will sound, and a still small voice will declare: "This is the Day of Judgment."

Congregation

Today we pass before You as the flock passes before the shepherd.

Wine Cup
Germany
Late 19th c.

Life and death are twins that dwell together; they cling to each other and cannot be separated. They are joined by the two extremes of a frail bridge over which all created beings travel. Life is the entrance; death is the exit. Life builds; death demolishes. Life sows; death reaps. Life plants, and death uproots. Know that yesterday shall never come back; nor should you say: "I shall do it tomorrow." Hasten to do your task every day, for death may at any time send forth its arrow-like lightning (Bahya ibn Pekuda, 11th century, Spain).

Reader

Judge us with mercy as we come before You.

Cantor and Choir

בְּרֹאשׁ הַשָּׁנָה יִכָּתֵבוּן וּבְיוֹם צוֹם כִּפּוּר יֵחָתֵמוּן.
כַּמָּה יַעַבְרוּן וְכַמָּה יִבָּרֵאוּן, מִי יִחְיֶה וּמִי יָמוּת,
מִי יָנוּחַ וּמִי יָנוּעַ, מִי יַשְׁקִיט וּמִי יִטָּרֵף, מִי יַעֲנִי
וּמִי יַעֲשִׁיר, מִי יִשָּׁפֵל וּמִי יָרוּם.
וּתְשׁוּבָה וּתְפִלָּה וּצְדָקָה
מַעֲבִירִין אֶת־רֹעַ הַגְּזֵרָה.

Reader

On Rosh Hashanah our destiny is written; at the end of Yom Kippur it is sealed:
How many will be born? How many will pass away? Who will live? Who will
die? Who will rest? Who will wander? Who will know peace? Who will be
troubled? Who will be needy? Who will be content? Who will be humbled?
Who will be exalted?

Congregation

May our repentance, prayer, and charity influence the ultimate decree.

Reader

For we are but dust, fragile vessels, easily broken.

Congregation

We are passing shadows, fleeting clouds, vanishing dreams.

Reader

וְאַתָּה הוּא מֶלֶךְ אֵל חַי וְקַיָּם!

But You, O God, are the Eternal One of all time and space.

All rise; ark is opened

Reader

We sanctify Your Name on earth, even as the heavens declare Your glory. Filled with awe before the wonder of life, we sing Your praise with words of the prophet:

All sing

Ka-dosh, ka-dosh, ka-dosh, A-do-nai
tse-va-ot, me-lo chol ha-a-rets ke-vo-do.

קָדוֹשׁ, קָדוֹשׁ, קָדוֹשׁ
יְיָ צְבָאוֹת,
מְלֹא כָל־הָאָרֶץ כְּבוֹדוֹ.

Holy, holy, holy is the Lord of hosts; the whole earth is filled with God's glory.

Cantor

אַדִּיר אַדִּירֵנוּ, יְיָ אֲדֹנֵינוּ, מָה־אַדִּיר שִׁמְךָ בְּכָל־הָאָרֶץ!

Source of our strength, Lord our God, how majestic is Your presence in all the earth! Blessed is the glory of God in heaven and earth.

All sing

Ba-ruch ke-vod A-do-nai mi-me-ko-mo.

בָּרוּךְ כְּבוֹד־יְיָ מִמְּקוֹמוֹ.

Cantor

אֶחָד הוּא אֱלֹהֵינוּ, הוּא אָבִינוּ, הוּא מַלְכֵּנוּ, הוּא מוֹשִׁיעֵנוּ;
וְהוּא יַשְׁמִיעֵנוּ בְּרַחֲמָיו לְעֵינֵי כָל־חָי:

God alone is our Creator, our Ruler, our Helper; and God is revealed in works of love in the sight of all the living. The Lord will reign forever; your God, O Zion, from generation to generation. Halleluyah.

All Sing

Yim-loch A-do-nai le-o-lam, E-lo-ha-yich
Tsi-yon, le-dor va-dor. Ha-le-lu-yah!

יִמְלֹךְ יְיָ לְעוֹלָם,
אֱלֹהַיִךְ צִיּוֹן,
לְדֹר וָדֹר. הַלְלוּיָהּ!

Reader

לְדוֹר וָדוֹר נַגִּיד גָּדְלֶךָ, וּלְנֵצַח נְצָחִים קְדֻשָּׁתְךָ נַקְדִּישׁ.
וְשִׁבְחֲךָ, אֱלֹהֵינוּ, מִפִּינוּ לֹא יָמוּשׁ לְעוֹלָם וָעֶד.
בָּרוּךְ אַתָּה, יְיָ, הָאֵל הַקָּדוֹשׁ.

To all generations we will make known Your greatness, and to all eternity
proclaim Your holiness. Your praise shall never depart from our lips. We praise
You, the God of holiness.

Ark is closed; all are seated

The *Kedushah* prayer is based upon the mystic experience of the prophet Isaiah. We
are told that while standing in the Jerusalem Temple, God summoned him to bring
a message of justice, truth, and mercy to the people of Israel. He responded:
"I am ready, send me" *(Isaiah 6:1-8)*.

93

SZL
DE

Reader

וּבְכֵן תֵּן פַּחְדְּךָ, יְיָ אֱלֹהֵינוּ, עַל כָּל־מַעֲשֶׂיךָ, וְאֵימָתְךָ
עַל כָּל־מַה־שֶּׁבָּרָאתָ. וְיֵעָשׂוּ כֻלָּם אֲגֻדָּה אֶחָת
לַעֲשׂוֹת רְצוֹנְךָ בְּלֵבָב שָׁלֵם, כְּמוֹ שֶׁיָּדַעְנוּ, יְיָ אֱלֹהֵינוּ,
שֶׁהַשָּׁלְטוֹן לְפָנֶיךָ, עֹז בְּיָדְךָ וּגְבוּרָה בִּימִינֶךָ, וְשִׁמְךָ
נוֹרָא עַל כָּל־מַה־שֶּׁבָּרָאתָ.

Now, O God, fill our hearts with reverence for all the wonders of Your creation. Unite us to fashion the time when fear and despair will be banished from every human heart.

Congregation

Now, O God, fill us with honor for those who support the hopes of the fallen with gentle, generous hands. May we be counted among them.

Reader

Now, O God, hasten the day when the just will see and rejoice that cruelty and selfishness have vanished like smoke, that arrogance and greed are banished from earth.

הָאֵל הַקָּדוֹשׁ נִקְדַּשׁ בִּצְדָקָה. בָּרוּךְ אַתָּה, יְיָ,
הַמֶּלֶךְ הַקָּדוֹשׁ

Be praised, O God, exalted in holiness, sanctified by righteousness.

Kedushat Ha-yom, or "Sanctification of the Day," is a prayer included in all holy day services. Composed during the 7th century C.E., it expresses the faith that every *mitzvah,* every kind deed, just action, and meaningful celebration of life is regarded by God and brings blessing to humanity.

Reader

אֱלֹהֵינוּ וֵאלֹהֵי אֲבוֹתֵינוּ, יַעֲלֶה וְיָבֹא וְיִזָּכֵר זִכְרוֹנֵנוּ
וְזִכְרוֹן כָּל־עַמְּךָ בֵּית יִשְׂרָאֵל לְפָנֶיךָ, לְטוֹבָה לְחֵן
לְחֶסֶד וּלְרַחֲמִים, לְחַיִּים וּלְשָׁלוֹם בְּיוֹם הַזִּכָּרוֹן הַזֶּה.

God of all ages, answer the prayers of Your people, Israel, on this Day of Remembrance. Strengthen our powers for kindness and caring, for compassion and love, for life and peace.

Reader

זָכְרֵנוּ, יְיָ אֱלֹהֵינוּ, בּוֹ לְטוֹבָה.

Congregation

This day, remember us for goodness.

Choir

Amen.

Reader

וּפָקְדֵנוּ בוֹ לִבְרָכָה.

Congregation

This day, mark us for blessing.

Choir

Amen.

Reader

וְהוֹשִׁיעֵנוּ בוֹ לְחַיִּים.

Congregation

This day, preserve us for life.

Choir

Amen.

Congregation

We give thanks that You have called us to Your service and sanctified us with Your mitzvot. Teach us to be satisfied with the gifts of Your goodness. Purify our hearts that we may serve You in truth. Let this (**Sabbath and**) Day of Remembrance bring renewal of purpose and peace to the people of Israel. Be praised, O God, who sanctifies (**the Sabbath,**) Israel, and this Day of Remembrance.

אֱלֹהֵינוּ וֵאלֹהֵי אֲבוֹתֵינוּ, (רְצֵה בִמְנוּחָתֵנוּ,) קַדְּשֵׁנוּ בְּמִצְוֹתֶיךָ וְתֵן חֶלְקֵנוּ בְּתוֹרָתֶךָ. שַׂבְּעֵנוּ מִטּוּבֶךָ, וְשַׂמְּחֵנוּ בִּישׁוּעָתֶךָ, (וְהַנְחִילֵנוּ, יְיָ אֱלֹהֵינוּ, בְּאַהֲבָה וּבְרָצוֹן שַׁבַּת קָדְשֶׁךָ, וְיָנוּחוּ בָה יִשְׂרָאֵל, מְקַדְּשֵׁי שְׁמֶךָ,) וְטַהֵר לִבֵּנוּ לְעָבְדְּךָ בֶּאֱמֶת, כִּי אַתָּה אֱלֹהִים אֱמֶת, וּדְבָרְךָ אֱמֶת וְקַיָּם לָעַד. בָּרוּךְ אַתָּה, יְיָ, מֶלֶךְ עַל כָּל־הָאָרֶץ, מְקַדֵּשׁ (הַשַּׁבָּת וְ) יִשְׂרָאֵל וְיוֹם הַזִּכָּרוֹן.

"We give thanks…" is the second prayer of the *Kedushat Ha-yom*. Also composed during the 7th century C.E., its theme of "sanctity" is drawn from the Hebrew, *kadosh*, meaning "holy," "separate," or "unique." Rabbi Solomon Schecter (1848-1915) comments that "the holiness of Israel is dependent on their acting in such a way as to become God-like" (*Aspects of Rabbinic Theology*, p. 202).

(When Rosh Hashanah falls on Sabbath)

All sing

Yis-me-chu be-ma-le-chu-te-cha
Sho-me-rei, sho-me-rei, sho-me-rei
Sha-bat ve-ko-re-ei o-neg Sha-bat.
(repeat)

יִשְׂמְחוּ בְמַלְכוּתְךָ שׁוֹמְרֵי שַׁבָּת
וְקוֹרְאֵי עֹנֶג.

Am me-ka-de-shei she-vi-i
Me-ka-de-shei she-vi-i
Ku-lam yis-be-u ve-yit-an-gu
Mi-tu-ve-cha.
(refrain)

עַם מְקַדְּשֵׁי שְׁבִיעִי
כֻּלָּם יִשְׂבְּעוּ וְיִתְעַנְּגוּ מִטּוּבֶךָ.

Ve-ha-she-vi-i ra-tsi-ta bo ve-ki-dash-to,
Chem-dat ya-mim o-to ka-ra-ta,
Zei-cher le-ma-a-sei ve-rei-sheet.
(refrain)

וְהַשְּׁבִיעִי רָצִיתָ בּוֹ וְקִדַּשְׁתּוֹ.
חֶמְדַּת יָמִים אוֹתוֹ קָרָאתָ, זֵכֶר
לְמַעֲשֵׂה בְרֵאשִׁית.

They who keep the Sabbath and call it a delight shall rejoice in Your dominion.
All who hallow the seventh day shall be gladdened by Your goodness. This day
is Israel's festival of the spirit, sanctified and blessed by You, the most precious
of days, a symbol of the joy of creation.

Yis-me-chu, which celebrates the joy of the Sabbath, is the poetic work of David
Abudraham, 14th century Spain. Jewish tradition teaches that "The Sabbath was
given for the study of the Torah"; that "it was given for pleasure"; that it was given
"as a sign between God and the children of Israel"; that "more than the Jews have
kept the Sabbath; the Sabbath has preserved the Jewish people" *(Pesikta Rabbati 22,
Exodus 31:17,* and Ahad Ha-am, 1856-1927).

Reader

רְצֵה, יְיָ אֱלֹהֵינוּ, בְּעַמְּךָ יִשְׂרָאֵל, וּתְפִלָּתָם בְּאַהֲבָה
תְקַבֵּל, וּתְהִי לְרָצוֹן תָּמִיד עֲבוֹדַת יִשְׂרָאֵל עַמֶּךָ.
בָּרוּךְ אַתָּה, יְיָ, שֶׁאוֹתְךָ לְבַדְּךָ בְּיִרְאָה נַעֲבוֹד.

May we, Your people Israel, be worthy in our deeds and our prayer. Wherever we live, wherever we seek You—in this land, in Zion restored, in all lands—You are our God, whom alone we serve in reverence.

HODA-AH—WE GIVE THANKS

Congregation

We give thanks for the gift of life, wonder beyond words; the awareness of soul, our light within; the world around us, so filled with beauty; and the richness of the earth, which day by day sustains us. For all these gifts and more, we thank and bless You, the Source of all goodness.

מוֹדִים אֲנַחְנוּ לָךְ, שָׁאַתָּה הוּא יְיָ אֱלֹהֵינוּ וֵאלֹהֵי אֲבוֹתֵינוּ
לְעוֹלָם וָעֶד. צוּר חַיֵּינוּ, מָגֵן יִשְׁעֵנוּ, אַתָּה הוּא לְדוֹר וָדוֹר.
וְכֹל הַחַיִּים יוֹדוּךָ סֶּלָה, וִיהַלְלוּ אֶת שִׁמְךָ בָּאֱמֶת, הָאֵל
יְשׁוּעָתֵנוּ וְעֶזְרָתֵנוּ סֶלָה. בָּרוּךְ אַתָּה, יְיָ, הַטּוֹב שִׁמְךָ וּלְךָ נָאֶה
לְהוֹדוֹת.

(For comment, see p. 62)

Reader

שִׂים שָׁלוֹם, טוֹבָה וּבְרָכָה, חֵן וָחֶסֶד וְרַחֲמִים, עָלֵינוּ
וְעַל כָּל־יִשְׂרָאֵל עַמֶּךָ. בָּרְכֵנוּ אָבִינוּ, כֻּלָּנוּ כְּאֶחָד,
בְּאוֹר פָּנֶיךָ, כִּי בְאוֹר פָּנֶיךָ נָתַתָּ לָּנוּ, יְיָ אֱלֹהֵינוּ,
תּוֹרַת חַיִּים, וְאַהֲבַת חֶסֶד, וּצְדָקָה וּבְרָכָה וְרַחֲמִים,
וְחַיִּים וְשָׁלוֹם. וְטוֹב בְּעֵינֶיךָ לְבָרֵךְ אֶת־עַמְּךָ יִשְׂרָאֵל
בְּכָל־עֵת וּבְכָל־שָׁעָה בִּשְׁלוֹמֶךָ.

Grant us peace, Your most precious gift, O Eternal source of peace, and enable
Israel to be its messenger unto the peoples of the earth. Bless our country that it
may ever be a stronghold of peace, and its advocate in the council of nations.
May contentment reign within its borders, health and happiness within its
homes. Strengthen the bonds of friendship among the inhabitants of all lands.
Plant virtue in every soul, and may the love of Your name hallow every home
and every heart.

Cantor and Choir

בְּסֵפֶר חַיִּים בְּרָכָה וְשָׁלוֹם וּפַרְנָסָה טוֹבָה נִזָּכֵר
וְנִכָּתֵב לְפָנֶיךָ, אֲנַחְנוּ וְכָל־עַמְּךָ בֵּית יִשְׂרָאֵל,
לְחַיִּים טוֹבִים וּלְשָׁלוֹם. בָּרוּךְ אַתָּה, יְיָ, עוֹשֵׂה הַשָּׁלוֹם.

May we, and all Israel, be inscribed in the Book of Life for blessing, sustenance
and peace. Be praised, O God, Giver of peace.

(For comment, see p. 63)

Havdalah Spice Box
Eastern Europe
19th c.

"How can I love…" is from Ruth F. Brin, *Harvest: Collected Poems and Prayers*, *p. 141*. "May the words…" is taken from *Psalms 19*.

How can I love You, who are so far away?
How can I know You, whose face I have not seen?
How can I approach You, when I am laden with guilt?

I can love some of Your creatures, and so love something
　　of You.
I can know some of Your world, and so know something
　　of You.
I can approach You with repentance and prayer and
　　righteous deeds,
But I can do none of these, my God, without Your help.

Help me to love You and know You and pray to You
That this my existence may become a life,
A life that like a leaf in the afternoon sun
Reflects Your great and golden light.

All sing

יִהְיוּ לְרָצוֹן אִמְרֵי־פִי וְהֶגְיוֹן לִבִּי לְפָנֶיךָ, יְיָ, צוּרִי
וְגוֹאֲלִי.

Yi-he-yu le-ra-tzon im-rei-fi, ve-heg-yon li-bi le-fa-ne-cha,
A-do-nai, tzu-ri ve-go-a-li.

May the words of my mouth, and the meditations of my heart, be acceptable to
You, my Rock and my Redeemer.

Congregation rises as ark is opened

Congregation

אָבִינוּ מַלְכֵּנוּ, שְׁמַע קוֹלֵנוּ.

Avinu Malkeinu, she-ma ko-lei-nu.
Avinu Malkeinu, hear our prayer.

אָבִינוּ מַלְכֵּנוּ, חַדֵּשׁ עָלֵינוּ שָׁנָה טוֹבָה.

Avinu Malkeinu, cha-desh a-lei-nu sha-nah to-vah.
Avinu Malkeinu, grant us a New Year of goodness.

אָבִינוּ מַלְכֵּנוּ, חֲמוֹל עָלֵינוּ וְעַל עוֹלָלֵינוּ וְטַפֵּנוּ.

Avinu Malkeinu, cha-mol a-lei-nu ve-al o-la-lei-nu ve-ta-pei-nu.
Avinu Malkeinu, have mercy upon us and upon our children.

אָבִינוּ מַלְכֵּנוּ, כַּלֵּה דֶּבֶר וְחֶרֶב וְרָעָב מֵעָלֵינוּ.

Avinu Malkeinu, ka-lei de-ver, ve-che-rev, ve-ra-av mei-a-lei-nu.
Avinu Malkeinu, rid us of pestilence, war and famine.

אָבִינוּ מַלְכֵּנוּ, כַּלֵּה כָּל־צַר וּמַשְׂטִין מֵעָלֵינוּ.

Avinu Malkeinu, ka-lei kol tsar u-mas-tin mei-a-lei-nu.
Avinu Malkeinu, rid us of all hatred and oppression.

אָבִינוּ מַלְכֵּנוּ, כָּתְבֵנוּ בְּסֵפֶר חַיִּים טוֹבִים.

Avinu Malkeinu, kot-vei-nu be-sei-fer cha-yim to-vim.
Avinu Malkeinu, inscribe us for blessing in the Book of Life.

אָבִֽינוּ מַלְכֵּֽנוּ, מַלֵּא יָדֵֽינוּ מִבִּרְכוֹתֶֽיךָ.

Avinu Malkeinu, ma-lei ya-dei-nu mi-bir-cho-te-cha.
Avinu Malkenu, fill our hands with generous deeds.

אָבִֽינוּ מַלְכֵּֽנוּ, חַדֵּשׁ עָלֵֽינוּ שָׁנָה טוֹבָה.

Avinu Malkeinu, cha-desh a-lei-nu sha-nah to-vah
Avinu Malkeinu, grant us a New Year of goodness.

אָבִֽינוּ מַלְכֵּֽנוּ, חָנֵּֽנוּ וַעֲנֵֽנוּ, כִּי אֵין בָּֽנוּ מַעֲשִׂים, עֲשֵׂה
עִמָּֽנוּ צְדָקָה וָחֶֽסֶד וְהוֹשִׁיעֵֽנוּ.

Avinu Malkeinu, cho-nei-nu va-a-nei-nu, ki ein ba-nu ma-a-sim,
a-sei i-ma-nu tse-da-kah va-che-sed, ve-ho-shi-ei-nu.
Avinu Malkeinu, be gracious and answer us. Treat us generously and with
kindness, and help us.

All sing

Avinu Malkeinu,
cho-nei-nu va-a-nei-nu (2)
ki ein ba-nu ma-a-sim

A-sei i-ma-nu tse-da-kah va-che-sed (2)
ve-ho-shi-ei-nu.

Avinu Malkeinu,
cho-nei-nu va-a-nei-nu (2)
ki ein ba-nu ma-a-sim.

אָבִֽינוּ מַלְכֵּֽנוּ, חָנֵּֽנוּ וַעֲנֵֽנוּ,
כִּי אֵין בָּֽנוּ מַעֲשִׂים, עֲשֵׂה
עִמָּֽנוּ צְדָקָה וָחֶֽסֶד וְהוֹשִׁיעֵֽנוּ.

(For comment, see p. 66)

Torah Crown
United States
20th c.

Some scholars date the public reading of Torah as early as Ezra, 420 B.C.E. *(Nehemiah 8),* which forms the selected Haftarah for this Rosh Hashanah service. Others believe that the practice originated in the early synagogue, 320 B.C.E. The Torah is divided into a yearly cycle of weekly readings. Each *parashah,* "weekly portion" is read and studied on Mondays, Thursdays and Shabbat. Every holy day also has its assigned Torah portion. Reading Torah is the heart of Jewish worship. "None compares…" is from *Psalms 86:8.* "The Lord, the Lord…" is from *Exodus 34:6-7.*

Reader

אֵין כָּמְוֹךָ בָאֱלֹהִים, יְיָ, וְאֵין כְּמַעֲשֶׂיךָ. מַלְכוּתְךָ
מַלְכוּת כָּל־עוֹלָמִים וּמֶמְשַׁלְתְּךָ בְּכָל־דּוֹר וָדֹר.

None compares to You, O God, and nothing equals the mystery and majesty of Your works.

Congregation

Before You we stand in awe.

Reader

Turn now toward us, O God, as we turn toward You.

Cantor and Choir

יְיָ, יְיָ אֵל רַחוּם וְחַנּוּן, אֶרֶךְ אַפַּיִם וְרַב־חֶסֶד וֶאֱמֶת,
נֹצֵר חֶסֶד לָאֲלָפִים, נֹשֵׂא עָוֹן וָפֶשַׁע וְחַטָּאָה וְנַקֵּה.

The Lord, the Lord God, is merciful and gracious, endlessly patient, loving, and true, showing mercy to thousands, forgiving iniquity, transgression, and sin, and granting pardon.

אE אE - שׁלום

Torah is taken from ark

Reader

הָבוּ גְדֶל לֵאלֹהֵינוּ וּתְנוּ כָבוֹד לַתּוֹרָה.

Let us declare the greatness of our God and give honor to the Torah.

All sing

כִּי מִצִּיּוֹן תֵּצֵא תוֹרָה, וּדְבַר־יְיָ מִירוּשָׁלָיִם.

Ki mi-tsi-yon tei-tsei To-rah (2)
u-de-var A-do-nai mi-ru-sha-la-yim.

Torah will come from Zion, the word of God from Jerusalem.

בָּרוּךְ שֶׁנָּתַן תּוֹרָה לְעַמּוֹ יִשְׂרָאֵל בִּקְדֻשָּׁתוֹ.

Ba-ruch she-na-tan To-rah, To-rah (2)
Le-a-mo Yis-ra-eil bi-ke-du-sha-to.

Praised be the One, who has given the Torah to Israel.

שְׁמַע יִשְׂרָאֵל: יְיָ אֱלֹהֵינוּ, יְיָ אֶחָד!

She-ma Yis-ra-eil: A-do-nai E-lo-hei-nu
A-do-nai E-chad!

Hear, O Israel: the Lord is our God, the Lord is One!

Reader

בֵּית יַעֲקֹב: לְכוּ, וְנֵלְכָה בְּאוֹר יְיָ.

O house of Jacob, let us walk in the light of our God.

All sing as Torah is carried through the congregation

Le-cha a-do-nai, ha-ge-du-la
ve-ha-ge-vu-ra ve-ha-tif-e-ret,
ve-ha-nei-tsach, ve-ha-hod,
ki chol ba-sha-ma-yim u-va-a-retz, (2)
le-cha, A-do-nai, ha-mam-la-cha
ve-ha-mit-na-sei le-chol le-rosh.

לְךָ, יְיָ, הַגְּדֻלָּה וְהַגְּבוּרָה
וְהַתִּפְאֶרֶת וְהַנֵּצַח וְהַהוֹד, כִּי
כֹל בַּשָּׁמַיִם וּבָאָרֶץ, לְךָ יְיָ
הַמַּמְלָכָה וְהַמִּתְנַשֵּׂא לְכֹל
לְרֹאשׁ.

Yours, Lord, is the greatness, the power, the glory, the victory, and the majesty;
for all that is in heaven and earth is Yours. Yours is the dominion, O Lord; You
are supreme over all.

Ro-me-mu A-do-nai, ro-me-mu (2)
Ro-me-mu A-do-nai Elo-hei-nu
A-do-nai Elo-hei-nu, ro-me-mu.
(repeat)

רוֹמְמוּ יְיָ אֱלֹהֵינוּ,

Ve-hish-ta-cha-vu, le-har kod-sho, (4)

וְהִשְׁתַּחֲווּ לְהַר קָדְשׁוֹ,

A-do-nai Elo-hei-nu, ro-me-mu.

יְיָ אֱלֹהֵינוּ.

Exalt and worship our God; bow down at God's holy mountain.

"Let us declare…" is from *Psalms 34:4;* "Torah will come from Zion…" is from
Isaiah 2:3. The *hakafah,* or "processional walk with the Torah," dates to the early
synagogue and dramatizes that the Torah is not the exclusive possession of a special
"priest" class of the Jewish people but belongs to the entire Jewish community.
Le-cha… is from *I Chronicles 29:11. Ro-me-mu…* is from *Psalms 99:5, 9.*

Mizrach 39.16
(An art piece hung on Eastern wall facing Jerusalem)
Subject: Binding of Isaac
Europe 19th c.
John R. Forsman, Photographer
From the Collection of the Hebrew Union College
Skirball Museum

The blessings before and after the reading of Torah date from the 1st century B.C.E. They state the belief that the people of Israel has been "chosen" for the privilege of receiving the Torah, and that loyalty to its study and values assures the Jewish people's survival.

Ark is closed; all are seated as the Torah is prepared for reading.

READING OF TORAH

Reader

The Torah portion we read on this Rosh Hashanah morning tells the story of a parent's call to sacrifice a child. Abraham's faith is tested by God, and some would say God is tested by Abraham. Taking his only and beloved son, Isaac, he climbs Mt. Moriah. Believing that the God of Israel rejects human sacrifice, Abraham puts his faith to the test. As he raises his arm to plunge the knife into Isaac's flesh, a voice calls out: "Do not raise your hand against the boy, for now I know that you fear God...." In Isaac's place a ram is offered, and to this day the Shofar sounds recall the test and ask: Is our faith strong enough to guarantee the survival of our children and our children's children?

Blessings before the reading

Ba-re-chu et A-do-nai ha-me-vo-rach!   בָּרְכוּ אֶת יְיָ הַמְבֹרָךְ!
Ba-ruch A-do-nai ha-me-vo-rach
le-o-lam va-ed.   בָּרוּךְ יְיָ הַמְבֹרָךְ לְעוֹלָם וָעֶד!

Ba-ruch a-ta, A-do-nai E-lo-hei-nu, me-lech   בָּרוּךְ אַתָּה, יְיָ אֱלֹהֵינוּ, מֶלֶךְ
ha-o-lam, a-sher ba-char ba-nu mi-kol   הָעוֹלָם, אֲשֶׁר בָּחַר־בָּנוּ מִכָּל־
ha-a-mim, ve-na-tan la-nu et To-ra-to.   הָעַמִּים וְנָתַן־לָנוּ אֶת־תּוֹרָתוֹ.
Ba-ruch a-ta A-do-nai, no-tein ha-To-rah.   בָּרוּךְ אַתָּה, יְיָ, נוֹתֵן הַתּוֹרָה.

Praise the Lord, to whom our praise is due! Praised be the Lord, to whom our praise is due, now and forever! Blessed is the Lord our God, Ruler of the universe, who has chosen us from all peoples by giving us the Torah. Be praised, O God, Giver of the Torah.

"Binding of Isaac," Manuscript 5.23
Amsterdam 1602 woodcut
Marvin Rand, Photographer
From the Collection of the Hebrew Union College
Skirball Museum

Jewish tradition records that *Genesis 21* is to be read on the first day of Rosh Hashanah, and *Genesis 22* on the second day. Most Reform Jewish congregations celebrate one Rosh Hashanah day, as prescribed by Torah *(Leviticus 23:23-25),* and read *Genesis 22* or the *Akeda,* "Abraham's test." The tale of God's trial of Abraham's faith symbolizes the testing of each person's life against the question: will our deeds match the values, ethics, beliefs we piously proclaim? The mention of the ram at the conclusion of the Biblical story signals the celebration that Abraham has passed his test of faith, and foreshadows the blowing of the ram's horn, or Shofar, which follows the Torah service.

The *Akeda,* Abraham's test:

Genesis 22:1-19

וַיְהִי אַחַר הַדְּבָרִים הָאֵלֶּה וְהָאֱלֹהִים נִסָּה אֶת־אַבְרָהָם וַיֹּאמֶר
אֵלָיו אַבְרָהָם וַיֹּאמֶר הִנֵּנִי: וַיֹּאמֶר קַח־נָא אֶת־בִּנְךָ אֶת־
יְחִידְךָ אֲשֶׁר־אָהַבְתָּ אֶת־יִצְחָק וְלֶךְ־לְךָ אֶל־אֶרֶץ הַמֹּרִיָּה
וְהַעֲלֵהוּ שָׁם לְעֹלָה עַל אַחַד הֶהָרִים אֲשֶׁר אֹמַר אֵלֶיךָ: וַיַּשְׁכֵּם
אַבְרָהָם בַּבֹּקֶר וַיַּחֲבֹשׁ אֶת־חֲמֹרוֹ וַיִּקַּח אֶת־שְׁנֵי נְעָרָיו אִתּוֹ
וְאֵת יִצְחָק בְּנוֹ וַיְבַקַּע עֲצֵי עֹלָה וַיָּקָם וַיֵּלֶךְ אֶל־הַמָּקוֹם אֲשֶׁר־
אָמַר־לוֹ הָאֱלֹהִים: בַּיּוֹם הַשְּׁלִישִׁי וַיִּשָּׂא אַבְרָהָם אֶת־עֵינָיו
וַיַּרְא אֶת־הַמָּקוֹם מֵרָחֹק: וַיֹּאמֶר אַבְרָהָם אֶל־נְעָרָיו שְׁבוּ־לָכֶם
פֹּה עִם־הַחֲמוֹר וַאֲנִי וְהַנַּעַר נֵלְכָה עַד־כֹּה וְנִשְׁתַּחֲוֶה וְנָשׁוּבָה
אֲלֵיכֶם:

Some time afterward, God put Abraham to the test. God said to him, "Abraham,"
and he answered, "Here I am." And God said, "Take your son, your favored one,
Isaac, whom you love, and go to the land of Moriah, and offer him there as a
burnt offering on one of the heights that I will point out to you." So early next
morning, Abraham saddled his ass and took with him two of his servants and
his son Isaac. He split the wood for the burnt offering, and he set out for the place
of which God had told him. On the third day Abraham looked up and saw the
place from afar. Then Abraham said to his servants, "You stay here with the ass.
The boy and I will go up there; we will worship and we will return to you."

וַיִּקַּח אַבְרָהָם אֶת־עֲצֵי הָעֹלָה וַיָּשֶׂם עַל־יִצְחָק בְּנוֹ
וַיִּקַּח בְּיָדוֹ אֶת־הָאֵשׁ וְאֶת־הַמַּאֲכֶלֶת וַיֵּלְכוּ שְׁנֵיהֶם יַחְדָּו:
וַיֹּאמֶר יִצְחָק אֶל־אַבְרָהָם אָבִיו וַיֹּאמֶר אָבִי וַיֹּאמֶר הִנֶּנִּי בְנִי
וַיֹּאמֶר הִנֵּה הָאֵשׁ וְהָעֵצִים וְאַיֵּה הַשֶּׂה לְעֹלָה: וַיֹּאמֶר אַבְרָהָם
אֱלֹהִים יִרְאֶה־לּוֹ הַשֶּׂה לְעֹלָה בְּנִי וַיֵּלְכוּ שְׁנֵיהֶם יַחְדָּו:

Abraham took the wood for the burnt offering and put it on his son Isaac. He himself took the firestone and the knife; and the two walked off together. Then Isaac said to his father Abraham, "Father!" And he answered, "Yes, my son." And he said, "Here are the firestone and the wood; but where is the sheep for the burnt offering?" And Abraham said, "God will see to the sheep for the burnt offering, my son." And the two of them walked on together.

וַיָּבֹ֗אוּ אֶֽל־הַמָּקוֹם֮ אֲשֶׁ֣ר אָֽמַר־ל֣וֹ הָֽאֱלֹהִים֒ וַיִּ֨בֶן שָׁ֤ם אַבְרָהָם֙ אֶת־
הַמִּזְבֵּ֔חַ וַֽיַּעֲרֹ֖ךְ אֶת־הָֽעֵצִ֑ים וַֽיַּעֲקֹד֙ אֶת־יִצְחָ֣ק בְּנ֔וֹ וַיָּ֤שֶׂם אֹתוֹ֙
עַל־הַמִּזְבֵּ֔חַ מִמַּ֖עַל לָֽעֵצִֽים: וַיִּשְׁלַ֤ח אַבְרָהָם֙ אֶת־יָד֔וֹ וַיִּקַּ֖ח אֶת־הַֽמַּֽאֲכֶ֑לֶת
לִשְׁחֹ֖ט אֶת־בְּנֽוֹ: וַיִּקְרָ֨א אֵלָ֜יו מַלְאַ֤ךְ יְהוָֹה֙ מִן־הַשָּׁמַ֔יִם וַיֹּ֖אמֶר
אַבְרָהָ֣ם ׀ אַבְרָהָ֑ם וַיֹּ֖אמֶר הִנֵּֽנִי: וַיֹּ֗אמֶר אַל־תִּשְׁלַ֤ח יָֽדְךָ֙ אֶל־הַנַּ֔עַר
וְאַל־תַּ֥עַשׂ ל֖וֹ מְא֑וּמָה כִּ֣י ׀ עַתָּ֣ה יָדַ֗עְתִּי כִּֽי־יְרֵ֤א אֱלֹהִים֙ אַ֔תָּה וְלֹ֥א חָשַׂ֛כְתָּ
אֶת־בִּנְךָ֥ אֶת־יְחִֽידְךָ֖ מִמֶּֽנִּי: וַיִּשָּׂ֨א אַבְרָהָ֜ם אֶת־עֵינָ֗יו וַיַּרְא֙ וְהִנֵּה־אַ֔יִל אַחַ֕ר
נֶֽאֱחַ֥ז בַּסְּבַ֖ךְ בְּקַרְנָ֑יו וַיֵּ֣לֶךְ אַבְרָהָ֗ם וַיִּקַּ֤ח אֶת־הָאַ֨יִל֙ וַיַּֽעֲלֵ֣הוּ לְעֹלָ֔ה תַּ֖חַת
בְּנֽוֹ: וַיִּקְרָ֧א אַבְרָהָ֛ם שֵֽׁם־הַמָּק֥וֹם הַה֖וּא יְהוָֹ֣ה ׀ יִרְאֶ֑ה אֲשֶׁר֙ יֵֽאָמֵ֣ר
הַיּ֔וֹם בְּהַ֥ר יְהוָֹ֖ה יֵֽרָאֶֽה:

They arrived at the place of which God had told him. Abraham built an altar there; he laid out the wood; he bound his son Isaac; he laid him on the altar, on top of the wood. And Abraham picked up the knife to slay his son. Then an angel of the Lord called to him from heaven: "Abraham! Abraham!" And he answered, "Here I am." And he said, "Do not raise your hand against the boy, or do anything to him. For now I know that you fear God, since you have not withheld your son, your favored one, from Me." When Abraham looked up, his eye fell upon a ram, caught in the thicket by its horns. So Abraham went and took the ram and offered it up as a burnt offering in place of his son. And Abraham named that site Adonai-yireh, whence the present saying, "On the mount of the Lord there is vision."

Blessings after the reading of Torah

Ba-ruch a-ta, A-do-nai E-lo-hei-nu,
me-lech ha-o-lam, a-sher na-tan la-nu
To-rat e-met, ve-cha-yei o-lam na-ta
be-to-chei-nu. Ba-ruch a-ta, A-do-nai,
no-tein ha-To-rah.

בָּרוּךְ אַתָּה, יְיָ אֱלֹהֵינוּ, מֶלֶךְ
הָעוֹלָם, אֲשֶׁר נָתַן־לָנוּ תּוֹרַת אֱמֶת
וְחַיֵּי עוֹלָם נָטַע בְּתוֹכֵנוּ.
בָּרוּךְ אַתָּה, יְיָ, נוֹתֵן הַתּוֹרָה.

Blessed is the Lord our God, Ruler of the universe, who has given us the
Torah of truth, implanting within us eternal life. Be praised, O Lord, Giver
of the Torah.

HAGBAHAH—LIFTING THE TORAH

All rise and sing as the Torah is held high

Ve-zot ha-To-rah a-sher sam Mo-sheh
li-fe-nei be-nei Yis-ra-eil, al pi A-do-nai
be-yad Mo-sheh.

וְזֹאת הַתּוֹרָה אֲשֶׁר־שָׂם מֹשֶׁה
לִפְנֵי בְּנֵי יִשְׂרָאֵל, עַל־ פִּי יְיָ
בְּיַד־מֹשֶׁה.

This is the Torah that Moses placed before the people of Israel to fulfill the
word of God.

(All are seated as Torah is rolled and wrapped.)

"This is the Torah..." is from *Deuteronomy 44:44,* a statement made just before
Moses' retelling of the revelation of Torah at Mt. Sinai. The tradition of *hagbahah,*
or "lifting" the Torah, allows the congregation to share its contents just as the people
of Israel witnessed its revelation at Sinai. The custom of *gelilah* or "rolling up"
the scroll is regarded as a special honor.

Reader

Our Haftarah recalls the first Rosh Hashanah celebration after the return of Jewish exiles to Jerusalem from Babylonian exile in 420 B.C.E. Led by Ezra and Nehemiah, they gathered as we do now, to hear the wisdom of Torah and to renew their commitment to the covenant of their people.

Blessings before the reading

בָּרוּךְ אַתָּה, יְיָ אֱלֹהֵינוּ, מֶלֶךְ הָעוֹלָם, אֲשֶׁר בָּחַר
בִּנְבִיאִים טוֹבִים וְרָצָה בְדִבְרֵיהֶם הַנֶּאֱמָרִים בֶּאֱמֶת.
בָּרוּךְ אַתָּה, יְיָ, הַבּוֹחֵר בַּתּוֹרָה וּבְמֹשֶׁה עַבְדּוֹ
וּבְיִשְׂרָאֵל עַמּוֹ וּבִנְבִיאֵי הָאֱמֶת וָצֶדֶק.

Praised is the Lord our God, Ruler of the universe, who has chosen faithful prophets to speak words of truth. Praised is the Lord, for the revelation of Torah, for God's servant, Moses, and for our prophets of truth and righteousness.

Haftarah means "completion" and refers to selected readings drawn from the Prophets and recited after the Torah is read. By the 2nd Century C.E. the rabbis had designated Haftarah readings for each Sabbath and all holy days. The choice of the Haftarah portion was usually made because of its relationship to the theme of the Torah portion.

Nehemiah 8:1-3, 9-10

וַיִּגַּע הַחֹדֶשׁ הַשְּׁבִיעִי וּבְנֵי יִשְׂרָאֵל בְּעָרֵיהֶם: וַיֵּאָסְפוּ כָל־הָעָם
כְּאִישׁ אֶחָד אֶל־הָרְחוֹב אֲשֶׁר לִפְנֵי שַׁעַר־ הַמָּיִם
וַיֹּאמְרוּ לְעֶזְרָא הַסֹּפֵר לְהָבִיא אֶת־סֵפֶר תּוֹרַת מֹשֶׁה
אֲשֶׁר־צִוָּה יְהוָה אֶת־יִשְׂרָאֵל: וַיָּבִיא עֶזְרָא הַכֹּהֵן אֶת־הַתּוֹרָה
לִפְנֵי הַקָּהָל מֵאִישׁ וְעַד־אִשָּׁה וְכֹל מֵבִין לִשְׁמֹעַ בְּיוֹם
אֶחָד לַחֹדֶשׁ הַשְּׁבִיעִי: וַיִּקְרָא־בוֹ לִפְנֵי הָרְחוֹב אֲשֶׁר | לִפְנֵי
שַׁעַר־ הַמַּיִם מִן־הָאוֹר עַד־מַחֲצִית הַיּוֹם נֶגֶד הָאֲנָשִׁים
וְהַנָּשִׁים וְהַמְּבִינִים וְאָזְנֵי כָל־הָעָם אֶל־סֵפֶר הַתּוֹרָה:

When the seventh month arrived—the Israelites being settled in their towns—the entire people assembled as one person in the square before the Water Gate, and they asked Ezra the scribe to bring the scroll of the Torah of Moses with which the Lord had charged Israel. On the first day of the seventh month, Ezra the priest brought the Torah before the congregation, men and women and all who could listen with understanding. He read from it, facing the square before the Water Gate, from the first light until midday, to the men and the women and those who could understand; the ears of all the people were given to the scroll of the Torah.

וַיֹּאמֶר נְחֶמְיָה הוּא הַתִּרְשָׁתָא וְעֶזְרָא הַכֹּהֵן ׀ הַסֹּפֵר וְהַלְוִיִּם
הַמְּבִינִים אֶת־הָעָם לְכָל־הָעָם הַיּוֹם קָדֹשׁ־הוּא לַיהוָה
אֱלֹהֵיכֶם אַל־תִּתְאַבְּלוּ וְאַל־תִּבְכּוּ כִּי בוֹכִים כָּל־הָעָם כְּשָׁמְעָם
אֶת־דִּבְרֵי הַתּוֹרָה: וַיֹּאמֶר לָהֶם לְכוּ אִכְלוּ מַשְׁמַנִּים וּשְׁתוּ
מַמְתַקִּים וְשִׁלְחוּ מָנוֹת לְאֵין נָכוֹן לוֹ כִּי־קָדוֹשׁ הַיּוֹם לַאֲדֹנֵינוּ
וְאַל־תֵּעָצֵבוּ כִּי־חֶדְוַת יְהוָה הִיא מָעֻזְּכֶם:

Then Nehemiah the governor, and Ezra the priestly scribe, and the Levites who taught the people, said to them: "This day is holy to the Lord your God; do not mourn or weep." For all the people had been weeping when they heard the words of the Torah. Then he said to them: "Go, eat choice foods and drink sweet drinks and send portions to whoever has nothing prepared, for the day is holy to our Lord. Do not be sad, for your rejoicing in the Lord is the source of your strength."

Reader

בָּרוּךְ אַתָּה, יְיָ אֱלֹהֵינוּ, מֶלֶךְ הָעוֹלָם, צוּר כָּל־
הָעוֹלָמִים, צַדִּיק בְּכָל־הַדּוֹרוֹת, הָאֵל הַנֶּאֱמָן,
הָאוֹמֵר וְעוֹשֶׂה, הַמְדַבֵּר וּמְקַיֵּם, שֶׁכָּל־דְּבָרָיו אֱמֶת
וָצֶדֶק.

עַל הַתּוֹרָה וְעַל הָעֲבוֹדָה וְעַל הַנְּבִיאִים (וְעַל יוֹם
הַשַּׁבָּת הַזֶּה) וְעַל יוֹם הַזִּכָּרוֹן הַזֶּה, שֶׁנָּתַתָּ לָּנוּ, יְיָ
אֱלֹהֵינוּ, (לִקְדֻשָּׁה וְלִמְנוּחָה) לְכָבוֹד וּלְתִפְאָרֶת, עַל
הַכֹּל, יְיָ אֱלֹהֵינוּ, אֲנַחְנוּ מוֹדִים לָךְ, וּמְבָרְכִים אוֹתָךְ.
יִתְבָּרַךְ שִׁמְךָ בְּפִי כָּל־חַי תָּמִיד לְעוֹלָם וָעֶד. וּדְבָרְךָ
אֱמֶת וְקַיָּם לָעַד. בָּרוּךְ אַתָּה, יְיָ, מֶלֶךְ עַל כָּל־הָאָרֶץ,
מְקַדֵּשׁ (הַשַּׁבָּת וְ) יִשְׂרָאֵל וְיוֹם הַזִּכָּרוֹן.

We give thanks for the Torah, for the privilege of worship, for the prophets, and
for this (**Shabbat and**) Day of Remembrance. Be praised, O God, who sanctifies (**Shabbat,**) Israel and the Day of Remembrance.

Jewish prayers and blessings are most often expressed in the plural, emphasizing
the connection of each individual to the community. "In our age, in which the true
meaning of every word is encompassed by delusion and falsehood, and the original
intention of the human glance is stifled by tenacious mistrust, it is of decisive importance to find again the genuineness of speech and existence as We.... Human
beings will not persist in existence if they do not learn anew to persist in it as a
genuine We" *(Martin Buber, 1878-1965).*

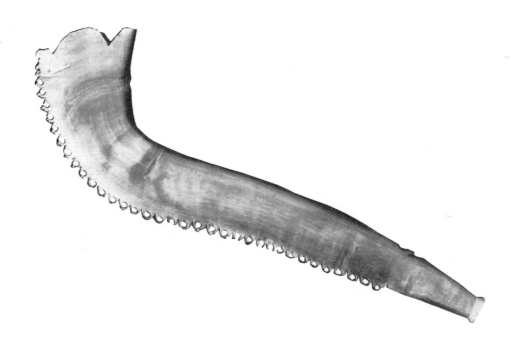

Shofar 52.19
Europe 18th-19th c. horn
John R. Forsman, Photographer
From the Collection of the Hebrew Union College
Skirball Museum

The name *Rosh Hashanah* is not mentioned in the Torah. The Biblical name for our holy day is *Yom Teruah,* or "a day of blowing the horn" *(Numbers 29:1).* Among the ancients, loud noises were used to drive away the powers of evil. For the people of Israel, blowing the Shofar, the ram's horn, was meant to banish all forces of corruption and all selfish impulses, and to awaken Jews to their covenant with God. Two of the Shofar sounds, *tekiah* and *teruah,* are indicated in the Torah *(Numbers 10:5-7);* the broken sound of *shevarim* was added by the rabbis and is noted in the Talmud, *(Rosh Hashanah 34a).* The Shofar service is divided into three sections celebrating God's majesty *(Malchuyot),* God's Power to remember the covenant made with Israel *(Zichronot),* and God's promise that one day the Shofar will sound for the redemption of all humanity in an era of tranquility and peace *(Shofarot).*

Reader

Shofar sounds on Rosh Hashanah speak a powerful message: "Arise from your slumber, you who are asleep; wake up...measure your accomplishments, your failings, and repent...You who forget the truth because of passing vanities... look into your souls, amend your ways, improve your deeds."

Choir

הַיּוֹם הֲרַת עוֹלָם. הַיּוֹם יַעֲמִיד בַּמִּשְׁפָּט כָּל־יְצוּרֵי עוֹלָמִים אִם כְּבָנִים אִם כַּעֲבָדִים. אִם כְּבָנִים, רַחֲמֵנוּ כְּרַחֵם אָב עַל בָּנִים. וְאִם כַּעֲבָדִים, עֵינֵינוּ לְךָ תְלוּיוֹת עַד שֶׁתְּחָנֵּנוּ וְתוֹצִיא כָאוֹר מִשְׁפָּטֵנוּ, אִם קָדוֹשׁ.

Today the world is born. Today all creatures stand in judgment, the high and mighty, the innocent and helpless. Judge us with compassion. We look to You for mercy. Enlighten our way, O holy and awesome God.

"Shofar sounds..." is from Moses Maimonides, 1135-1204, *Mishnah Torah, Laws of Repentance, 3-4.* "Today the world is born..." has its basis in Rabbi Elazar's observation that the world was created on the first day of Tishre *(Rosh Hashanah 10b).*

Reader

מִן הַמֵּצַר קָרָאתִי יָהּ, עָנָנִי בַמֶּרְחָב יָהּ.

קוֹלִי שָׁמָעְתָּ, אַל תַּעְלֵם אָזְנְךָ לְרַוְחָתִי לְשַׁוְעָתִי.

רֹאשׁ דְּבָרְךָ אֱמֶת, וּלְעוֹלָם כָּל־מִשְׁפַּט צִדְקֶךָ.

עֲרֹב עַבְדְּךָ לְטוֹב, אַל יַעַשְׁקֻנִי זֵדִים.

שָׂשׂ אָנֹכִי עַל אִמְרָתֶךָ, כְּמוֹצֵא שָׁלָל רָב.

טוּב טַעַם וָדַעַת לַמְּדֵנִי, כִּי בְמִצְוֹתֶיךָ הֶאֱמָנְתִּי.

נִדְבוֹת פִּי רְצֵה נָא יְיָ, וּמִשְׁפָּטֶיךָ לַמְּדֵנִי.

Out of the depths do we call unto You, O God. We lift troubled hearts to You.

Centuries ago, the stirring sounds of the Shofar at Mount Sinai proclaimed our covenant with You. There we promised allegiance to Your commandments. There we pledged ourselves to become a light of justice, a beacon of hope to all peoples. Now, as we prepare to hear the solemn sounds of the Shofar once again, let them stir us to struggle against the forces of evil within us and in the world. May they summon us to fashion justice, compassion, and love enough to heal suspicion and hatred, callousness and falsehood, selfishness and greed. To You, O God, do we turn.

Congregation

May the day soon dawn when the Shofar will sound for the redemption of all humanity.

"Out of the depths..." is a combination of seven verses from *Psalms 118:5; Lamentations 3:56; Psalms 119:160, 122, 162, 66* and *108*. The statement "Out of the depths..." is followed by the arrangement of the verses into an acrostic, so that the first letters of each verse spell out the words *K'RA SaTaN*, or "banish Satan." The sounding of the Shofar is meant to urge loyalty to God and the banishing of all evil from society and from the human heart.

Responsively

אַשְׁרֵי הָעָם יוֹדְעֵי תְרוּעָה, יְיָ בְּאוֹר פָּנֶיךָ יְהַלֵּכוּן.

Blessed are those who cherish the sounds of Shofar; they walk in Your light, O God.

Righteousness and justice are the foundation of Your rule. Mercy and truth go before You.

You uplift the fallen. You urge us to ennoble Your dominion with compassion for all Your creatures.

You are sovereign over all. Your splendor spans all time and space.

You are first and last. Who can fathom the wonder of Your power?

You are in each generous pulse of life.

You are in the alphabet we weave into healing words of caring and kindness.

Rule us with patience, forgiveness and love.

בָּרוּךְ אַתָּה, יְיָ, מֶלֶךְ עַל כָּל־ הָאָרֶץ, מְקַדֵּשׁ (הַשַׁבָּת וְ)
יִשְׂרָאֵל וְיוֹם הַזִּכָּרוֹן.

Be praised, O God, Sovereign over all, who sanctifies (**the Sabbath**) Israel and this Day of Remembrance.

Mal-chu-yot, or "Sovereignty," is the first section of the Shofar service.

Reader

We praise You, O God, for the privilege of hearing the Shofar.

Congregation

בָּרוּךְ אַתָּה, יְיָ אֱלֹהֵינוּ, מֶלֶךְ הָעוֹלָם, אֲשֶׁר קִדְּשָׁנוּ
בְּמִצְוֹתָיו וְצִוָּנוּ לִשְׁמוֹעַ קוֹל שׁוֹפָר.

Ba-ruch a-ta, A-do-nai Elo-hei-nu, me-lech ha-olam, a-sher ki-de-sha-nu be-mits-vo-tav, ve-tsi-va-nu, lish-mo-ah kol Sho-far.

Be praised O Lord our God, Ruler of the Universe, who has enabled us to attain holiness through the religious duty of hearing the Shofar.

בָּרוּךְ אַתָּה, יְיָ אֱלֹהֵינוּ, מֶלֶךְ הָעוֹלָם, שֶׁהֶחֱיָנוּ וְקִיְּמָנוּ
וְהִגִּיעָנוּ לַזְּמַן הַזֶּה.

Ba-ruch a-ta, A-do-nai E-lo-hei-nu, me-lech ha-o-lam, she-he-che-ya-nu, ve-ki-ye-ma-nu, ve-hi-gi-a-nu la-ze-man ha-zeh.

Be praised, O God, who has kept us in life, sustained us, and enabled us to reach this festive season.

The *mitzvah,* or commandment for blowing the Shofar, is found in the Torah: "The Lord spoke to Moses, saying: Speak to the Israelite people thus: In the seventh month, on the first day of the month, you shall observe complete rest, a sacred occasion commemorated with the loud blasts of the horn" *(Leviticus 23:23-24).*

The Shofar is sounded

Tekiah Shevarim-Teruah	תקיעה שברים־תרועה
Tekiah	תקיעה
Tekiah Teruah Tekiah	תקיעה תרועה תקיעה
Tekiah Shevarim Tekiah	תקיעה שברים תקיעה

All sing

אֲרֶשֶׁת שְׂפָתֵינוּ יֶעֱרַב לְפָנֶיךָ, אֵל רָם וְנִשָּׂא, מֵבִין
וּמַאֲזִין מַבִּיט וּמַקְשִׁיב לְקוֹל תְּקִיעָתֵנוּ, וּתְקַבֵּל
בְּרַחֲמִים וּבְרָצוֹן סֵדֶר מַלְכִיּוֹתֵינוּ.

A-re-shet se-fa-tei-nu
ye-e-rav le-fa-ne-cha,
Eil ram ve-ni-sa, (2)
mei-vin u-ma-a-zin, ma-bit
u-mak-shiv le-kol te-ki-a-tei-nu,
u-te-ka-beil be-ra-cha-mim, be-ra-cha-mim
u-ve-ra-tzon sei-der mal-chu-yo-tei-nu.

O God, accept the offering of our lips, the sounds of the Shofar. Hear us with
love and favor as we proclaim Your rule.

Defining the sounds of the Shofar, scholar, Max Arzt comments that "we are awak-
ened by the awesome *tekiah* sound to the multiple dangers that threaten human life
and make it so precarious. The weird *shevarim-teruah* notes which follow serve
to remind us that...life is frequently the bearer of tragedy and frustrations....
(Then) we are lifted to the heights of hope as we hear the *tekiah gedolah,* the pro-
longed concluding blast. This hope is one of redemption—the redemption...from
inner and outer 'drives' that threaten to efface (our) divine image...the liberation
of all...from exploitation and tyranny" *(Justice and Mercy, pp. 153-154).*

Torah Valance 59.39
Germany 1704
Erich Huckley, Photographer
From the Collection of the Hebrew Union College
Skirball Museum

Zichronot, the second section of the Shofar service, celebrates the faith that nothing is lost, no good deed, no noble intention, no act of kindness or love. God holds it all, weighs it all. We are the accumulation of our deeds, our memories. We are cursed or blessed by them.

Responsively

אַתָּה זוֹכֵר מַעֲשֵׂה עוֹלָם וּפוֹקֵד כָּל־יְצוּרֵי קֶדֶם.

You remember the fathomless depths of space, the formless beginnings of creation.

Nothing is hidden from You. Remind us that we are Yours.

You remember Your covenant with our people. Instruct us in its wisdom that we may remove all shallowness from our lives and fulfill Your sacred purposes.

Nothing is hidden from You. Remind us that we are Yours.

You remember the fate of nations, the anguish of our people tormented and tortured by cruelty, their bravery in defying dark despair with bright visions of justice, mercy and peace.

Nothing is hidden from You. Remind us that we are Yours.

You remember each of us. Our acts, our schemes, our thoughts and desires, our failure and merits come before You this day.

Nothing is hidden from You. Every noble act is a sign of Your goodness. Remind us that we are Yours.

בָּרוּךְ אַתָּה, יְיָ, זוֹכֵר הַבְּרִית.

Be praised, O God, who remembers the covenant made with our people. Let the sounds of the Shofar remind us that we are Yours.

125

The Shofar is sounded

Tekiah Shevarim-Teruah Tekiah	תקיעה שברים־תרועה תקיעה
Tekiah Shevarim Tekiah	תקיעה שברים תקיעה
Tekiah Teruah Tekiah	תקיעה תרועה תקיעה

All sing

אֲרֶשֶׁת שְׂפָתֵינוּ יֶעֱרַב לְפָנֶיךָ, אֵל רָם וְנִשָּׂא, מֵבִין
וּמַאֲזִין מַבִּיט וּמַקְשִׁיב לְקוֹל תְּקִיעָתֵנוּ, וּתְקַבֵּל
בְּרַחֲמִים וּבְרָצוֹן סֵדֶר זִכְרוֹנוֹתֵינוּ.

A-re-shet se-fa-tei-nu
ye-e-rav le-fa-ne-cha,
Eil ram ve-ni-sa, (2)
mei-vin u-ma-a-zin, ma-bit
u-mak-shiv le-kol te-ki-a-tei-nu,
u-te-ka-beil be-ra-cha-mim,
be-ra-cha-mim
u-ve-ra-tzon
sei-der zich-ro-no-tei-nu.

O God, accept the offering of our lips, the sounds of the Shofar. Hear us with love and favor, O God of remembrance.

For the Shofar of Rosh Hashanah, whose purpose it is to rouse the purely Divine... no artificially constructed piece of work may be sounded. It must be an instrument in its natural form (naturally hollow), with life given to it by the breath of a person, speaking to the spirit of a person. For you cannot attain to God by artificial means or by artifice. (Samson Raphael Hirsch, 1808-1888)

Reader

אַתָּה נִגְלֵיתָ עַל הַר סִינַי לְלַמֵּד לְעַמְּךָ תּוֹרָה וּמִצְוֹת,

Gathered at Sinai, our people heard Your voice amidst the blasts of the Shofar. There they became a people of Torah, sent forth to live those laws through which humanity shall endure and not die.

Congregation

Today, the Shofar stirs us with the truth that we live by the spirit of our ancient covenant. Its sounds rouse us from indifference. They summon us to fulfill the prophet's words, "Cease to do evil, learn to do good, devote yourselves to justice, aid the oppressed, defend the cause of the needy."

Reader

God of all generations, let us see the day when the great Shofar of liberation will be heard, when the shackles of suffering will be broken, and banners of righteousness, compassion, and peace will be raised over all the world and over Jerusalem.

בָּרוּךְ אַתָּה, יְיָ, שׁוֹמֵעַ קוֹל תְּרוּעַת עַמּוֹ יִשְׂרָאֵל בְּרַחֲמִים.

Be praised, O God, who, in mercy, hears the triumphant sounds of the Shofar.

In this third section of the Shofar service, known as *Shofarot*, "Shofar sounds," we are transported back to Mount Sinai and to the moment when the people of Israel accepted the Torah, promising to "teach it diligently to their children." The fulfillment of such loyalty promises to bring about the day when the "great Shofar of liberation will be sounded..." and the *tekiah gedolah* will announce the redemption of all humanity. "Cease to do evil..." is from *Isaiah 1:16-17.*

The Shofar is sounded

| Tekiah Shevarim-Teruah | תקיעה שברים־תרועה |
| Tekiah | תקיעה |

| Tekiah Shevarim Tekiah | תקיעה שברים תקיעה |

| Tekiah Teruah Tekiah Gedolah | תקיעה תרועה תקיעה |
| | גדולה |

Choir

הַלְלוּיָהּ.

הַלְלוּ אֵל בְּקׇדְשׁוֹ, הַלְלוּהוּ בִּרְקִיעַ עֻזּוֹ.
הַלְלוּהוּ בִגְבוּרֹתָיו, הַלְלוּהוּ כְּרֹב גֻּדְלוֹ.
הַלְלוּהוּ בְּתֵקַע שׁוֹפָר, הַלְלוּהוּ בְּנֵבֶל וְכִנּוֹר.
הַלְלוּהוּ בְּתֹף וּמָחוֹל, הַלְלוּהוּ בְּמִנִּים וְעֻגָב.
הַלְלוּהוּ בְצִלְצְלֵי־שָׁמַע, הַלְלוּהוּ בְּצִלְצְלֵי תְרוּעָה.
כֹּל הַנְּשָׁמָה תְּהַלֵּל יָהּ
הַלְלוּיָהּ.

Hallelujah. Praise God in the sanctuary. Praise God in the sky, the Lord's stronghold. Praise for mighty acts. Praise God for exceeding greatness. Praise God with blasts of the Shofar. Praise God with the harp and lyre, with timbrel and dance, with lute and pipe. Praise God with resounding cymbals, with loud, clashing cymbals. Let all that breathes praise the Lord. Hallelujah.

Hallelujah, "Praise God in the sanctuary. . ." from *Psalms 150,* was sung in the Temple and contains a description of the various musical instruments used by the ancients, including the Shofar.

Reader

אֱלֹהֵֽינוּ וֵאלֹהֵי אֲבוֹתֵֽינוּ, קַבֶּל־נָא בְּרַחֲמִים אֶת־תְּפִלָּתֵֽנוּ בְּעַד
אַרְצֵֽנוּ וּמֶמְשַׁלְתָּהּ. שְׁלַח רוּחֲךָ עַל כָּל־תּוֹשְׁבֵי אַרְצֵֽנוּ וְטַע בֵּין
בְּנֵי הָאֻמּוֹת וְהָאֱמוּנוֹת הַשּׁוֹנוֹת הַשּׁוֹכְנִים בָּהּ אַהֲבָה וְאַחֲוָה שָׁלוֹם
וְרֵעוּת. וְקַיֵּם בִּמְהֵרָה חֲזוֹן נְבִיאֶֽיךָ: לֹא יִשָּׂא גוֹי אֶל גּוֹי חֶֽרֶב
וְלֹא יִלְמְדוּ עוֹד מִלְחָמָה.

Our God, and God of our people, as we enter this New Year, accept our prayers on behalf of our nation and troubled world. Banish all hatred and bigotry, injustice and indifference. Bless those who aid the poor, heal the sick, and care for those who have lost their way.

Congregation

May this New Year bring blessings upon our land. Enlighten with wisdom all who have been chosen to serve. Forge bonds of friendship among all peoples. Let the day soon come when "nation shall not lift up sword against nation, nor learn war any more."

Since the first exile into Babylonia (586 B.C.E.) when the prophet Jeremiah instructed the people: "Seek the welfare of the city to which I have exiled you and pray to God on its behalf…" *(Jeremiah 29:7)*, Jews have included prayers for the welfare of the government as a part of their worship. "Nation shall not lift…" is from *Isaiah 2:4.*

All rise as Torah is lifted and ark is opened.

Reader

וַאֲנִי זֹאת בְּרִיתִי אוֹתָם, אָמַר יְיָ: רוּחִי אֲשֶׁר עָלֶיךָ, וּדְבָרַי
אֲשֶׁר־שַׂמְתִּי בְּפִיךָ, לֹא־יָמוּשׁוּ מִפִּיךָ וּמִפִּי זַרְעֲךָ וּמִפִּי זֶרַע
זַרְעֲךָ, אָמַר יְיָ, מֵעַתָּה וְעַד־עוֹלָם.

"This is My covenant with you," says the Lord. "Let not My spirit, and the words that I have put in your mouth, depart from you, nor from your children or their children, from this time forth and forever."

All sing

הוֹדוֹ עַל אֶרֶץ וְשָׁמָיִם, וַיָּרֶם קֶרֶן לְעַמּוֹ, תְּהִלָּה לְכָל־
חֲסִידָיו, לִבְנֵי יִשְׂרָאֵל עַם קְרוֹבוֹ. הַלְלוּיָהּ!

Ho-do al e-rets ve-sha-ma-yim, ve-ya-rem ke-ren le-a-mo, te-hi-la le-chol
cha-si-dav, li-ve-nei Yis-ra-eil, am ke-ro-vo. Ha-le-lu-yah!

God's splendor covers heaven and earth; God is the Source of Israel's strength, the praise of the faithful, the hope of those who draw near to serve. Halleluyah!

"This is the covenant...," from *Isaiah 59:21,* was incorporated into the first prayer book by Amram Gaon who headed the academy at Sura in Babylonia during the 9th century. The phrase, "words I have put in your mouth," was taken to refer to the Torah. "God's splendor..." is from *Psalms 148:13-14.* "It is a tree of life..." is a collection of verses on the importance of Torah taken from *Psalms 19:8-10* and *Proverbs 4:2, 3:12, 17.*

IT IS A TREE OF LIFE

Reader

God's Torah is perfect, renewing life;
God's teachings are enduring,
Making wise the simple.

תּוֹרַת יְיָ תְּמִימָה, מְשִׁיבַת נָפֶשׁ;
עֵדוּת יְיָ נֶאֱמָנָה, מַחְכִּימַת פֶּתִי;

God's precepts are just,
Rejoicing the heart;
God's commandments are lucid,
Giving light to the eyes.

פִּקּוּדֵי יְיָ יְשָׁרִים, מְשַׂמְּחֵי־לֵב;
מִצְוַת יְיָ בָּרָה, מְאִירַת עֵינָיִם;

God's word is pure, enduring forever;
God's judgments are true,
And altogether just.

יִרְאַת יְיָ טְהוֹרָה, עֹמֶדֶת לָעַד;
מִשְׁפְּטֵי יְיָ אֱמֶת, צָדְקוּ יַחְדָּו.

כִּי לֶקַח טוֹב נָתַתִּי לָכֶם,
תּוֹרָתִי אַל־תַּעֲזֹבוּ.

Behold, a good doctrine has been given you, My Torah; do not forsake it. It is a tree of life to those who hold it fast, and all who cling to it find happiness. Its ways are ways of pleasantness, and all its paths are peace. Return us to You, O God, and we shall return. Renew our days as of old.

All sing

Eits cha-yim hi la-ma-cha-zi-kim ba,
ve-to-me-che-ha me-u-shar.
De-re-che-ha da-re-chei no-am,
ve-chol ne-ti-vo-te-ha sha-lom.

עֵץ־חַיִּים הִיא לַמַּחֲזִיקִים בָּהּ,
וְתֹמְכֶיהָ מְאֻשָּׁר: דְּרָכֶיהָ דַרְכֵי־
נֹעַם, וְכָל־נְתִיבֹתֶיהָ שָׁלוֹם.
הֲשִׁיבֵנוּ יְיָ אֵלֶיךָ, וְנָשׁוּבָה.
חַדֵּשׁ יָמֵינוּ כְּקֶדֶם.

Ha-shi-vei-nu A-do-nai ei-le-cha
ve-na-shu-va.
Cha-deish ya-mei-nu ke-ke-dem.

Ark is closed; all are seated

ROSH HASHANAH MORNING SERMON

All rise; ark is opened

All sing

A-lei-nu le-sha-bei-ach la-a-don
ha-kol,
la-teit ge-du-lah le-yo-tseir
be-rei-sheet,
she-lo a-sa-nu ke-go-yei
ha-a-ra-tsot,
ve-lo sa-ma-nu ke-mish-pe-chot
ha-a-da-mah,
she-lo sam chel-kei-nu ka-hem,
ve-go-ra-lei-nu ke-chol ha-mo-nam.

עָלֵינוּ לְשַׁבֵּחַ לַאֲדוֹן הַכֹּל,
לָתֵת גְּדֻלָּה לְיוֹצֵר בְּרֵאשִׁית,
שֶׁלֹּא עָשָׂנוּ כְּגוֹיֵי הָאֲרָצוֹת,
וְלֹא שָׂמָנוּ כְּמִשְׁפְּחוֹת הָאֲדָמָה;
שֶׁלֹּא שָׂם חֶלְקֵנוּ כָּהֶם,
וְגֹרָלֵנוּ כְּכָל־הֲמוֹנָם.

Let us adore the ever-living God, rendering praise to the Creator of all, who chose us from all peoples, singling us out for sacred service, assigning us to a unique destiny.

Va-a-nach-nu ko-re-im u-mish-ta-cha-vim
u-mo-dim
li-fe-nei me-lech ma-le-chei
ha-me-la-chim, ha-ka-dosh ba-ruch Hu.

וַאֲנַחְנוּ כֹּרְעִים וּמִשְׁתַּחֲוִים
וּמוֹדִים לִפְנֵי מֶלֶךְ מַלְכֵי
הַמְּלָכִים, הַקָּדוֹשׁ בָּרוּךְ הוּא.

We bow the head in reverence and worship the God of all, the Holy One whom we praise.

(For comment, see p. 68)

Congregation

May the time not be distant, O God, when Your name shall be worshiped in all the earth, when unbelief shall disappear and error be no more. Fervently, we pray that the day may come when all shall turn to You in love, when corruption and evil shall give way to integrity and goodness, when superstition shall no longer enslave the mind, nor idolatry blind the eye, when all who dwell on earth shall know that You alone are God. O may all, created in Your image, become one in spirit and one in friendship, forever united in Your service.

Then shall a new day of peace dawn on earth, and the word of Your prophet be fulfilled: "God will reign for ever and ever."

All sing

Ve-ne-e-mar: "Ve-ha-ya A-do-nai
le-me-lech al kol ha-a-rets;
ba-yom ha-hu yi-he-yeh A-do-nai
e-chad u-she-mo e-chad."

וְנֶאֱמַר: "וְהָיָה יְיָ לְמֶלֶךְ
עַל־כָּל־הָאָרֶץ;
בַּיּוֹם הַהוּא יִהְיֶה
יְיָ אֶחָד וּשְׁמוֹ אֶחָד."

And it has been said: "God shall reign over all the earth; on that day the Eternal shall be One, and God's name shall be One."

(For comment, see p. 69)

Reader

You give us loved ones, and they become the strength of our life, the light of our eyes. And when they are taken from us, we are overwhelmed with sorrow and loneliness. In these precious Rosh Hashanah hours we look to You for comfort. Help us, O God, to see life as through windows that open on eternity. Let us understand that love abides, that our years are more than grass that withers, more than flowers that fade. For our loved ones continue to live. Their attainments have become our inheritance; their ideals, our challenge. We recall them now. They live in our hearts as a sacred blessing.

"Memorial prayers. . . bring comfort and consolation. The Kaddish. . . is not so much a prayer for the dead as the exaltation of God, who has given us so many blessings." (Rabbi Edgar F. Magnin, 1890-1984, served as spiritual leader of Wilshire Boulevard Temple for sixty-nine years.)

All rise

Yit-ga-dal ve-yit-ka-dash she-mei ra-ba
be-al-ma di-ve-ra chi-re-u-tei, ve-yam-lich
mal-chu-tei
be-cha-yei-chon u-ve-yo-mei-chon
u-ve-cha-yei de-chol beit Yis-ra-eil,
ba-a-ga-la u-vi-ze-man ka-riv, ve-i-me-ru:
a-mein.

יִתְגַּדַּל וְיִתְקַדַּשׁ שְׁמֵהּ רַבָּא
בְּעָלְמָא דִּי־בְרָא כִרְעוּתֵהּ,
וְיַמְלִיךְ מַלְכוּתֵהּ בְּחַיֵּיכוֹן
וּבְיוֹמֵיכוֹן וּבְחַיֵּי דְכָל־בֵּית
יִשְׂרָאֵל, בַּעֲגָלָא וּבִזְמַן קָרִיב,
וְאִמְרוּ: אָמֵן.

Ye-hei she-mei ra-ba me-va-rach le-a-lam
u-le-al-mei al-ma-ya.

יְהֵא שְׁמֵהּ רַבָּא מְבָרַךְ לְעָלַם
וּלְעָלְמֵי עָלְמַיָּא.

Yit-ba-rach ve-yish-ta-bach, ve-yit-pa-ar
ve-yit-ro-mam ve-yit-na-sei,
ve-yit-ha-dar ve-yit-a-leh ve-yit-ha-lal
she-mei de-ku-de-sha, be-rich hu,
le-ei-la min kol bi-re-cha-ta ve-shi-ra-ta
tush-be-cha-ta ve-ne-che-ma-ta,
da-a mi-ran be-al-ma,
ve-i-me-ru: amein.

יִתְבָּרַךְ וְיִשְׁתַּבַּח, וְיִתְפָּאַר
וְיִתְרוֹמַם וְיִתְנַשֵּׂא, וְיִתְהַדָּר
וְיִתְעַלֶּה וְיִתְהַלָּל שְׁמֵהּ
דְּקוּדְשָׁא, בְּרִיךְ הוּא, לְעֵלָּא
מִן־כָּל־בִּרְכָתָא וְשִׁירָתָא,
תֻּשְׁבְּחָתָא וְנֶחֱמָתָא דַּאֲמִירָן
בְּעָלְמָא, וְאִמְרוּ: אָמֵן.

Ye-hei she-la-ma ra-ba
min she-ma-ya ve-cha-yim
a-lei-nu ve-al kol Yis-ra-eil
ve-i-me-ru: a-mein.

יְהֵא שְׁלָמָא רַבָּא מִן־שְׁמַיָּא
וְחַיִּים עָלֵינוּ וְעַל־כָּל־יִשְׂרָאֵל,
וְאִמְרוּ: אָמֵן.

O-seh sha-lom bi-me-ro-mav, hu ya-a-seh
sha-lom a-lei-nu
ve-al kol Yis-ra-eil
ve-i-me-ru: a-mein.

עֹשֶׂה שָׁלוֹם בִּמְרוֹמָיו, הוּא
יַעֲשֶׂה שָׁלוֹם עָלֵינוּ וְעַל־
כָּל־יִשְׂרָאֵל
וְאִמְרוּ: אָמֵן.

Havdalah Spice Box
Portugal
Mid-19th c.

"Judaism...teaches us to understand death as part of the Divine pattern of the universe. Actually we could not have our sensitivity without fragility. Mortality is the tax that we pay for the privilege of love, thought, creative work—the toll on the bridge of being from which clods of earth and snow-peaked mountain summits are exempt. Just because we are human, we are prisoners of the years, yet that very prison is the room of discipline in which we, driven by the urgency of time, create" (Rabbi Joshua Loth Liebman, 1907-1948).

May God's great name be magnified and made holy in the world created according to Divine will. May God soon establish a reign of justice and peace during our life and days, and during the lifetime of the whole house of Israel. And let us say, Amen.

May God's great name be blessed now and forever.

May the name of the Holy One be blessed, praised, glorified, exalted, extolled, honored, magnified, and celebrated, even though God is above and beyond all the blessings, songs, praises, and consolations that are spoken in the world. And let us say, Amen.

May there be great peace from heaven and life for us and all Israel. And let us say, Amen.

May the One who makes peace in the heavens make peace for us and for all Israel. And let us say, Amen.

MEDITATIONS
FOR THE
TEN DAYS OF REPENTANCE

Havdalah Spice Box
Central Europe
Cir. 1860

The period of ten days between Rosh Hashanah and Yom Kippur, known as *Aseret Yemei Teshuvah,* or "The Ten Days of Repentance," was established by the Talmudic rabbis as a time for *heshbon ha-nefesh,* or "self-scrutiny." A part of each day was to be spent in meditation, providing the opportunity for taking stock of one's deeds, confessing one's sins, and seeking forgiveness for them.

MEDITATIONS FOR THE TEN DAYS OF REPENTANCE

I

These High Holy Days are the mountain peaks from which I can survey the hills and valleys of my life. From here I see the road of years winding its way. I have known bright places of worthiness and joy, and dark, tangled jungles of failure and disappointment.

Teach me, O God, to judge with honesty the landscape of my life. Lead me to repent the wrongs I have done to others and to forgive them for injuring me. Let the power of repentance set me, again, on the path toward You, that in doing Your will for generosity and love, for justice and truth, my journey through life may become a blessing.

II

O God, during these Days of Awe fill me with a new appreciation of life. Give me the wisdom to keep my body strong and my mind free from all misleading illusions. Banish all evil intentions from my heart. Remove all vain pride from my spirit. Grant me discernment that I may discover You in all my achievements, and let me always be eager to do Your will. You have given me abundant gifts, invaluable treasures for life and love. May my deeds always match the promises You have placed within my power to accomplish.

III

God of repentance and renewal, take away my shame. Lift my anxiety. Absolve me of my sin, and enable me to pray with gladness of heart. Strengthen me to pursue a life filled with carrying out Your commandments. Grant me days for bringing happiness to others, hours for spreading goodness and mercy in the world. Save me from arrogance, falsehood and greed. Rescue me when I stumble toward postures of indifference and insensitivity. Illumine my eyes that I may walk with righteous causes, and guide my feet on paths of caring and love.

"O God, during these…" is adapted from *High Holy Day Prayer Book, Yom Kippur,* Jewish Reconstructionist Society, pp. 332-335. "God of repentance…" is adapted from a prayer by Rabbi Abraham Isaac Kook (1865–1935), from *The Yom Kippur Anthology, pp. 53-54.*

IV

O Lord our God, all people pray to You. They piously assure You of their devotion. But what do their prayers mean? What does it matter whether I do this or that? Who am I that I should believe that my prayers are necessary? When I say, "God," I know that I speak of the Only, Eternal, Omnipotent, All-Knowing and Inconceivable One, of Whom I neither can nor should make for myself an image; on Whom I neither may nor can make any demand; Who will fulfill my most fervent prayer, or ignore it; and yet I pray as each one prays who is alive; and yet I pray for mercies, miracles and fulfillments. I pray, for I do not want to lose the elation of communion with You.

V

Praised are You
For what no eye has seen
No ear has heard
But has arisen in our hearts
Since You first spoke Your word to us.

Praised are You
For all those who support each other
Who give comfort and light
Who in their secret way make life easier to bear...
Who honor the stranger in their midst
Who speak the truth when others are silent
Who leave the corners of their fields...

Praised be You for all
Who only hunger for Your rule to be made manifest
Praised are You.

"O Lord our God..." is adapted from *Moderne Psalmen* by composer Arnold Schoenberg, as found in *The Language of Faith,* edited by Nahum N. Glatzer, pp. 82-83. "Praised are You...," by Huub Oosterhuis, as found in *On Wings Of Awe,* edited by Rabbi Richard N. Levy, pp. 272-273.

VI

Lord of the universe, whose rule extends everywhere, for You are the foundation of all that is, give me a heart of truth, a heart that is virtuous and pure, that I might do Your will with reverent Jewish intention. May my deeds be worthy as a dwelling place for Your glory. And, wherever I journey, may the paths of my life be charted with the wisdom of Your Torah. Cling to me, O God, as I reach out to You. Reconcile me to my mistakes and failures. Forgive my sins, and send me forth, renewed, to serve You with truth and love.

VII

God, Whom Abraham discovered in pleading the cause of justice for the sinners of Sodom and Gomorrah; Whom lonely Jacob encountered on a ladder stretching from earth to heaven; Whom Moses found in the mystery of the burning bush; Whom Isaiah discovered as the champion of justice for victims of hunger and oppression; Whom Micah found in the command to reject all "windy, baseless falsehoods"; Whom Amos met in the demand to "hate evil and love good"; use me now as You used them. Place within me courage to fuel my convictions, patience to suffer the derision of others, and light enough to find Your way of wisdom and gentle peace.

VIII

I am resolved to do Your will, O God, but how? Evil urges trap me, glib words flow from my mouth, but deeds are left undone. Idle play snares me. I bend to greed. I use my talents to swell my self-importance. So speak to me now. Return me to You. Guide my feet to find Your Torah of truth. Compel me to pursue Your will for generosity, kindness, mercy, and love. Guide me back to You.

"Lord of the universe..." is based on a prayer in *Likkute Tefilot,* a collection of meditations ascribed to Rabbi Nachman of Bratzlav of the Ukraine, 1772-1811. "God, Whom Abraham..." contains references to *Genesis 18:22-32, 28:10-19; Exodus 3:1-6; Isaiah 1; Micah 2:11;* and *Amos 5:15.* "I am resolved..." is adapted from a meditation by Judah Leon Moscato of Italy, 16th century.

IX

God, whose word created all the vast harmony of stars and space, open Your lips within me. Send words to me from Your place—words of healing for those in pain; words of support for those who have fallen; words of truth for those who deceive others and themselves; words of compassion for the lonely; words of patience for those who stumble into sin; words of understanding for those who surround their weaknesses with high fences of indifference; and words of courage for those who have lost their faith. Give such words to me that I may transform myself with them and find You, Author of all, speaking through my every breath.

X

O Lord, my God, approaching Yom Kippur, I confess my sins. Forgive them. For stubbornness of heart, deceiving others, insincerity, slander, and arrogance, forgive me. For hasty judgments, gossiping, envy, and prejudice, forgive me. For neglecting to measure my deeds against the ethical demands of Your Torah tradition and for failing to enrich myself with its wisdom, forgive me. Pardon my fears and confusions. Return me to You. Nurture me with Your love. Renew me for Your promises.

"God, whose word..." is based on a mystical meditation by Rabbi Nachman of Bratzlav of the Ukraine, 1772-1811.

PRAYER FOR VISITING THE GRAVES OF LOVED ONES

O Lord our God, it is hard to sing of oneness when our world is not complete, when those who once brought wholeness to our lives have gone, and nothing but memory can fill the emptiness their passing leaves behind. Yet, in these moments of memory, we feel a bond that is stronger than death. We know that we are not alone. Our beloved......continue(s) to live in our hearts. We feel (his, her, their) echo within our words and thoughts, and in all that we are and will become. Standing at this (these) grave(s) during this sacred season of the New Year, we give thanks for the consolation of memory. May our deeds of charity and love always do honor to those we have loved and lost, and may the memory of our beloved......be a constant source of blessing. We praise You, O God, for the generous gift of life.

(It is customary to recite the prayer, *El molei rachamim,* found on p. 385, and then the *Kaddish* prayer found on p. 386.)

Visiting the graves of relatives during the period of the High Holy Days is a custom among Jews and is mentioned in Joseph Caro's (1488-1575) compendium of Jewish law and practice known as *Shulchan Aruch.* See *Orach Chayim 581:4.*

YOM KIPPUR EVENING
HOME SERVICE

(Set table festively with white cloth, flowers, holiday challah and candles for lighting. Members of family may wish to prepare special readings. These may take the place of any of those suggested below. It is also customary for members of the family to make a contribution to some worthy cause before Yom Kippur begins, in fulfillment of the statement, "But repentance, prayer and charity temper judgment's severe decree.")

READINGS FOR
YOM KIPPUR

—1—

In the Torah it is written: And this shall be to you for all time: In the seventh month, on the tenth day of the month, you shall afflict your souls; and you shall do no manner of work, for...on this day atonement shall be made for you to cleanse you of all your sins...It shall be a sabbath of complete rest for you, and you shall afflict your souls; it is a law for all time.

—2—

All our secrets are known to You, O Lord. We cannot even fool ourselves. Lying is a vain exercise; Help us not even to try. How could we deceive You within us, at once forming and knowing our most secret thoughts?

We live in a world of illusion. We think we are separate, alone, cut off, misunderstood, unwanted. We forget we are part of Your glory, each of us a unique ray of Your Light.

As we live our lives, help us to remember what we often forget: We need one another, we each are part of the other, and some place, so well known yet so secret, we may find our true solace in You.

3

Just as the hand, held before the eye, can hide the tallest mountain, so the routine of everyday life keeps us from seeing the vast radiance and the secret wonders that fill the world. *Yom Kippur* is for removing the hand before our eyes and letting our hearts fill with awe and our mouths with thanksgiving to God.

The purpose of Yom Kippur is to become a *baal teshuvah*, to master repentance. *Teshuvah* means "returning" or "repairing" ourselves. We begin to accomplish *teshuvah* when we confess our failure to span the distance between conscience and conduct, between standards we profess and actions we perform. That is the purpose of Yom Kippur. This day we struggle to close the gap between what we are and want to be, between our promise and our conduct.

"In the Torah..." is taken from *Leviticus 16:29-31*. "All our secrets..." is from *Seder Eliyahu Rabbah*.

(Light Candles)

Reader

Yom Kippur lights
Illuminate the boundaries of a long day of judgment.

This sacred Sabbath is
For looking inward,
For teaching our hearts to love,
For turning our passions to peace.

May these lights
Expose all fear of self-truth,
Brighten our quest for goodness,
And fire our will to build a better world.

בָּרוּךְ אַתָּה, יְיָ אֱלֹהֵינוּ, מֶלֶךְ הָעוֹלָם, אֲשֶׁר קִדְּשָׁנוּ
בְּמִצְוֹתָיו וְצִוָּנוּ לְהַדְלִיק נֵר שֶׁל (שַׁבָּת וְשֶׁל) יוֹם
הַכִּפּוּרִים.

Ba-ruch a-ta, A-do-nai Elo-hei-nu, me-lech ha-o-lam, a-sher ki-de-sha-nu
be-mits-vo-tav, vi-tsi-va-nu le-had-lik ner shel (**Shabbat ve-shel...**)
Yom ha-kippurim.

Be praised, O Lord our God, Ruler of the Universe, who hallows us with
mitzvot and commands us to kindle the lights of (**Shabbat and**) Yom Kippur.

Everyone

בָּרוּךְ אַתָּה, יְיָ אֱלֹהֵינוּ, מֶלֶךְ הָעוֹלָם, שֶׁהֶחֱיָנוּ וְקִיְּמָנוּ
וְהִגִּיעָנוּ לַזְּמַן הַזֶּה.

Ba-ruch a-ta, A-do-nai E-lo-hei-nu, me-lech ha-o-lam, she-he-che-ya-nu
ve-ki-ye-ma-nu ve-hi-gi-a-nu la-zman ha-zeh.

Be praised, O Lord our God, Ruler of the Universe, who has kept us alive,
sustained us, and permitted us to reach this moment of joy.

BLESSING FOR MEAL

Everyone

בָּרוּךְ אַתָּה, יְיָ אֱלֹהֵינוּ, מֶלֶךְ הָעוֹלָם, הַמּוֹצִיא לֶחֶם
מִן הָאָרֶץ.

Ba-ruch a-ta, A-do-nai Elo-hei-nu, me-lech ha-olam, ha-mo-tzi le-chem min
ha-a-retz.

Be praised, O Lord our God, Ruler of the Universe, who brings forth bread
from the earth.

YOM KIPPUR
EVENING SERVICE

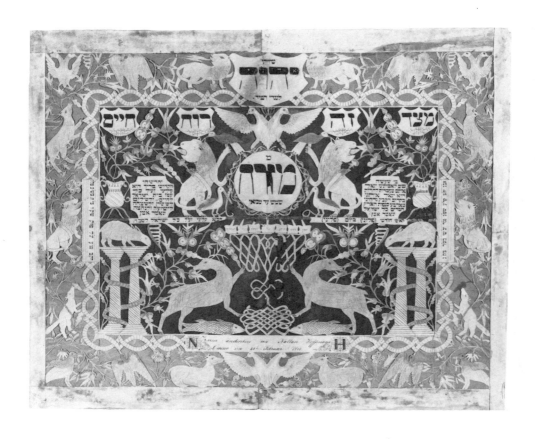

Mizrach 39.39
(An art piece hung on Eastern wall facing Jerusalem)
Odessa, Russia 1890
Marvin Rand, Photographer
From the Collection of the Hebrew Union College
Skirball Museum

"Open to Me...," God says to the Jewish people on Yom Kippur, meaning that if you make an opening of repentance for Me, even if it is as narrow as the point of a needle, I will make it wide for you and forgive you for your sins. God says: "Though you be far from Me, I will draw you near and absolve you—if you will come toward Me" *(Song of Songs Rabbah 5:2, Midrash Tehillim to Psalms 120:7).*

A Silent Prayer

Will You accept our prayers, forgive our wrongs, though we sin again and again?

O Lord, on this evening of Yom Kippur, I bring all my regrets before You. You know my desires, my hopes, my best intentions. You know my deeds. You know the sacred powers for life and love which You have placed in me as a gracious gift. With all my breath I praise You for them.

Forgive me my failures and my sins during this past year. Too often I have wasted opportunities for helping others; or, shackled by habit, I have cheated myself or wounded others. Cure me of my jealousies, my prejudices, my weaknesses on the bewildering border of temptation.

All the vows I make tonight and throughout Yom Kippur Day, I intend to fulfill. Strengthen my resolve. Awaken me in moments of apathy and forgetfulness. Urge me toward my noblest aspirations. Fill me with gentleness, generosity and love.

Answer my prayers. Speak through my heart and hands. Look past my failures. Forgive me. Forgive all of us. Pardon me. Pardon all of us.

Part of Torah Ark Decalogue 30.13 A-B
Marcus Illions. United States
Early 20th c.
From the Collection of the Hebrew Union College
Skirball Museum

The origins of the words and music of *Kol Nidre,* "All vows," are obscure. While an early version of the prayer is found within the Talmud as a formula for annulling promises, it is unclear when it was fused into a ritual for Yom Kippur evening. Despite those sages who objected to it on grounds that it provided an excuse for not fulfilling vows, its formula and music have remained irrepressible. Among American Reform Jews in the late 19th century, the prayer was dropped and replaced by *Psalm 130.* It was mentioned but not included in the *Union Prayer Book II* when it was revised (1945), and finally included in *Gates of Repentance* (1978). The special appeal of *Kol Nidre* may derive from the blunt honesty of the statement it makes. It articulates the realization that our lives are a patchwork of divided ambitions, best intentions, successes and failures. On Yom Kippur we ask forgiveness for not always living up to our expectations...and God's. We pray that *Kol Nidre,* "all our vows," might be considered forgiven if, after trying, we "fail" to fulfill them.

Reader

אַשְׁרֵי יוֹשְׁבֵי בֵיתֶךָ, עוֹד יְהַלְלוּךָ סֶּלָה.

Fortunate are those who enter Your house of prayer,
They shall praise You.
Fortunate are the people who gather here,
And whose God of forgiveness summons them.

All rise as ark is opened. Those unable to stand for the duration of the Kol Nidre may remain seated.

Choir

רַחוּם וְחַנּוּן יְיָ, אֶרֶךְ אַפַּיִם וְרַב חָסֶד.

טוֹב יְיָ לַכֹּל, וְרַחֲמָיו עַל כָּל־מַעֲשָׂיו.

אוֹר זָרֻעַ לַצַּדִּיק, וּלְיִשְׁרֵי־לֵב שִׂמְחָה.

God is gracious and compassionate, patient and merciful,
Nurturing of all creatures, caring for all creation
Light is sown for the righteous, joy for the upright in heart.

"Fortunate are those…" is from *Psalms 84:5*. "God is gracious…" is a composite from *Psalms 103:8, 145:9 and 97:11*.

Responsively

Kol Nidre. How sacred this moment. How filled with memories, some sweet, some bitter. Bearing them all, we stand now on holy ground.

We come with all our vows, those of yesterday and those for tomorrow.

We bring our broken promises, all our lofty intentions.

We seek Your pardon; may we merit Your forgiveness.

עֲבֵרוֹת שֶׁבֵּין אָדָם לַמָּקוֹם, יוֹם הַכִּפּוּרִים מְכַפֵּר.
עֲבֵרוֹת שֶׁבֵּין אָדָם לַחֲבֵרוֹ, אֵין יוֹם הַכִּפּוּרִים מְכַפֵּר
עַד שֶׁיְּרַצֶּה אֶת־חֲבֵרוֹ.

For transgressions against God, Yom Kippur atones; but for transgressions of one human being against another, Yom Kippur does not atone until they have made peace with one another.

God of Israel, in our weakness, strengthen us.

God of Israel, when we falter, support us.

God of Israel, pardon the vows we have failed to keep.

Return us in full repentance to You.

"Forgive the transgressions..." is from *Numbers 14:19-20.* Upon reaching a new juncture in time, a Jew is to recite the blessing *she-he-che-ya-nu,* "who has kept us in life...."

Kol Nidre is chanted

כָּל־נִדְרֵי וֶאֱסָרֵי וַחֲרָמֵי וְקוֹנָמֵי וְכִנּוּיֵי וְקִנּוּסֵי
וּשְׁבוּעוֹת, דִּנְדַרְנָא וּדְאִשְׁתַּבַּעְנָא וּדְאַחֲרִימְנָא
וְדַאֲסַרְנָא עַל נַפְשָׁתָנָא, מִיּוֹם כִּפּוּרִים זֶה עַד יוֹם
כִּפּוּרִים הַבָּא עָלֵינוּ לְטוֹבָה, כֻּלְּהוֹן אַחֲרַטְנָא בְהוֹן,
כֻּלְּהוֹן יְהוֹן שָׁרָן, שְׁבִיקִין שְׁבִיתִין, בְּטֵלִין וּמְבֻטָּלִין,
לָא שְׁרִירִין וְלָא קַיָּמִין. נִדְרָנָא לָא נִדְרֵי, וֶאֱסָרָנָא לָא
אֱסָרֵי, וּשְׁבוּעָתָנָא לָא שְׁבוּעוֹת.

Let all our vows and oaths, all the promises we make and the obligations we incur to You, O God, between this Yom Kippur and the next, be null and void should we, after honest effort, find ourselves unable to fulfill them. Then may we be absolved of them.

Reader

סְלַח נָא לַעֲוֹן הָעָם הַזֶּה כְּגֹדֶל חַסְדֶּךָ, וְכַאֲשֶׁר נָשָׂאתָ
לָעָם הַזֶּה מִמִּצְרַיִם וְעַד הֵנָּה.

Forgive the transgressions of our people. With loving kindness support us, even as You have sustained us from Egypt until now.

Choir

"I have pardoned you according to your word," says the Lord.

וַיֹּאמֶר יְיָ: "סָלַחְתִּי כִּדְבָרֶךָ."

All Sing

בָּרוּךְ אַתָּה, יְיָ אֱלֹהֵינוּ, מֶלֶךְ הָעוֹלָם, שֶׁהֶחֱיָנוּ וְקִיְּמָנוּ
וְהִגִּיעָנוּ לַזְּמַן הַזֶּה.

Ba-ruch a-ta, A-do-nai E-lo-hei-nu, me-lech ha-olam, she-he-che-ya-nu, ve-ki-ye-ma-nu, ve-hi-gi-a-nu la-ze-man ha-zeh.

Be praised, O God, who has kept us in life, sustained us, and enabled us to reach this sacred occasion.

Torah scrolls are returned to ark

All sing

Ba-re-chu et A-do-nai ha-me-vo-rach.

בָּרְכוּ אֶת־יְיָ הַמְבֹרָךְ!

Ba-ruch A-do-nai ha-me-vo-rach
le-o-lam va-ed.

בָּרוּךְ יְיָ הַמְבֹרָךְ לְעוֹלָם וָעֶד!

Be praised, O God, to whom our praise is due.
Praised be the Lord, to whom our praise is due, now and forever

MA-ARIV ARAVIM—CREATOR OF EVENING

Reader

בָּרוּךְ אַתָּה, יְיָ אֱלֹהֵינוּ, מֶלֶךְ הָעוֹלָם, אֲשֶׁר בִּדְבָרוֹ
מַעֲרִיב עֲרָבִים. בְּחָכְמָה פּוֹתֵחַ שְׁעָרִים, וּבִתְבוּנָה
מְשַׁנֶּה עִתִּים, וּמַחֲלִיף אֶת־הַזְּמַנִּים, וּמְסַדֵּר אֶת־
הַכּוֹכָבִים בְּמִשְׁמְרוֹתֵיהֶם בָּרָקִיעַ כִּרְצוֹנוֹ. בּוֹרֵא יוֹם
וָלַיְלָה, גּוֹלֵל אוֹר מִפְּנֵי חֹשֶׁךְ וְחֹשֶׁךְ מִפְּנֵי אוֹר,
וּמַעֲבִיר יוֹם וּמֵבִיא לָיְלָה, וּמַבְדִּיל בֵּין יוֹם וּבֵין
לָיְלָה, יְיָ צְבָאוֹת שְׁמוֹ. אֵל חַי וְקַיָּם, תָּמִיד יִמְלוֹךְ
עָלֵינוּ, לְעוֹלָם וָעֶד. בָּרוּךְ אַתָּה, יְיָ, הַמַּעֲרִיב עֲרָבִים.

Congregation

Be praised, O God, by whose will the shadows of evening fall and the gates of
morning are opened. Creator of heaven and earth, we praise You for the day
and its work and for the night and its rest.

(For comment, see p. 79)

Reader

אַהֲבַת עוֹלָם בֵּית יִשְׂרָאֵל עַמְּךָ אָהָבְתָּ: תּוֹרָה
וּמִצְוֹת, חֻקִּים וּמִשְׁפָּטִים אוֹתָנוּ לִמַּדְתָּ.

With eternal love You have sustained our people.

Congregation

Your commandments give meaning to our lives and length to our days. Let
Your love never depart from our hearts.

Reader

בָּרוּךְ אַתָּה, יְיָ, אוֹהֵב עַמּוֹ יִשְׂרָאֵל.

Be praised, O God, Source of love, the One and Eternal of time and space.

All sing

She-ma Yis-ra-eil: A-do-nai   שְׁמַע יִשְׂרָאֵל: יְיָ אֱלֹהֵינוּ, יְיָ אֶחָד!
E-lo-hei-nu, A-do-nai E-chad.

Ba-ruch sheim ke-vod   בָּרוּךְ שֵׁם כְּבוֹד מַלְכוּתוֹ לְעוֹלָם וָעֶד!
mal-chu-to le-o-lam va-ed.

Hear, O Israel: the Lord is our God, the Lord is One:
Blessed is God's glorious power forever and ever.

Ark is closed; all are seated

(For comment, see p. 46)

Congregation

Ve-a-hav-ta eit A-do-nai E-lo-he-cha,
be-chol le-va-ve-cha, u-ve-chol
naf-she-cha, u-ve-chol me-o-de-cha.
Ve-ha-yu ha-de-va-rim ha-ei-leh, a-sher
a-no-chi me-tsa-ve-cha ha-yom, al
le-va-ve-cha. Ve-shi-nan-tam le-va-ne-cha,
ve-di-bar-ta bam be-shiv-te-cha
be-vei-te-cha u-ve-lech-te-cha va-de-rech
u-ve-shoch-be-cha u-ve-ku-me-cha.
U-ke-shar-tam le-ot al ya-de-cha, ve-ha-yu
le-to-ta-fot bein ei-ne-cha, U-che-tav-tam
al me-zu-zot bei-te-cha u-vish-a-re-cha.

Le-ma-an tiz-ke-ru, va-a-si-tem et kol
mits-vo-tai, vi-hi-yi-tem ke-do-shim
lei-lo-hei-chem. A-ni A-do-nai
E-lo-hei-chem: a-sher ho-tsei-ti e-te-chem
mei-e-rets Mits-ra-yim, li-hi-yot la-chem
lei-lo-him. A-ni A-do-nai E-lo-hei-chem.

וְאָהַבְתָּ אֵת יְיָ אֱלֹהֶיךָ בְּכָל־
לְבָבְךָ וּבְכָל־נַפְשְׁךָ וּבְכָל־
מְאֹדֶךָ.
וְהָיוּ הַדְּבָרִים הָאֵלֶּה, אֲשֶׁר אָנֹכִי
מְצַוְּךָ הַיּוֹם, עַל־לְבָבֶךָ. וְשִׁנַּנְתָּם
לְבָנֶיךָ, וְדִבַּרְתָּ בָּם בְּשִׁבְתְּךָ
בְּבֵיתֶךָ, וּבְלֶכְתְּךָ בַדֶּרֶךְ,
וּבְשָׁכְבְּךָ וּבְקוּמֶךָ. וּקְשַׁרְתָּם לְאוֹת
עַל־יָדֶךָ, וְהָיוּ לְטֹטָפֹת בֵּין עֵינֶיךָ.
וּכְתַבְתָּם עַל־מְזֻזוֹת בֵּיתֶךָ,
וּבִשְׁעָרֶיךָ.

לְמַעַן תִּזְכְּרוּ וַעֲשִׂיתֶם אֶת־כָּל־
מִצְוֹתָי, וִהְיִיתֶם קְדֹשִׁים
לֵאלֹהֵיכֶם. אֲנִי יְיָ אֱלֹהֵיכֶם, אֲשֶׁר
הוֹצֵאתִי אֶתְכֶם מֵאֶרֶץ מִצְרַיִם
לִהְיוֹת לָכֶם לֵאלֹהִים. אֲנִי יְיָ
אֱלֹהֵיכֶם.

You shall love the Lord your God with all your heart, with all your soul, and with all your might. And these words which I command you this day shall be upon your heart. You shall teach them diligently to your children and shall speak of them when you sit in your house, when you walk by the way, when you lie down, and when you rise up. You shall bind them for a sign upon your hand, and they shall be for frontlets between your eyes. You shall write them upon the doorposts of your house and upon your gates, that you may remember and do all my commandments and be holy unto your God.

(For comment, see p. 48)

Reader

We hold all of this to be true: the Lord is our God, and we are Israel, devoted to God's service. We were redeemed from Egypt to liberate the oppressed and to bring hope to those who wait in darkness.

Congregation

When our people stood at the shore of freedom's sea, they proclaimed their faith, as we do now, with a song of praise.

All sing

Mi cha-mo-cha ba-ei-lim, A-do-nai?
Mi ka-mo-cha, ne-dar ba-ko-desh,
no-ra te-hi-lot, o-sei fe-leh?

מִי־כָמֹכָה בָּאֵלִם, יְיָ?
מִי כָּמֹכָה, נֶאְדָּר בַּקֹּדֶשׁ,
נוֹרָא תְהִלֹּת, עֹשֵׂה פֶלֶא?

Who is like You, Eternal One, among the gods that are worshiped? Who is like You, majestic in holiness, awesome in splendor, doing wonders?

Cantor

מַלְכוּתְךָ רָאוּ בָנֶיךָ, בּוֹקֵעַ יָם לִפְנֵי מֹשֶׁה; "זֶה אֵלִי!" עָנוּ
וְאָמְרוּ:

Your redeemed people sang of Your power as the sea opened before Moses: "This is my God! God will reign forever and ever."

All sing

"A-do-nai yim-loch le-o-lam va-ed."

"יְיָ יִמְלֹךְ לְעֹלָם וָעֶד!"

Reader

וְנֶאֱמַר: "כִּי־פָדָה יְיָ אֶת יַעֲקֹב, וּגְאָלוֹ מִיַּד חָזָק מִמֶּנּוּ." בָּרוּךְ
אַתָּה, יְיָ, גָּאַל יִשְׂרָאֵל.

O God, as You have redeemed Israel from powers of oppression, liberate all who are persecuted. Be praised, Redeemer of Israel.

(For comment, see p. 48)

Reader

*Cause us, O Lord, to lie down
each night in peace, and to arise
each morning to life. Spread over us
Your shelter of peace.*

הַשְׁכִּיבֵנוּ, יְיָ אֱלֹהֵינוּ,
לְשָׁלוֹם, וְהַעֲמִידֵנוּ, מַלְכֵּנוּ,
לְחַיִּים. וּפְרוֹשׂ עָלֵינוּ
סֻכַּת שְׁלוֹמֶךָ,

This has been our evening prayer for centuries. Assaulted by persecution and slaughter, our people resisted despair and lifted their voices in praise. Our night and morning prayers for a world without enemies, without hunger, poverty, suffering and fear, have foundered against the resistance of selfishness and cynicism, and yet we pray. With hearts trembling, we dare to yearn for peace.

Congregation

For our evening prayer is a triumph over darkness and disappointment. Our prayer is a song of hope and attachment to You, O God.

Reader

בָּרוּךְ אַתָּה, יְיָ, הַפּוֹרֵשׂ סֻכַּת שָׁלוֹם עָלֵינוּ, וְעַל־כָּל־עַמּוֹ
יִשְׂרָאֵל, וְעַל־יְרוּשָׁלָיִם.

Be praised, O God, who spreads over us a shelter of peace, whispering that one day all the dark forces of evil will be defeated and peace will prevail for us, for the people of Israel, for all peoples, and over Jerusalem.

(For comment, see p. 51)

164

Choir

כִּי בַיּוֹם הַזֶּה יְכַפֵּר עֲלֵיכֶם, לְטַהֵר אֶתְכֶם; מִכֹּל
חַטֹּאתֵיכֶם לִפְנֵי יְיָ תִּטְהָרוּ.

For on this day God will grant atonement to you and cleanse you from all your sins. Before God shall you be pure.

When Yom Kippur occurs on Shabbat

VE-SHA-ME-RU—KEEPING THE SABBATH

All sing

Ve-sha-me-ru ve-nei Yis-ra-eil et
ha-sha-bat, la-a-sot et ha-sha-bat
le-do-ro-tam, be-rit o-lam. Bei-ni u-vein
be-nei Yis-ra-eil ot hi le-o-lam. Ki
shei-shet ya-mim a-sa A-do-nai
et-ha-sha-ma-yim ve-et ha-a-rets
u-va-yom ha-she-vi-i sha-vat
va-yi-na-fash.

וְשָׁמְרוּ בְנֵי־יִשְׂרָאֵל אֶת־הַשַּׁבָּת,
לַעֲשׂוֹת אֶת־הַשַּׁבָּת לְדֹרֹתָם
בְּרִית עוֹלָם. בֵּינִי וּבֵין בְּנֵי
יִשְׂרָאֵל אוֹת הִיא לְעֹלָם, כִּי
שֵׁשֶׁת יָמִים עָשָׂה יְיָ אֶת־הַשָּׁמַיִם
וְאֶת־הָאָרֶץ, וּבַיּוֹם הַשְּׁבִיעִי
שָׁבַת וַיִּנָּפַשׁ.

The people of Israel shall keep the Sabbath, observing the Sabbath in every generation as a covenant for all time. It is a sign forever between Me and the people of Israel, for in six days the Eternal God made heaven and earth, and on the seventh day God rested from all the work of creation.

"For on this day…," from *Leviticus 16:30,* contains the promise of forgiveness for sins when complete repentance has been made. *Ve-sha-me-ru…* is from *Exodus 31:16-17.*

A Silent Meditation for the Amidah

To pray means to bring God back into the world. On the Days of Awe, we cry out of the depth of our disconcerted souls, a prayer of redemption: Deepen our reverence of You that we may bond together to do Your will with a full heart. Great is the power of prayer, for it expands the presence of God in the world.

Reader

אֲדֹנָי, שְׂפָתַי תִּפְתָּח, וּפִי יַגִּיד תְּהִלָּתֶךָ.

Eternal God, open our lips, that our mouths may declare Your glory.

Amidah means "standing" and is the third section of the service. On the weekday this section, also known as *Tefilah,* "the Prayer," contains nineteen prayers. On the Sabbath and Holy Days the first three and last three prayers of this section are retained, and a special "Sanctification of the Day" is added. According to tradition the *Amidah* was written by the rabbis of the Great Assembly and made an official part of Jewish worship by Rabban Gamliel, head of the Yavneh Academy in about 100 C.E.

Cantor

Ba-ruch a-ta, A-do-nai, E-lo-hei-nu
vei-lo-hei a-vo-tei-nu, E-lo-hei Av-ra-ham,
E-lo-hei Yits-chak, vei-lo-hei Ya-a-kov:
ha-eil ha-ga-dol, ha-gi-bor ve-ha-no-ra, Eil
el-yon, go-meil cha-sa-dim to-vim,
ve-ko-nei ha-kol, ve-zo-cheir cha-se-dei
a-vot, u-mei-vi ge-u-lah li-ve-nei
ve-nei-hem le-man-an she-mo, be-a-ha-va.

בָּרוּךְ אַתָּה, יְיָ אֱלֹהֵינוּ
וֵאלֹהֵי אֲבוֹתֵינוּ, אֱלֹהֵי
אַבְרָהָם, אֱלֹהֵי יִצְחָק,
וֵאלֹהֵי יַעֲקֹב: הָאֵל הַגָּדוֹל,
הַגִּבּוֹר וְהַנּוֹרָא, אֵל עֶלְיוֹן.
גּוֹמֵל חֲסָדִים טוֹבִים,
וְקוֹנֵה הַכֹּל, וְזוֹכֵר חַסְדֵי
אָבוֹת, וּמֵבִיא גְאֻלָּה לִבְנֵי
בְנֵיהֶם, לְמַעַן שְׁמוֹ, בְּאַהֲבָה.

All sing

Zoch-rei-nu le-cha-yim, me-lech
cha-feitz ba-cha-yim, ve-cho-te-vei-nu
be-sei-fer ha-cha-yim, le-ma-a-ne-cha
Elo-him cha-yim.

זָכְרֵנוּ לְחַיִּים, מֶלֶךְ חָפֵץ
בַּחַיִּים, וְכָתְבֵנוּ בְּסֵפֶר הַחַיִּים,
לְמַעַנְךָ אֱלֹהִים חַיִּים.

Cantor

Me-lech o-zeir u-mo-shi-a u-ma-gein.
Ba-ruch a-ta A-do-nai, ma-gein
Av-ra-ham.

מֶלֶךְ עוֹזֵר וּמוֹשִׁיעַ וּמָגֵן.
בָּרוּךְ אַתָּה, יְיָ, מָגֵן אַבְרָהָם.

Responsively

Source of all being, we turn to You as did our fathers and mothers in ancient days.

They knew You in their hearts; they sought You in their lives.

On this Yom Kippur eve we embrace their quest for lives fulfilled with acts of caring and love, deeds of loyalty to our people, and faith.

O God of life, may we merit inscription in Your Book of Life.

(For comment, see p. 54)

Reader

אַתָּה גִּבּוֹר לְעוֹלָם, אֲדֹנָי, מְחַיֵּה הַכֹּל אַתָּה, רַב
לְהוֹשִׁיעַ.
מְכַלְכֵּל חַיִּים בְּחֶסֶד, מְחַיֵּה הַכֹּל בְּרַחֲמִים רַבִּים.
סוֹמֵךְ נוֹפְלִים, וְרוֹפֵא חוֹלִים, וּמַתִּיר אֲסוּרִים,
וּמְקַיֵּם אֱמוּנָתוֹ לִישֵׁנֵי עָפָר.
מִי כָמוֹךָ, בַּעַל גְּבוּרוֹת, וּמִי דוֹמֶה לָּךְ, מֶלֶךְ מֵמִית
וּמְחַיֶּה וּמַצְמִיחַ יְשׁוּעָה? מִי כָמוֹךָ אַב הָרַחֲמִים,
זוֹכֵר יְצוּרָיו לְחַיִּים בְּרַחֲמִים? וְנֶאֱמָן אַתָּה לְהַחֲיוֹת
הַכֹּל. בָּרוּךְ אַתָּה, יְיָ, מְחַיֵּה הַכֹּל.

Congregation

God of eternal might, through us send help to the fallen, healing to the sick, freedom to the captive; confirm Your faithfulness to those who sleep in the dust. For You are mindful in mercy of all Your creatures. We praise You, the Source of life.

YOU ARE HOLY

Reader

אַתָּה קָדוֹשׁ וְשִׁמְךָ קָדוֹשׁ, וּקְדוֹשִׁים בְּכָל־יוֹם
יְהַלְלוּךָ סֶּלָה.

Congregation

You are holy beyond compare, and we seek You each day by uplifting our lives with deeds of holiness.

Ark is closed; all are seated

(For comment, see p. 56)

168

Reader

וּבְכֵן תֵּן פַּחְדְּךָ, יְיָ אֱלֹהֵינוּ, עַל כָּל־מַעֲשֶׂיךָ,

וּבְכֵן תֵּן כָּבוֹד, יְיָ, לְעַמֶּךָ, תְּהִלָּה לִירֵאֶיךָ וְתִקְוָה לְדוֹרְשֶׁיךָ,

וּבְכֵן צַדִּיקִים יִרְאוּ וְיִשְׂמָחוּ וְתִמְלֹךְ אַתָּה, יְיָ,

לְבַדְּךָ עַל כָּל־מַעֲשֶׂיךָ, כַּכָּתוּב בְּדִבְרֵי קָדְשֶׁךָ:

יִמְלֹךְ יְיָ לְעוֹלָם, אֱלֹהַיִךְ צִיּוֹן, לְדֹר וָדֹר, הַלְלוּיָהּ!

O Lord, our God, may reverence for all creation fill our hearts. Inspire with courage those who seek a time when violence and injustice will be no more.

May we be counted among them.

Strengthen the resolve of those who work for the time when wickedness will vanish like smoke and the rule of arrogance and tyranny will be banished from earth.

May we be counted among them.

Let the day come soon when all humanity will be gathered under a banner of peace and exalt You with deeds of righteousness and words of love on their lips.

May we be counted among them.

(For comment, see p. 58)

Cantor and Choir

קָדוֹשׁ אַתָּה וְנוֹרָא שְׁמֶךָ, וְאֵין אֱלוֹהַּ מִבַּלְעָדֶיךָ, כַּכָּתוּב:

וַיִּגְבַּהּ יְיָ צְבָאוֹת בַּמִּשְׁפָּט, וְהָאֵל הַקָּדוֹשׁ נִקְדַּשׁ בִּצְדָקָה.

בָּרוּךְ אַתָּה, יְיָ, הַמֶּלֶךְ הַקָּדוֹשׁ.

You are holy; awe inspiring is Your name. There is no God but You, as is written: The Lord is exalted by justice and sanctified by righteousness. Be praised, O God, who rules in holiness.

(For comment on *Kadosh A-ta,* see p. 60.) "Our God, and God of our people..." is the fourth, or middle, prayer of the *Amidah.* It assures the worshiper that God will pardon the sins of those who examine their deeds and commit themselves to repentance.

KEDUSHAT HA-YOM—SANCTIFICATION OF THIS DAY

Responsively

אֱלֹהֵינוּ וֵאלֹהֵי אֲבוֹתֵינוּ, מְחַל לַעֲוֹנוֹתֵינוּ בְּיוֹם
(הַשַּׁבָּת הַזֶּה וּבְיוֹם) הַכִּפּוּרִים הַזֶּה;

Our God, and God of our people, You have given us this (**Sabbath and**) Yom Kippur Day that we might seek forgiveness for our sins.

Lead us to search the inner recesses of our hearts.

Arouse us to examine all our thoughts and deeds.

Purify our hearts that we may serve You in truth.

Be praised, O God, who year after year lovingly extends forgiveness to us, and to the people of Israel, sanctifying (**the Sabbath**) Israel and this Yom Kippur Day.

Cantor and Choir

Ba-ruch a-ta, A-do-nai, Me-lech mo-cheil
ve-so-lei-ach, la-a-vo-no-tei-nu,
ve-la-a-vo-not a-mo beit Yis-ra-eil,
u-ma-a-vir ash-mo-tei-nu be-chol
sha-nah ve-sha-nah,

בָּרוּךְ אַתָּה, יְיָ, מֶלֶךְ
מוֹחֵל וְסוֹלֵחַ לַעֲוֹנוֹתֵינוּ
וְלַעֲוֹנוֹת עַמּוֹ בֵּית יִשְׂרָאֵל,
וּמַעֲבִיר אַשְׁמוֹתֵינוּ בְּכָל־
שָׁנָה וְשָׁנָה,

All sing

Me-lech al kol ha-a-retz, me-ka-deish
(**ha-Sha-bat v**...) Yis-ra-eil, v'yom
ha-Ki-pu-rim.

מֶלֶךְ עַל כָּל־הָאָרֶץ, מְקַדֵּשׁ
(הַשַּׁבָּת וְ) יִשְׂרָאֵל וְיוֹם
הַכִּפּוּרִים.

171

Reader

רְצֵה, יְיָ אֱלֹהֵינוּ, בְּעַמְּךָ יִשְׂרָאֵל, וּתְפִלָּתָם בְּאַהֲבָה תְקַבֵּל,
וּתְהִי לְרָצוֹן תָּמִיד עֲבוֹדַת יִשְׂרָאֵל עַמֶּךָ.
בָּרוּךְ אַתָּה, יְיָ, שֶׁאוֹתְךָ לְבַדְּךָ בְּיִרְאָה נַעֲבוֹד.

Look with favor, O God, upon us, and may our worship and deeds be acceptable
to You. Be praised, O God, whom alone we serve in reverence.

HODA-AH—WE GIVE THANKS

Congregation

מוֹדִים אֲנַחְנוּ לָךְ, שָׁאַתָּה הוּא יְיָ אֱלֹהֵינוּ וֵאלֹהֵי אֲבוֹתֵינוּ
לְעוֹלָם וָעֶד. צוּר חַיֵּינוּ, מָגֵן יִשְׁעֵנוּ, אַתָּה הוּא לְדוֹר וָדוֹר.
נוֹדֶה לְךָ וּנְסַפֵּר תְּהִלָּתֶךָ, עַל־חַיֵּינוּ הַמְּסוּרִים בְּיָדֶךָ, וְעַל־
נִשְׁמוֹתֵינוּ הַפְּקוּדוֹת לָךְ, וְעַל־נִסֶּיךָ שֶׁבְּכָל־יוֹם עִמָּנוּ, וְעַל־
נִפְלְאוֹתֶיךָ וְטוֹבוֹתֶיךָ שֶׁבְּכָל־עֵת, עֶרֶב וָבֹקֶר וְצָהֳרָיִם. הַטּוֹב
כִּי לֹא־כָלוּ רַחֲמֶיךָ, וְהַמְרַחֵם: כִּי־לֹא תַמּוּ חֲסָדֶיךָ, מֵעוֹלָם
קִוִּינוּ לָךְ.

We gratefully acknowledge, O Lord our God, that You are our Creator and
Preserver, the Rock of our lives and our protecting Shield. We give thanks to
You for our lives, which are in Your hand, for our souls which are in Your
keeping; for Your wondrous providence and Your continuous goodness, which
You bestow upon us day by day. Truly, Your mercies never fail, and Your loving
kindness never ceases. Therefore do we put our trust in You. Be praised,
O God, to whom our thanks are due.

(For comment, see p. 62)

Reader

שָׁלוֹם רָב עַל־יִשְׂרָאֵל עַמְּךָ וְעַל־כָּל־הָעַמִּים תָּשִׂים לְעוֹלָם,
כִּי אַתָּה הוּא מֶלֶךְ אָדוֹן לְכָל־הַשָּׁלוֹם. וְטוֹב בְּעֵינֶיךָ לְבָרֵךְ
אֶת־עַמְּךָ יִשְׂרָאֵל וְאֶת־כָּל־הָעַמִּים בְּכָל־עֵת וּבְכָל־שָׁעָה
בִּשְׁלוֹמֶךָ.

Bless us and all Israel, Your people, with peace and goodness, mercy and
compassion. Bless us with the light of Torah, for You have given us a heritage
of love and commandments for kindness, charity and peace.

Cantor and Choir

בְּסֵפֶר חַיִּים בְּרָכָה וְשָׁלוֹם וּפַרְנָסָה טוֹבָה נִזָּכֵר
וְנִכָּתֵב לְפָנֶיךָ, אֲנַחְנוּ וְכָל־עַמְּךָ בֵּית יִשְׂרָאֵל, לְחַיִּים
טוֹבִים וּלְשָׁלוֹם. בָּרוּךְ אַתָּה, יְיָ, עוֹשֵׂה הַשָּׁלוֹם.

Reader

May our deeds be worthy before You, and may we, and all Israel, be inscribed
in the Book of Life for blessing, sustenance and peace. Be praised, O God,
Source of peace.

(For comment, see p. 63)

173

Torah Ark Curtain Spiegel 159.20
Germany 18th c.
Erich Hockley, Photographer
From the Collection of the Hebrew Union College
Skirball Museum

Judaism teaches that the first step of repentance is *vidu-i,* or "confession." On Yom Kippur we are to admit our failings, specify them, not gloss over them with general pieties. The ancient rabbis prescribed the repetition of the *vidu-i* at each service for Yom Kippur Day *(Yoma 87b).* "Return to Me..." is from *Isaiah 44:22.* The prayers of confession are offered in the plural, underscoring the understanding that "no one sins in a social vacuum; all of society is partly responsible for the transgressions of the individual" (Abraham Milgram, *Jewish Worship, p. 249*).

Reader

אֱלֹהֵינוּ וֵאלֹהֵי אֲבוֹתֵינוּ, מְחַל לַעֲוֹנוֹתֵינוּ בְּיוֹם
(הַשַּׁבָּת הַזֶּה וּבְיוֹם) הַכִּפּוּרִים הַזֶּה; מְחֵה וְהַעֲבֵר
פְּשָׁעֵינוּ וְחַטֹּאתֵינוּ מִנֶּגֶד עֵינֶיךָ, כָּאָמוּר: " שׁוּבָה אֵלַי,
כִּי גְאַלְתִּיךָ."

Our God and God of our people, pardon our transgressions on this **(Sabbath day and on this)** Yom Kippur Day. Forgive our sins as You have promised: "Return to Me with deeds of loving-kindness and faithfulness, and I will embrace You."

All rise

Cantor and Choir

אֱלֹהֵינוּ וֵאלֹהֵי אֲבוֹתֵינוּ, תָּבוֹא לְפָנֶיךָ תְּפִלָּתֵנוּ וְאַל
תִּתְעַלַּם מִתְּחִנָּתֵנוּ, שֶׁאֵין אֲנַחְנוּ עַזֵּי פָנִים וּקְשֵׁי עֹרֶף
לוֹמַר לְפָנֶיךָ, יְיָ אֱלֹהֵינוּ וֵאלֹהֵי אֲבוֹתֵינוּ, צַדִּיקִים
אֲנַחְנוּ וְלֹא חָטָאנוּ, אֲבָל אֲנַחְנוּ חָטָאנוּ. חָטָאנוּ,
עָוִינוּ, פָּשַׁעְנוּ.

Our God, and God of our people, may our prayers be acceptable before You. Hear our plea for pardon, for we are not so stubborn as to say that we are perfect and have not sinned. We confess our wrongs. We have sinned. We have transgressed. We have done perversely.

All are seated

175

Kiddush Cup 18.21
Germany 18th c.
Marvin Rand, Photographer
From the Collection of the Hebrew Union College
Skirball Museum

Jews are to measure the worth of their lives by the *mitzvot,* the "commandments" or "deeds," they perform. Torah commentator, Rashi (1040-1105, France) observed that "human beings come into the world naked and leave naked. After all their work, they carry nothing away—except for the impact of the deeds they leave behind." Rashi's contention is that when we miss the opportunity of fulfilling a *mitzvah* or accidentally neglect our responsibilities or deliberately refuse to pursue them, then we betray the legacy we will leave to our loved ones and community. For that reason we are called upon to confess our neglect on Yom Kippur and to resolve that we will turn our sins of selfishness into sensitivity and our wrongdoings into deeds of kindness, generosity and love.

SARNU—WE HAVE NEGLECTED YOUR COMMANDMENTS

Responsively

סַרְנוּ מִמִּצְוֹתֶיךָ וּמִמִּשְׁפָּטֶיךָ הַטּוֹבִים וְלֹא שָׁוָה לָנוּ.
וְאַתָּה צַדִּיק עַל כָּל־הַבָּא עָלֵינוּ, כִּי אֱמֶת עָשִׂיתָ
וַאֲנַחְנוּ הִרְשָׁעְנוּ.

We have neglected Your commandments, and it has brought us no benefit. We have spurned Your summons for generosity and goodness, for justice and understanding, and have not profited.

What shall we say before You? What excuses shall we utter? For You know all the secrets of our hearts. Nothing is hidden from You.

So let us judge ourselves honestly. Help us to search our souls. Expose us to our failings. Lift the veil from our wrongdoing. Conceal no vanity or selfishness from our confession.

Pardon our transgressions. Grant us atonement for all the sins we have sinned against You.

Responsively, Reader, then Congregation

עַל חֵטְא שֶׁחָטָאנוּ לְפָנֶיךָ בְּאֹנֶס וּבְרָצוֹן,.

Al cheit she-cha-ta-nu...For **Acts** of wrongdoing committed under stress or by choice, forgive us.

עַל חֵטְא שֶׁחָטָאנוּ לְפָנֶיךָ בִּבְלִי דָעַת.

Al cheit she-cha-ta-nu...For **Blunders** committed unintentionally, forgive us.

עַל חֵטְא שֶׁחָטָאנוּ לְפָנֶיךָ בְּגִלּוּי עֲרָיוֹת,.

Al cheit she-cha-ta-nu...For **Glibly** condoning immorality out of self-interest, forgive us.

עַל חֵטְא שֶׁחָטָאנוּ לְפָנֶיךָ בְּדַעַת וּבְמִרְמָה.

Al cheit she-cha-ta-nu...For **Deceiving** others and ourselves, forgive us.

עַל חֵטְא שֶׁחָטָאנוּ לְפָנֶיךָ בְּהַרְהוֹר הַלֵּב,.

Al cheit she-cha-ta-nu...For **Harnessing** our hearts to selfish thoughts, forgive us.

עַל חֵטְא שֶׁחָטָאנוּ לְפָנֶיךָ בְּוְעִידַת זְנוּת.

Al cheit she-cha-ta-nu...For **Vainly** seeking out flattering advice and not the truth, forgive us.

עַל חֵטְא שֶׁחָטָאנוּ לְפָנֶיךָ בְּזָדוֹן וּבִשְׁגָגָה,.

Al cheit she-cha-ta-nu...For **Zealously** defending our stubbornness and errors, forgive us.

עַל חֵטְא שֶׁחָטָאנוּ לְפָנֶיךָ בְּחִלּוּל הַשֵּׁם.

Al cheit she-cha-ta-nu...For **Choosing** to profane God's name by dealing unfairly with others, forgive us.

עַל חֵטְא שֶׁחָטָאנוּ לְפָנֶיךָ בְּטֻמְאַת שְׂפָתָיִם

Al cheit she-cha-ta-nu...For **Trading** hurtful rumors and gossip, forgive us.

עַל חֵטְא שֶׁחָטָאנוּ לְפָנֶיךָ בְּיוֹדְעִים וּבְלֹא יוֹדְעִים.

Al cheit she-cha-ta-nu...For **Yielding** to wrongdoing wittingly and unwittingly, forgive us.

All sing

Ve-al ku-lam, E-lo-ah se-li-chot,
se-lach la-nu, me-chal la-nu
ka-per la-nu.

וְעַל כֻּלָּם, אֱלוֹהַּ סְלִיחוֹת,
סְלַח־לָנוּ, מְחַל־לָנוּ,
כַּפֶּר־לָנוּ.

For all our failings, O God of forgiveness, pardon us, help us, grant us atonement.

"Consider three things, and you will avoid sin: Above you is an all-seeing eye, an all-hearing ear, and a record of all your acts" *(Avot 3:1)*. So taught the ancient rabbis. Indifference and insensitivity, pride and selfishness lead us to sin. On Yom Kippur we confess all wrongdoings in the hope that in saying them we will distance ourselves from them and find forgiveness for them.

Reader

אֱלֹהֵינוּ וֵאלֹהֵי אֲבוֹתֵינוּ, אַל תַּעַזְבֵנוּ וְאַל תִּטְּשֵׁנוּ
וְאַל תַּכְלִימֵנוּ, וְאַל תָּפֵר בְּרִיתְךָ אִתָּנוּ. קָרְבֵנוּ
לְתוֹרָתֶךָ, לַמְּדֵנוּ מִצְוֹתֶיךָ, הוֹרֵנוּ דְרָכֶיךָ, הַט לִבֵּנוּ
לְיִרְאָה אֶת־שְׁמֶךָ, וּמוֹל אֶת־לְבָבֵנוּ לְאַהֲבָתֶךָ, וְנָשׁוּב
אֵלֶיךָ בֶּאֱמֶת וּבְלֵב שָׁלֵם.

Our God and God of our people, do not abandon us or allow us to shame ourselves through neglect of Your sacred covenant. Draw us to the study of Torah, engage us in fulfilling Your commandments. Teach us Your ways that we may prosper in kindness, grow rich in wisdom, and confirm our faith with deeds of reverence, righteousness, truth, and mercy.

Congregation

Turn us to You in sincerity and love. For Your sake and ours, hear our prayers and forgive our failings.

Cantor and Choir

שְׁמַע קוֹלֵנוּ, יְיָ אֱלֹהֵינוּ, חוּס וְרַחֵם עָלֵינוּ, וְקַבֵּל
בְּרַחֲמִים וּבְרָצוֹן אֶת־תְּפִלָּתֵנוּ. הֲשִׁיבֵנוּ יְיָ אֵלֶיךָ
וְנָשׁוּבָה, חַדֵּשׁ יָמֵינוּ כְּקֶדֶם.

Hear our prayers, O Lord our God. Care about us. Save us. In mercy and compassion accept our plea for forgiveness. Return us to You, O God, and we shall return. Renew our days as of old.

"Do not abandon us..." is a compilation of verses taken from poems of confession created during the Middle Ages and placed within High Holy Day prayer books. "Hear our prayers..." may date from the 16th century. "Return us...." is from *Lamentations 5:21*. Jewish tradition recognizes the power of regret, of admitting faults and repairing the wrongs we do to others and to ourselves. The tradition teaches that *te-shuvah*, or "repentance," lengthens a person's life *(Yoma 86b)*.

Congregation rises as ark is opened

Congregation

אָבְינוּ מַלְכֵּנוּ, שְׁמַע קוֹלֵנוּ.

Avinu Malkeinu, she-ma ko-lei-nu.
Avinu Malkeinu, hear our prayer.

אָבְינוּ מַלְכֵּנוּ, חָטָאנוּ לְפָנֶיךָ.

Avinu Malkeinu, cha-ta-nu le-fa-ne-cha.
Avinu Malkeinu, we have sinned against You.

אָבְינוּ מַלְכֵּנוּ, חֲמוֹל עָלֵינוּ וְעַל עוֹלָלֵינוּ וְטַפֵּנוּ.

Avinu Malkeinu, cha-mol a-lei-nu ve-al o-la-lei-nu ve-ta-pei-nu.
Avinu Malkeinu, have mercy upon us and upon our children.

אָבְינוּ מַלְכֵּנוּ, כַּלֵּה דֶּבֶר וְחֶרֶב וְרָעָב מֵעָלֵינוּ.

Avinu Malkeinu, ka-lei de-ver, ve-che-rev, ve-ra-av mei-a-lei-nu.
Avinu Malkeinu, rid us of pestilence, war and famine.

אָבְינוּ מַלְכֵּנוּ, כַּלֵּה כָּל־צַר וּמַשְׂטִין מֵעָלֵינוּ.

Avinu Malkeinu, ka-lei kol tsar u-mas-tin mei-a-lei-nu.
Avinu Malkeinu, rid us of all hatred and oppression.

אָבְינוּ מַלְכֵּנוּ, כָּתְבֵנוּ בְּסֵפֶר חַיִּים טוֹבִים.

Avinu Malkeinu, kot-vei-nu be-sei-fer cha-yim to-vim.
Avinu Malkeinu, inscribe us for blessing in the Book of Life.

אָבִינוּ מַלְכֵּנוּ, מַלֵּא יָדֵינוּ מִבִּרְכוֹתֶיךָ.

Avinu Malkeinu, ma-lei ya-dei-nu mi-bir-cho-te-cha.
Avinu Malkeinu, fill our hands with Your blessings.

אָבִינוּ מַלְכֵּנוּ, כָּתְבֵנוּ בְּסֵפֶר סְלִיחָה וּמְחִילָה.

Avinu Malkeinu, kot-vei-nu be-sei-fer se-li-cha u-me-chi-lah.
Avinu Malkeinu, inscribe us for blessing in the Book of forgiveness.

אָבִינוּ מַלְכֵּנוּ, חָנֵּנוּ וַעֲנֵנוּ, כִּי אֵין בָּנוּ מַעֲשִׂים,
עֲשֵׂה עִמָּנוּ צְדָקָה וָחֶסֶד וְהוֹשִׁיעֵנוּ.

Avinu Malkeinu, cho-nei-nu va-a-nei-nu, ki ein ba-nu ma-a-sim, a-sei
i-ma-nu tse-da-kah va-che-sed, ve-ho-shi-ei-nu.
Avinu Malkeinu, be gracious and answer us. Treat us generously and with
kindness, and help us.

All sing

Avinu Malkeinu,
cho-nei-nu va-a-nei-nu (2)
ki ein ba-nu ma-a-sim.

A-sei i-ma-nu tse-da-kah va-che-sed (2)
ve-ho-shi-ei-nu.

Avinu Malkeinu,
cho-nei-nu va-a-nei-nu (2)
ki ein ba-nu ma-a-sim.

אָבִינוּ מַלְכֵּנוּ, חָנֵּנוּ וַעֲנֵנוּ,
כִּי אֵין בָּנוּ מַעֲשִׂים, עֲשֵׂה
עִמָּנוּ צְדָקָה וָחֶסֶד וְהוֹשִׁיעֵנוּ.

All are seated

(For comment, see p. 66)

Mizrach 39.1
(An art piece hung on the Eastern wall facing Jerusalem)
Moses Henry, Ohio 1850
Marvin Rand, Photographer
From the Collection of the Hebrew Union College
Skirball Museum

"Kol Nidre is repeated...." The custom of repeating the prayer three times is common in most synagogues. Each time, the congregation recalls the promise of God to forgive sins, a promise which was given to the Israelites during their wanderings in the Sinai desert. "The whole Israelite community and the stranger residing among them shall be forgiven, for it happened to the entire people through error" *(Numbers 15:26)*. "Kol Nidre..." is by modern Hebrew poet Zev Falk and translated by Stanley Schacter.

Kol Nidre is repeated as instrumental solo

Kol Nidre…
All the vows on our lips,
the burdens in our hearts,
the pent-up regrets about
which we brooded and spoke
through prayers without end
on last Yom Kippur Day
did not change our way of life,
did not bring deliverance
in the year that has gone.
From mountain peaks of fervor
we fell to common ways
at the close of the fast.

Will You hear our regret?
Will You open our prison,
release us from shackles of habit?
Will You accept our prayers,
forgive our wrongs,
though we sin again and again?

In moments of weakness
we do not remember
promises of Yom Kippur Day.
Recall that we easily forget;
take only our heart's intent;
Forgive us, pardon us.

כָּל־נִדְרֵי שְׂפָתֵינוּ, קַבָּלוֹת שֶׁבְּלִבֵּנוּ
וְהִרְהוּרֵי הַתְּשׁוּבָה שֶׁהָגִינוּ וּבִטַּאנוּ
בְּאַלְפֵי תְפִלּוֹתֵינוּ בְּיוֹם כִּפּוּר שֶׁהָיָה
לֹא שִׁנּוּ אְרַח חַיֵּינוּ,
לֹא הֵבִיאוּ גְאֻלָּתֵנוּ
בַּשָּׁנָה שֶׁנִּסְתַּיְּמָה.
מִמְּרוֹמֵי הִתְלַהֲבוּתֵנוּ
אֶל חֻלִּין הֻרְגַּלְנוּ
שַׁבְנוּ מִיָּד עִם נְעִילָה.

הֲתִשְׁמַע חֲרָטָתֵנוּ, אִם תַּתִּיר אֶת־מַאֲסָרֵנוּ
בִּידֵי יֵצֶר שֶׁל שִׁגְרָה?

הֲתִרְצֶה תְפִלָּתֵנוּ לְכַפֵּר עַל פְּשָׁעֵינוּ
אַף אִם נָשׁוּב וְנֶחֱטָא?

דַּע כִּי בִּשְׁעַת חֻלְשָׁתֵנוּ לֹא נִזְכֹּר מוֹדָעָתֵנוּ
מִיּוֹם כִּפּוּר שֶׁהָיָה.
תִּתְחַשֵּׁב בְּשִׁכְחָתֵנוּ וּתְקַבֵּל כַּוָּנוֹתֵינוּ
לִסְלִיחָה וְלִמְחִילָה.

YOM KIPPUR EVENING SERMON

All rise, ark is opened

All sing

A-lei-nu le-sha-bei-ach la-a-don
ha-kol,
la-teit ge-du-lah le-yo-tseir
be-rei-sheet,
she-lo a-sa-nu ke-go-yei
ha-a-ra-tsot,
ve-lo sa-ma-nu ke-mish-pe-chot
ha-a-da-mah,
she-lo sam chel-kei-nu ka-hem,
ve-go-ra-lei-nu ke-chol ha-mo-nam.

עָלֵינוּ לְשַׁבֵּחַ לַאֲדוֹן הַכֹּל,
לָתֵת גְּדֻלָּה לְיוֹצֵר בְּרֵאשִׁית,
שֶׁלֹּא עָשָׂנוּ כְּגוֹיֵי הָאֲרָצוֹת,
וְלֹא שָׂמָנוּ כְּמִשְׁפְּחוֹת הָאֲדָמָה;
שֶׁלֹּא שָׂם חֶלְקֵנוּ כָּהֶם,
וְגֹרָלֵנוּ כְּכָל־הֲמוֹנָם.

Let us adore the ever-living God, rendering praise to the Creator of all, who chose us from all peoples, singling us out for sacred service, assigning us to a unique destiny.

Va-a-nach-nu ko-re-im u-mish-ta-cha-vim
u-mo-dim
lif-nei me-lech mal-chei
ha-me-la-chim, ha-ka-dosh ba-ruch Hu.

וַאֲנַחְנוּ כֹּרְעִים וּמִשְׁתַּחֲוִים
וּמוֹדִים לִפְנֵי מֶלֶךְ מַלְכֵי
הַמְּלָכִים, הַקָּדוֹשׁ בָּרוּךְ הוּא.

We bow the head in reverence and worship the God of all, the Holy One whom we praise.

(For comment, see p. 68)

Reader and Congregation

Eternal God, we face the morrow with hope made stronger by the vision of Your rule: a world where poverty and war are banished, where injustice and hate are no more. Teach us to share the pain of others, to heed Your call for justice, to pursue the blessing of peace. Help us, O God, to gain victory over evil and to bring nearer the day when all the world shall be one.

Cantor

Ve-ne-e-mar: "Ve-ha-ya A-do-nai
le-me-lech al kol ha-a-rets;

וְנֶאֱמַר: "וְהָיָה יְיָ לְמֶלֶךְ
עַל כָּל־הָאָרֶץ.

All sing

ba-yom ha-hu yi-he-yeh A-do-nai
e-chad u-she-mo e-chad."

בַּיּוֹם הַהוּא יִהְיֶה יְיָ אֶחָד וּשְׁמוֹ אֶחָד."

And it has been said: "God shall reign over all the earth; on that day the Eternal shall be One, and God's name shall be One."

(For comment, see p. 69)

187

Havdalah Spice Box
Viennese
18th c.

"Judaism...teaches us to understand death as part of the Divine pattern of the universe. Actually we could not have our sensitivity without fragility. Morality is the tax that we pay for the privilege of love, thought, creative work—the toll on the bridge of being from which clods of earth and snow-peaked mountain summits are exempt. Just because we are human, we are prisoners of the years, yet that very prison is the room of discipline in which we, driven by the urgency of time, create." (Rabbi Joshua Loth Liebman, 1907-1948).

Reader

Death diminishes us. It severs us from those whose presence enriched our days with joy and love. It robs us of those whose courage and wisdom comforted us in times of despair, and lifted our spirits in moments of confusion and pain. Yet death is not the end. Those now beyond our reach live in memory. Their attainments have become our inheritance; their ideals our challenge. On this Yom Kippur evening, we ask forgiveness for those times when we may have hurt or disappointed those we loved and have lost. May our lives constantly testify to the highest values they cherished and to their continuing impact upon us. We recall them now. They live in our hearts as an abiding blessing.

All rise

Yit-ga-dal ve-yit-ka-dash she-mei ra-ba
be-al-ma di-ve-ra chi-re-u-tei, ve-yam-lich
mal-chu-tei
be-cha-yei-chon u-ve-yo-mei-chon
u-ve-cha-yei de-chol beit Yis-ra-eil,
ba-a-ga-la u-vi-ze-man ka-riv, ve-i-me-ru:
a-mein.

יִתְגַּדַּל וְיִתְקַדַּשׁ שְׁמֵהּ רַבָּא
בְּעָלְמָא דִּי־בְרָא כִרְעוּתֵהּ,
וְיַמְלִיךְ מַלְכוּתֵהּ בְּחַיֵּיכוֹן
וּבְיוֹמֵיכוֹן וּבְחַיֵּי דְכָל־בֵּית
יִשְׂרָאֵל, בַּעֲגָלָא וּבִזְמַן קָרִיב,
וְאִמְרוּ: אָמֵן.

Ye-hei she-mei ra-ba me-va-rach le-a-lam
u-le-al-mei al-ma-ya.

יְהֵא שְׁמֵהּ רַבָּא מְבָרַךְ לְעָלַם
וּלְעָלְמֵי עָלְמַיָּא.

Yit-ba-rach ve-yish-ta-bach, ve-yit-pa-ar
ve-yit-ro-mam ve-yit-na-sei,
ve-yit-ha-dar ve-yit-a-leh ve-yit-ha-lal
she-mei de-ku-de-sha, be-rich hu,
le-ei-la min kol bi-re-cha-ta ve-shi-ra-ta
tush-be-cha-ta ve-ne-che-ma-ta,
da-a mi-ran be-al-ma,
ve-i-me-ru: a-mein.

יִתְבָּרַךְ וְיִשְׁתַּבַּח, וְיִתְפָּאַר
וְיִתְרוֹמַם וְיִתְנַשֵּׂא, וְיִתְהַדָּר
וְיִתְעַלֶּה וְיִתְהַלָּל שְׁמֵהּ
דְּקוּדְשָׁא, בְּרִיךְ הוּא, לְעֵלָּא
מִן־כָּל־בִּרְכָתָא וְשִׁירָתָא,
תֻּשְׁבְּחָתָא וְנֶחֱמָתָא דַּאֲמִירָן
בְּעָלְמָא, וְאִמְרוּ: אָמֵן.

Ye-hei she-la-ma ra-ba
min she-ma-ya ve-cha-yim
a-lei-nu ve-al kol Yis-ra-eil
ve-i-me-ru: a-mein.

יְהֵא שְׁלָמָא רַבָּא מִן־שְׁמַיָּא
וְחַיִּים עָלֵינוּ וְעַל־כָּל־יִשְׂרָאֵל,
וְאִמְרוּ: אָמֵן.

O-seh sha-lom bi-me-ro-mav, hu ya-a-seh
sha-lom a-lei-nu
ve-al kol Yis-ra-eil
ve-i-me-ru: a-mein.

עֹשֶׂה שָׁלוֹם בִּמְרוֹמָיו, הוּא
יַעֲשֶׂה שָׁלוֹם עָלֵינוּ וְעַל־
כָּל־יִשְׂרָאֵל
וְאִמְרוּ: אָמֵן.

May God's great name be magnified and made holy in the world created according to Divine will. May God soon establish a reign of justice and peace during our life and days, and during the lifetime of the whole house of Israel. And let us say, Amen.

May God's great name be blessed now and forever.

May the name of the Holy One be blessed, praised, glorified, exalted, extolled, honored, magnified, and celebrated, even though God is above and beyond all the blessings, songs, praises, and consolations that are spoken in the world. And let us say, Amen.

May there be great peace from heaven and life for us and all Israel. And let us say, Amen.

May the One who makes peace in the heavens make peace for us and for all Israel. And let us say, Amen.

YOM KIPPUR
MORNING SERVICE

Havdalah Spice Box
Poland
18th c.

The Torah refers to Yom Kippur as "a day on which you shall afflict your souls" *(Leviticus 23:28, 32)*. Rabbinic tradition interpreted "afflict" as meaning a day of fasting and self-examination. Yom Kippur worship, as Rabbi Max Arzt points out, "is suffused with the belief that sin alienates a human being from God…and that the sinner is in desperate need of reconciliation and atonement." Yom Kippur worship leads us through repentance to the renewal of moral purpose and the bonds uniting us with our people and faith *(Yomah 37a; Justice and Mercy, pp. 192-193)*.

MEDITATION FOR YOM KIPPUR MORNING

A Silent Prayer

O Source of life, You have given us this Yom Kippur Day for repentance and renewal. Entering into its sacred prayers, I turn to You. I bring all my confusions, my uncertainties, all the storms and fears battering me, and I place them before You. For You know my heart's desires, and I seek to fulfill the best of them.

You have given me understanding to distinguish between good and evil, and freedom to choose between them. So often, out of complacency, I allow habit to subvert my best intentions. I choose selfishness and greed over acts of kindness and love. I yield to temptations, wasting my precious powers for growth and goodness.

O God, let the promise of this Yom Kippur Day be fulfilled in my life. May these hours from early morning to the setting of the sun be spent in earnest self scrutiny and reconciliation. Remove callousness and cynicism from my heart. Heal my fears and failings. Bring me back to You. Inscribe me in the Book of Life for blessing.

Cantor and Choir

שַׁחַר אֲבַקֶּשְׁךָ, צוּרִי וּמִשְׂגַּבִּי,
אֶעֱרוֹךְ לְפָנֶיךָ שַׁחְרִי וְגַם עַרְבִּי.
לִפְנֵי גְדֻלָּתְךָ אֶעֱמֹד וְאֶבָּהֵל,
כִּי עֵינְךָ תִרְאֶה כָּל מַחְשְׁבוֹת לִבִּי.
מַה־זֶּה אֲשֶׁר יוּכַל הַלֵּב וְהַלָּשׁוֹן
לַעֲשׂוֹת, וּמַה כֹּחַ רוּחִי בְּתוֹךְ קִרְבִּי?
הִנֵּה לְךָ תִיטַב זִמְרַת אֱנוֹשׁ; עַל כֵּן
אוֹדְךָ בְּעוֹד תִּהְיֶה נִשְׁמַת אֱלוֹהַּ בִּי.

Early will I seek You, God, my Rock and Refuge. I will place before You my mornings and evenings. I tremble before Your awesome power, for You know all the thoughts of my heart. What can I say or do? What is the potential of the spirit within me? My human song is pleasant to You. Therefore I give You thanks for placing Your spirit within me.

"Early will I seek You..." is a poem by Solomon ibn Gabirol of Spain, 1021-1058. "Happy are those..." is derived from *Psalms 85:5; 144:15, 145:18, 115:18.*

ASHREI—HAPPY ARE THOSE IN YOUR HOUSE

Responsively

אַשְׁרֵי יוֹשְׁבֵי בֵיתֶךָ; עוֹד יְהַלְלוּךָ סֶּלָה.
אַשְׁרֵי הָעָם שֶׁכָּכָה לּוֹ; אַשְׁרֵי הָעָם שֶׁיְיָ אֱלֹהָיו.

Happy are those who dwell in Your house, O God; they lift their hearts in prayer.

Let every living soul praise You and proclaim Your loving-kindness forever.

On this Yom Kippur Day we are called to our sanctuary by a summons as exalting as the everlasting hills.

On this Day of Awe we stand in God's presence seeking repentance, reconciliation and renewal of spirit.

What are we? A leaf in a storm, a fleeting moment in the tide of time, a whisper lost in the vastness of creation?

Yet we summon the courage to invoke the God of our destiny.

Today we confess our sins, confront our failures, our wrongdoings.

Today we seek to mend the evil we have done and to pray that we might be inscribed in the Book of Life for a year of blessing.

קָרוֹב יְיָ לְכָל־קֹרְאָיו, לְכֹל אֲשֶׁר יִקְרָאֻהוּ בֶאֱמֶת.
וַאֲנַחְנוּ נְבָרֵךְ יָהּ מֵעַתָּה וְעַד־עוֹלָם. הַלְלוּיָהּ.

For You, O God, are never distant from those who seek You. And we, fragile creatures of Your love, rise to praise You, infinite God of time and space.

All rise and sing

Ba-re-chu et A-do-nai ha-me-vo-rach.

בָּרְכוּ אֶת־יְיָ הַמְבֹרָךְ!

Ba-ruch A-do-nai ha-me-vo-rach
le-o-lam va-ed.

בָּרוּךְ יְיָ הַמְבֹרָךְ לְעוֹלָם וָעֶד!

Praise God, to whom our praise is due.
Praised be the Lord, to whom our praise is due, now and forever.

YOTZER OR—CREATOR OF LIGHT

Reader

בָּרוּךְ אַתָּה, יְיָ אֱלֹהֵינוּ, מֶלֶךְ הָעוֹלָם, יוֹצֵר אוֹר וּבוֹרֵא
חֹשֶׁךְ, עֹשֶׂה שָׁלוֹם וּבוֹרֵא אֶת־הַכֹּל. הַמֵּאִיר לָאָרֶץ וְלַדָּרִים
עָלֶיהָ בְּרַחֲמִים, וּבְטוּבוֹ מְחַדֵּשׁ בְּכָל־יוֹם תָּמִיד מַעֲשֵׂה
בְרֵאשִׁית. בָּרוּךְ אַתָּה, יְיָ, יוֹצֵר הַמְּאוֹרוֹת.

Congregation

Heaven and earth are the work of Your hands. You form light and darkness, renewing daily the wonder of creation. The mysteries of life and death,
of growth and decay reveal Your creative power. O God, the whole universe
is Your dwelling-place, a hymn to Your glory.

(For comment, see p. 79)

Reader

Great has been Your love for us. Our people put their trust in You, and You taught them laws for life. Be gracious also to us. Enlighten us with the wisdom of Torah. Inspire us to carry out Your will with deeds of mercy, justice and love. Lead us to lives enriched by faithfulness to Your teachings.

Congregation

You have sanctified us for Your service. You have drawn us to You in love. You have summoned us to proclaim Your unity.

Reader

בָּרוּךְ אַתָּה, יְיָ, הַבּוֹחֵר בְּעַמּוֹ יִשְׂרָאֵל בְּאַהֲבָה.

Be praised, O God, who in love has chosen our people Israel to serve You.

All sing

She-ma Yis-ra-eil: A-do-nai
E-lo-hei-nu, A-do-nai E-chad.

שְׁמַע יִשְׂרָאֵל: יְיָ אֱלֹהֵינוּ, יְיָ אֶחָד!

Ba-ruch sheim ke-vod
mal-chu-to le-o-lam va-ed.

בָּרוּךְ שֵׁם כְּבוֹד מַלְכוּתוֹ לְעוֹלָם וָעֶד!

Hear, O Israel: the Lord is our God, the Lord is One!
Blessed is God's glorious power forever and ever.

All are seated

———————————

(For comment, see p. 80)

199

Tik (Torah Container), Turkey 57.4
John R. Forsman, Photographer
From the Collection of the Hebrew Union College
Skirball Museum

The words "You shall love..." are from *Deuteronomy 6:4-9*. Together with *Deuteronomy 11:13-21* and *Numbers 15:37-41*, they form the traditional sections of the *Shema* as found in the *mezuzah* placed on the doorpost, and in the *tefilin*, or "phylacteries" worn on the hand and between the eyes during morning worship. "You shall love..." emphasizes the responsibility of parents to teach Torah to their children, and the obligation to practice the ethical and ritual traditions of Torah in every aspect of one's life.

Congregation

Ve-a-hav-ta eit A-do-nai E-lo-he-cha,
be-chol le-va-ve-cha, u-ve-chol
naf-she-cha, u-ve-chol me-o-de-cha.
Ve-ha-yu ha-de-va-rim ha-ei-leh, a-sher
a-no-chi me-tsa-ve-cha ha-yom, al
le-va-ve-cha. Ve-shi-nan-tam le-va-ne-cha,
ve-di-bar-ta bam be-shiv-te-cha
be-vei-te-cha u-ve-lech-te-cha va-de-rech
u-ve-shoch-be-cha u-ve-ku-me-cha.
U-ke-shar-tam le-ot al ya-de-cha, ve-ha-yu
le-to-ta-fot bein ei-ne-cha. U-che-tav-tam
al me-zu-zot bei-te-cha u-vish-a-re-cha.

Le-ma-an tiz-ke-ru, va-a-si-tem et kol
mits-vo-tai, vi-hi-yi-tem ke-do-shim
lei-lo-hei-chem. A-ni A-do-nai
E-lo-hei-chem: a-sher ho-tsei-ti e-te-chem
mei-e-rets Mits-ra-yim, li-hi-yot la-chem
lei-lo-him. A-ni A-do-nai E-lo-hei-chem.

וְאָהַבְתָּ אֵת יְיָ אֱלֹהֶיךָ בְּכָל־
לְבָבְךָ וּבְכָל־נַפְשְׁךָ וּבְכָל־
מְאֹדֶךָ.

וְהָיוּ הַדְּבָרִים הָאֵלֶּה, אֲשֶׁר אָנֹכִי
מְצַוְּךָ הַיּוֹם, עַל־לְבָבֶךָ. וְשִׁנַּנְתָּם
לְבָנֶיךָ, וְדִבַּרְתָּ בָּם בְּשִׁבְתְּךָ
בְּבֵיתֶךָ, וּבְלֶכְתְּךָ בַדֶּרֶךְ,
וּבְשָׁכְבְּךָ וּבְקוּמֶךָ. וּקְשַׁרְתָּם לְאוֹת
עַל־יָדֶךָ, וְהָיוּ לְטֹטָפֹת בֵּין עֵינֶיךָ.
וּכְתַבְתָּם עַל־מְזֻזוֹת בֵּיתֶךָ,
וּבִשְׁעָרֶיךָ.

לְמַעַן תִּזְכְּרוּ וַעֲשִׂיתֶם אֶת־כָּל־
מִצְוֹתָי, וִהְיִיתֶם קְדֹשִׁים
לֵאלֹהֵיכֶם. אֲנִי יְיָ אֱלֹהֵיכֶם, אֲשֶׁר
הוֹצֵאתִי אֶתְכֶם מֵאֶרֶץ מִצְרַיִם
לִהְיוֹת לָכֶם לֵאלֹהִים. אֲנִי יְיָ
אֱלֹהֵיכֶם.

You shall love the Lord your God with all your heart, with all your soul, and with all your might. And these words which I command you this day shall be upon your heart. You shall teach them diligently to your children, and shall speak of them when you sit in your house, when you walk by the way, when you lie down, and when you rise up. You shall bind them for a sign upon your hand, and they shall be for frontlets between your eyes. You shall write them upon the doorposts of your house and upon your gates, that you may remember and do all My commandments and be holy unto your God.

Responsively

True and enduring is Your saving power, O God.

> You have sustained our people in times of trouble and have been our refuge in all generations.

As You saved Israel from Egyptian bondage, send help to all who are broken and oppressed.

> As You lifted us out of suffering, send us to heal the hurts of others.

May Your law of love transform our words and deeds for goodness.

> O God, we glorify You now as did our people in ancient days.

All sing

Mi cha-mo-cha ba-ei-lim, A-do-nai?
Mi ka-mo-cha, ne-dar ba-ko-desh,
no-ra te-hi-lot, o-sei fe-leh?

מִי־כָמֹכָה בָּאֵלִם, יְיָ?
מִי כָּמֹכָה, נֶאְדָּר בַּקֹּדֶשׁ,
נוֹרָא תְהִלֹּת, עֹשֵׂה פֶלֶא?

Who is like You, Eternal One, among the gods that are worshiped? Who is like You, majestic in holiness, awesome in splendor, doing wonders?

Cantor

שִׁירָה חֲדָשָׁה שִׁבְּחוּ גְאוּלִים לְשִׁמְךָ עַל־שְׂפַת הַיָּם; יַחַד כֻּלָּם
הוֹדוּ וְהִמְלִיכוּ וְאָמְרוּ:

Those who were redeemed sang a new song to Your name. At the shore of the sea, saved from destruction, they proclaimed Your sovereign power: "God will reign forever and ever."

All sing

"A-do-nai yim-loch le-o-lam va-ed."

"יְיָ יִמְלֹךְ לְעֹלָם וָעֶד!"

Reader

צוּר יִשְׂרָאֵל, קוּמָה בְּעֶזְרַת יִשְׂרָאֵל, וּפְדֵה כִנְאֻמֶךָ יְהוּדָה
וְיִשְׂרָאֵל. גֹּאֲלֵנוּ, יְיָ צְבָאוֹת שְׁמוֹ, קְדוֹשׁ יִשְׂרָאֵל.
בָּרוּךְ אַתָּה, יְיָ, גָּאַל יִשְׂרָאֵל.

O Rock of Israel, redeem those who are oppressed and liberate those who are persecuted. Be praised, O God, Redeemer of Israel.

"True and enduring...." Jewish tradition affirms that God not only creates life but liberates humanity from bondage and oppression. This prayer, composed during the time of the Second Temple in Jerusalem, and known as *Ge-ulah,* "Liberation," recalls the words *mi cha-mo-cha,* sung by Miriam and the Israelites after their liberation from Egypt *(Mishnah, Tamid 5:1,* and *Exodus 15:11).*

All rise as ark is opened

Meditation before the Amidah

We are sojourners; our days on earth are a brief span. Time flows into the sea of eternity, and we ask: What is the meaning of our lives, our flickering fleeting light? In You, O Eternal One, we uncover the mystery of our being. Our souls reflect You as our yearnings and the faith of our people testify to Your power and love. Awaken us now to Your glory. Release us from sins of indifference, arrogance and hypocrisy. Touch our trembling souls with Your will for goodness, truth and beauty. Answer our longings and our prayers. For with You is the fountain of life; in Your light do we see light.

Reader

אֲדֹנָי, שְׂפָתַי תִּפְתָּח, וּפִי יַגִּיד תְּהִלָּתֶךָ.

Eternal God, open our lips that our mouths may declare Your glory.

Amidah means "standing" and is the third section of the service. On weekdays this section, also known as *Tefilah,* or "the Prayer," contains nineteen prayers. On the Sabbath and Holy Days the first three and last three prayers of the weekday section are retained, and a special "Sanctification of the Day" replaces the others. According to tradition, the *Amidah* was written by the rabbis of the Great Assembly and made an official part of Jewish worship by Rabban Gamliel, head of the Yavneh Academy in about 100 C.E.

Cantor

Ba-ruch a-ta, A-do-nai, E-lo-hei-nu
vei-lo-hei a-vo-tei-nu, E-lo-hei Av-ra-ham,
E-lo-hei Yits-chak, vei-lo-hei Ya-a-kov:
ha-eil ha-ga-dol, ha-gi-bor ve-ha-no-ra, Eil
el-yon, go-meil cha-sa-dim to-vim,
ve-ko-nei ha-kol, ve-zo-cheir cha-se-dei
a-vot, u-mei-vi ge-u-lah li-ve-nei
ve-nei-hem le-ma-an she-mo, be-a-ha-va.

All sing

Zoch-rei-nu le-cha-yim, me-lech
cha-feitz ba-cha-yim, ve-chot-vei-nu
be-sei-fer ha-cha-yim, le-ma-an-cha
Elo-him cha-yim.

Cantor

Me-lech o-zeir u-mo-shi-a u-ma-gein.
Ba-ruch a-ta A-do-nai, ma-gein
Av-ra-ham.

בָּרוּךְ אַתָּה, יְיָ אֱלֹהֵינוּ
וֵאלֹהֵי אֲבוֹתֵינוּ, אֱלֹהֵי
אַבְרָהָם, אֱלֹהֵי יִצְחָק,
וֵאלֹהֵי יַעֲקֹב: הָאֵל הַגָּדוֹל,
הַגִּבּוֹר וְהַנּוֹרָא, אֵל עֶלְיוֹן.
גּוֹמֵל חֲסָדִים טוֹבִים,
וְקוֹנֵה הַכֹּל, וְזוֹכֵר חַסְדֵי
אָבוֹת, וּמֵבִיא גְאֻלָּה לִבְנֵי
בְנֵיהֶם, לְמַעַן שְׁמוֹ, בְּאַהֲבָה.

זָכְרֵנוּ לְחַיִּים, מֶלֶךְ חָפֵץ
בַּחַיִּים, וְכָתְבֵנוּ בְּסֵפֶר הַחַיִּים,
לְמַעַנְךָ אֱלֹהִים חַיִּים.

מֶלֶךְ עוֹזֵר וּמוֹשִׁיעַ וּמָגֵן.
בָּרוּךְ אַתָּה, יְיָ, מָגֵן אַבְרָהָם.

Responsively

You are our God, even as You were the God of Abraham, Isaac and Jacob, the
God of Sarah, Rebekah, Leah and Rachel.

Their faith was strong that all humanity would one day be redeemed
from injustice, fear and pain.

As we remember their vision, remember us with the blessing of life.

O God of life, may we merit inscription in Your Book of Life.

(For comment, see p. 54)

Havdalah Spice Box
China
20th c.

The *Gevurot* prayer celebrates God's creative and renewing Power at work in all nature, as well as the human responsibility to embody and express that Power for creativity, healing, liberation and hope. Even in death, God's Power for life sustains the memory and contributions of loved ones in the minds and hearts of succeeding generations.

Reader

אַתָּה גִבּוֹר לְעוֹלָם, אֲדֹנָי, מְחַיֵּה הַכֹּל אַתָּה, רַב
לְהוֹשִׁיעַ. מְכַלְכֵּל חַיִּים בְּחֶסֶד, מְחַיֵּה הַכֹּל בְּרַחֲמִים
רַבִּים. סוֹמֵךְ נוֹפְלִים, וְרוֹפֵא חוֹלִים, וּמַתִּיר
אֲסוּרִים, וּמְקַיֵּם אֱמוּנָתוֹ לִישֵׁנֵי עָפָר. מִי כָמְוֹךָ, בַּעַל
גְבוּרוֹת, וּמִי דְוֹמֶה לָּךְ, מֶלֶךְ מֵמִית וּמְחַיֵּה וּמַצְמִיחַ
יְשׁוּעָה? מִי כָמְוֹךָ אַב הָרַחֲמִים, זוֹכֵר יְצוּרָיו לְחַיִּים
בְּרַחֲמִים? וְנֶאֱמָן אַתָּה לְהַחֲיוֹת הַכֹּל. בָּרוּךְ אַתָּה, יְיָ,
מְחַיֵּה הַכֹּל.

O God, the power of Your spirit sustains all creation. When we open our hearts
to You, we are filled with the strength to bear the afflictions of our kind
and to refuse them victory.

Congregation

May we be among those who lift up the fallen, who set free the captive, who
bring healing to the sick and help to those in need. And when we must walk
in the valley of the shadows, may Your light and love dispel our terror of the
darkness. Be praised, O God, for the gift of life.

Ark is closed; all are seated

Cantor and Choir

וּנְתַנֶּה תְּקֶף קְדֻשַּׁת הַיּוֹם כִּי הוּא נוֹרָא וְאָים. וּבוֹ
תִנָּשֵׂא מַלְכוּתֶךָ וְיִכּוֹן בְּחֶסֶד כִּסְאֶךָ וְתֵשֵׁב עָלָיו
בֶּאֱמֶת.

Reader

We proclaim the sacred power of this day, for it is wondrous and full of
dread. Today, O God, Your rule is exalted. Your glory is celebrated. You are
our Judge, our Conscience. You know our dreams and disappointments. We are
an open book before You.

Congregation

You remember all that we have forgotten, and today You measure our deeds
as the signature of our lives.

Choir

וּבְשׁוֹפָר גָּדוֹל יִתָּקַע וְקוֹל דְּמָמָה דַקָּה יִשָּׁמַע.
וּמַלְאָכִים יֵחָפֵזוּן וְחִיל וּרְעָדָה יֹאחֵזוּן וְיֹאמְרוּ: הִנֵּה
יוֹם הַדִּין.

Reader

The great Shofar will sound, and a voice will declare: "This is the Day
of Judgment."

Congregation

Today we pass before You as the flock passes before the shepherd.

(For comment, see p. 88)

Reader

Judge us with mercy as we come before You.

Cantor and Choir

בְּרֹאשׁ הַשָּׁנָה יִכָּתֵבוּן וּבְיוֹם צוֹם כִּפּוּר יֵחָתֵמוּן.
כַּמָּה יַעַבְרוּן וְכַמָּה יִבָּרֵאוּן, מִי יִחְיֶה וּמִי יָמוּת,
מִי יָנוּחַ וּמִי יָנוּעַ, מִי יַשְׁקִיט וּמִי יְטָרֵף, מִי יַעֲנִי
וּמִי יַעֲשִׁיר, מִי יִשָּׁפֵל וּמִי יָרוּם.
וּתְשׁוּבָה וּתְפִלָּה וּצְדָקָה
מַעֲבִירִין אֶת־רֹעַ הַגְּזֵרָה.

Reader

On Rosh Hashanah our destiny is written; at the end of Yom Kippur it is sealed:
How many will be born? How many will pass away? Who will live? Who will
die? Who will rest? Who will wander? Who will know peace? Who will be
troubled? Who will be needy? Who will be content? Who will be humbled?
Who will be exalted?

Congregation

May our repentance, prayer and charity influence the ultimate decree.

Reader

For we are but dust, fragile vessels, easily broken.

Congregation

We are passing shadows, fleeting clouds, vanishing dreams.

Reader

וְאַתָּה הוּא מֶלֶךְ אֵל חַי וְקַיָּם!

But You, O God, are the Eternal One of all time and space.

Ark is opened; all rise

Reader

נְקַדֵּשׁ אֶת־שִׁמְךָ בָּעוֹלָם כְּשֵׁם שֶׁמַּקְדִּישִׁים אוֹתוֹ
בִּשְׁמֵי מָרוֹם, כַּכָּתוּב עַל יַד נְבִיאֶךָ, וְקָרָא זֶה אֶל־זֶה
וְאָמַר:

We sanctify Your Name on earth. Filled with awe before the wonder of life, we sing Your praise:

All sing

Ka-dosh, ka-dosh, ka-dosh, A-do-nai
tse-va-ot, me-lo chol ha-a-rets ke-vo-do.

קָדוֹשׁ, קָדוֹשׁ, קָדוֹשׁ
יְיָ צְבָאוֹת,
מְלֹא כָל־הָאָרֶץ כְּבוֹדוֹ.

Holy, holy, holy is the Lord of hosts; the whole earth is filled with God's glory.

Cantor

אַדִּיר אַדִּירֵנוּ, יְיָ אֲדֹנֵינוּ, מָה־אַדִּיר שִׁמְךָ בְּכָל־הָאָרֶץ!

Source of our strength, Lord our God, how majestic is Your presence in all the earth!

All sing

Ba-ruch ke-vod A-do-nai mi-me-ko-mo.

בָּרוּךְ כְּבוֹד־יְיָ מִמְּקוֹמוֹ.

Blessed is the glory of God in heaven and earth.

Cantor

אֶחָד הוּא אֱלֹהֵינוּ, הוּא אָבִינוּ, הוּא מַלְכֵּנוּ, הוּא מוֹשִׁיעֵנוּ;
וְהוּא יַשְׁמִיעֵנוּ בְּרַחֲמָיו לְעֵינֵי כָּל־חָי:

God alone is our Creator, our Ruler, our Helper; and God is revealed in works of love in the sight of all the living.

All sing

Yim-loch A-do-nai le-o-lam, E-lo-ha-yich
Tsi-yon, le-dor va-dor. Ha-le-lu-yah!

יִמְלֹךְ יְיָ לְעוֹלָם,
אֱלֹהַיִךְ צִיּוֹן,
לְדֹר וָדֹר. הַלְלוּיָהּ!

The Lord will reign forever, your God,
O Zion, from generation to generation. Halleluyah.

Reader

לְדוֹר וָדוֹר נַגִּיד גָּדְלֶךָ, וּלְנֵצַח נְצָחִים קְדֻשָּׁתְךָ נַקְדִּישׁ.
וְשִׁבְחֲךָ, אֱלֹהֵינוּ, מִפִּינוּ לֹא יָמוּשׁ לְעוֹלָם וָעֶד.
בָּרוּךְ אַתָּה, יְיָ, הָאֵל הַקָּדוֹשׁ.

To all generations we will make known Your greatness. Your praise shall
never depart from our lips. We praise You, the God of holiness.

Ark is closed; all are seated

The *Kedushah* prayer is based upon the mystic experience of the prophet Isaiah.
We are told that while standing in the Jerusalem Temple, God summoned him to
bring a message of justice, truth and mercy to the people of Israel. He responded:
"I am ready; send me" *(Isaiah 6:1-8)*.

Reader

וּבְכֵן תֵּן פַּחְדְּךָ, יְיָ אֱלֹהֵינוּ, עַל כָּל־מַעֲשֶׂיךָ, וְאֵימָתְךָ
עַל כָּל־מַה־שֶּׁבָּרָאתָ. וְיֵעָשׂוּ כֻלָּם אֲגֻדָּה אַחַת לַעֲשׂוֹת
רְצוֹנְךָ בְּלֵבָב שָׁלֵם, כְּמוֹ שֶׁיָּדַעְנוּ, יְיָ אֱלֹהֵינוּ,
שֶׁהַשִּׁלְטוֹן לְפָנֶיךָ, עֹז בְּיָדְךָ וּגְבוּרָה בִּימִינֶךָ, וְשִׁמְךָ
נוֹרָא עַל כָּל־מַה־שֶּׁבָּרָאתָ.

Now, O God, fill our hearts with reverence for all the wonders of Your creation. Unite us to fashion the time when fear and despair will be banished from every human heart.

Congregation

Now, O God, fill us with honor for those who generously support the hopes of the helpless. May we be counted among them.

Reader

Now, O God, hasten the day when the just will see and rejoice that cruelty and selfishness have vanished like smoke, that arrogance and greed are banished from earth.

הָאֵל הַקָּדוֹשׁ נִקְדַּשׁ בִּצְדָקָה. בָּרוּךְ אַתָּה, יְיָ, הַמֶּלֶךְ הַקָּדוֹשׁ.

Congregation

Be praised, O God, exalted in holiness, sanctified by righteousness.

(For comment, see p. 58)

Reader

אֱלֹהֵֽינוּ וֵאלֹהֵי אֲבוֹתֵֽינוּ, יַעֲלֶה וְיָבֹא וְיִזָּכֵר זִכְרוֹנֵֽנוּ
וְזִכְרוֹן כָּל־עַמְּךָ בֵּית יִשְׂרָאֵל לְפָנֶֽיךָ, לְטוֹבָה לְחֵן
לְחֶֽסֶד וּלְרַחֲמִים, לְחַיִּים וּלְשָׁלוֹם בְּיוֹם הַכִּפּוּרִים
הַזֶּה.

God of all ages, answer the prayers of Your people, Israel, on this Yom Kippur Day. Strengthen our powers for kindness and caring, for compassion and love, for life and peace.

Reader

זָכְרֵֽנוּ, יְיָ אֱלֹהֵֽינוּ, בּוֹ לְטוֹבָה.

Congregation

This day, remember us for goodness.

Choir

Amen

Reader

וּפָקְדֵֽנוּ בוֹ לִבְרָכָה.

Congregation

This day, mark us for blessing.

Choir

Amen

Reader

וְהוֹשִׁיעֵֽנוּ בוֹ לְחַיִּים.

Congregation

This day, preserve us for life.

Choir

Amen

Havdalah Spice Box
Europe
19th c.

"Our God, and God of our people..." is the fourth, or middle prayer of the *Amidah*. It assures the worshiper that God will pardon the sins of those who examine their deeds and commit themselves to repentance. "For on this Yom Kippur day..." is from *Leviticus 16:30*.

Responsively

אֱלֹהֵינוּ וֵאלֹהֵי אֲבוֹתֵינוּ, מְחַל לַעֲוֹנוֹתֵינוּ בְּיוֹם
(הַשַּׁבָּת הַזֶּה וּבְיוֹם) הַכִּפּוּרִים הַזֶּה,

Our God, and God of our people, You have given us this (**Sabbath and**) Yom Kippur Day that we might seek forgiveness for our sins.

For none of us lives without sinning, without our failures, our regrets, our mistakes, our excesses.

Even when we seek to do our best, we err and spoil good intentions.

Our sins begin as a spider's web and grow into heavy ropes shackling us in harmful habits.

Sin roots in the neglect of loved ones; it thrives in selfishness; it flourishes in greed; it multiplies in stubborness and anger.

Sin knows no boundaries. Like the dust of our slander, which scatters with the winds, our sins fall like stones, injuring those who are near and far.

Yet, You have given us this Yom Kippur Day promising forgiveness.

You will cast away our sins if we regret them and correct them.

For You have promised, "Return to Me and I will blot out your sins. I will redeem you."

Choir

"כִּי בַיּוֹם הַזֶּה יְכַפֵּר עֲלֵיכֶם לְטַהֵר אֶתְכֶם; מִכֹּל
חַטֹּאתֵיכֶם לִפְנֵי יְיָ תִּטְהָרוּ."

For on this Yom Kippur Day, God will grant you atonement to purify you from all your sins. Before God will you be pure.

215

Reader

רְצֵה, יְיָ אֱלֹהֵינוּ, בְּעַמְּךָ יִשְׂרָאֵל, וּתְפִלָּתָם בְּאַהֲבָה
תְקַבֵּל, וּתְהִי לְרָצוֹן תָּמִיד עֲבוֹדַת יִשְׂרָאֵל עַמֶּךָ.
בָּרוּךְ אַתָּה, יְיָ, שֶׁאוֹתְךָ לְבַדְּךָ בְּיִרְאָה נַעֲבוֹד.

May we, Your people Israel, be worthy in our deeds and our prayer. Wherever we live, wherever we seek You—in this land, in Zion restored, in all lands— You are our God, whom alone we serve in reverence.

HODA-AH—WE GIVE THANKS

Congregation

We give thanks for the gift of life, wonder beyond words; the awareness of soul, our light within; the world around us, so filled with beauty; and the richness of the earth, which day by day sustains us. For all these gifts and more, we thank and bless You, the Source of all goodness.

מוֹדִים אֲנַחְנוּ לָךְ, שָׁאַתָּה הוּא יְיָ אֱלֹהֵינוּ וַאלֹהֵי אֲבוֹתֵינוּ
לְעוֹלָם וָעֶד. צוּר חַיֵּינוּ, מָגֵן יִשְׁעֵנוּ, אַתָּה הוּא לְדוֹר וָדוֹר.
וְכָל הַחַיִּים יוֹדוּךָ סֶּלָה, וִיהַלְלוּ אֶת שִׁמְךָ בֶּאֱמֶת, הָאֵל
יְשׁוּעָתֵנוּ וְעֶזְרָתֵנוּ סֶלָה. בָּרוּךְ אַתָּה, יְיָ, הַטּוֹב שִׁמְךָ וּלְךָ נָאֶה
לְהוֹדוֹת.

(For comment, see p. 62)

Reader

שִׂים שָׁלוֹם, טוֹבָה וּבְרָכָה, חֵן וָחֶסֶד וְרַחֲמִים, עָלֵינוּ
וְעַל כָּל־יִשְׂרָאֵל עַמֶּךָ. בָּרְכֵנוּ אָבִינוּ, כֻּלָּנוּ כְּאֶחָד,
בְּאוֹר פָּנֶיךָ, כִּי בְאוֹר פָּנֶיךָ נָתַתָּ לָנוּ, יְיָ אֱלֹהֵינוּ,
תּוֹרַת חַיִּים, וְאַהֲבַת חֶסֶד, וּצְדָקָה וּבְרָכָה וְרַחֲמִים,
וְחַיִּים וְשָׁלוֹם. וְטוֹב בְּעֵינֶיךָ לְבָרֵךְ אֶת־עַמְּךָ יִשְׂרָאֵל
בְּכָל־עֵת וּבְכָל־שָׁעָה בִּשְׁלוֹמֶךָ.

Grant us peace, Your most precious gift, O Eternal Source of peace, and
enable Israel to be its messenger unto the peoples of the earth. Bless our
country that it may ever be a stronghold of peace and its advocate in the council
of nations. May contentment reign within its borders, health and happiness
within its homes. Strengthen the bonds of friendship among the inhabitants
of all lands. Plant virtue in every soul, and may the love of Your name hallow
every home and every heart.

Cantor and Choir

בְּסֵפֶר חַיִּים בְּרָכָה וְשָׁלוֹם וּפַרְנָסָה טוֹבָה נִזָּכֵר
וְנִכָּתֵב לְפָנֶיךָ, אֲנַחְנוּ וְכָל־עַמְּךָ בֵּית יִשְׂרָאֵל, לְחַיִּים
טוֹבִים וּלְשָׁלוֹם. בָּרוּךְ אַתָּה, יְיָ, עוֹשֵׂה הַשָּׁלוֹם.

May we, and all Israel, be inscribed in the Book of Life for blessing, sustenance
and peace. Be praised, O God, Giver of peace.

Torah Breast Plate
United States
19th c.

Jewish tradition emphasizes God's forgiveness. No human being is abandoned because of wrongdoing. The gates of repentance are always open, and the study of Torah is the means through which one grows in wisdom, and is guided to deeds of charity, justice and love. The prophet Zechariah taught that God says, "Return to Me...and I will return to You" *(1.3).*

Reader

אֱלֹהֵינוּ וֵאלֹהֵי אֲבוֹתֵינוּ, מְחַל לַעֲוֹנוֹתֵינוּ בְּיוֹם
(הַשַּׁבָּת הַזֶּה וּבְיוֹם) הַכִּפּוּרִים הַזֶּה; מְחֵה וְהַעֲבֵר
פְּשָׁעֵינוּ וְחַטֹּאתֵינוּ מִנֶּגֶד עֵינֶיךָ, כָּאָמוּר: " שׁוּבָה אֵלַי,
כִּי גְאַלְתִּיךָ."

Our God and God of our people, pardon our transgressions on this **(Sabbath
day and on this)** Yom Kippur Day. Forgive our sins as You have promised:
"Return to Me with deeds of loving-kindness and faithfulness, and I will
embrace You."

All rise

Cantor and Choir

אֱלֹהֵינוּ וֵאלֹהֵי אֲבוֹתֵינוּ, תָּבוֹא לְפָנֶיךָ תְּפִלָּתֵנוּ וְאַל
תִּתְעַלַּם מִתְּחִנָּתֵנוּ, שֶׁאֵין אֲנַחְנוּ עַזֵּי פָנִים וּקְשֵׁי עֹרֶף
לוֹמַר לְפָנֶיךָ, יְיָ אֱלֹהֵינוּ וֵאלֹהֵי אֲבוֹתֵינוּ, צַדִּיקִים
אֲנַחְנוּ וְלֹא חָטָאנוּ, אֲבָל אֲנַחְנוּ חָטָאנוּ. חָטָאנוּ,
עָוִינוּ, פָּשַׁעְנוּ.

Our God, and God of our people, may our prayers be acceptable before You.
Hear our plea for pardon, for we are not so stubborn as to say that we are perfect
and have not sinned. We confess our wrongs. We have sinned. We have transgressed. We have done perversely.

All are seated

Reader

אַתָּה יוֹדֵעַ רָזֵי עוֹלָם, וְתַעֲלוּמוֹת סִתְרֵי כָּל חָי.

O Lord, You know all our ways, the words we speak, the thoughts we harbor, the deeds we do, and those left undone. There is no escaping from Your spirit, no fleeing from Your presence.

Congregation

The darkness is not too dark for You; night is as the light of day.

Reader

You know the truth about us. We have failed others, and others have failed us. We have cheated ourselves, and others have taken advantage of us.

Congregation

We are a community of regret. We bear not only our sins but those of our people as well. You have bound us to a single destiny. You are our Conscience, and we admit to You the alphabet of our sins.

Reader

In accents of sacred Yom Kippur tradition, we listen to the declaration of each failing and then repeat it in reverent confession.

"O Lord, You know all our ways..." is attributed to Rav (280 C.E.-352 C.E.), head of the Academy at Pumbedita in Babylonia. It forms one of the central prayers of the Yom Kippur confession. "The darkness..." is from *Psalms 139:12.* The *A-sham-nu* was composed during the 9th century C.E. in Babylonia and, like the *Al Cheit,* is an alphabetical confession of sins. The recitation incorporates repetition so that each failure can be heard and expressed. It is a custom to tap one's chest with a loosely made fist as a sign of regret as each sin is recited. Isaac Luria (1534-1572), a teacher of Jewish mysticism in Safed, once asked, "Why is it that our confession is arranged in the plural and not singular form? We say, 'We are sinful,' instead of 'I am sinful.' Because the people of Israel are as one body. When one sins, it hurts us all. We are responsible for one another." (Joseph H. Hertz, *Daily Prayer Book, p. 906).*

Cantor pronounces each sin. Congregation then repeats in Hebrew while meditating on the meaning of each human failing.

Cantor	Congregation	Meditation
אָשַׁמְנוּ	Asham-nu	We are sinful.
בָּגַדְנוּ	Ba-gad-nu	We are faithless.
גָּזַלְנוּ	Ga-zal-nu	We are cruel.
דִּבַּרְנוּ דֹפִי	Di-bar-nu do-fi	We are sarcastic.
הֶעֱוִינוּ	He-e-vi-nu	We are arrogant.
וְהִרְשַׁעְנוּ	Ve-hir-sha-nu	We are vicious.
זַדְנוּ	Zad-nu	We are fraudulent.
חָמַסְנוּ	Cha-mas-nu	We are vulgar.
טָפַלְנוּ שֶׁקֶר	Ta-fal-nu she-ker	We are dishonest.
יָעַצְנוּ רַע	Ya-atz-nu ra	We are deceptive.
כִּזַּבְנוּ	Ki-zav-nu	We are liars.
לַצְנוּ	Latz-nu	We are frivolous.
מָרַדְנוּ	Ma-rad-nu	We are rebellious.
נִאַצְנוּ	Ni-atz-nu	We are insulting.
סָרַרְנוּ	Sa-rar-nu	We are obstinate.
עָוִינוּ	Avi-nu	We are subverters.
פָּשַׁעְנוּ	Pa-sha-nu	We are offensive.
צָרַרְנוּ	Tza-rar-nu	We are hurtful.
קִשִּׁינוּ עֹרֶף	Ki-shi-nu o-ref	We are stubborn.
רָשַׁעְנוּ	Ra-sha-nu	We are unjust.
שִׁחַתְנוּ	Shi-chat-nu	We are corrupt.
תִּעַבְנוּ	Ti-av-nu	We are destructive.
תָּעִינוּ	Ta-i-nu	We are erratic.
תִּעְתָּעְנוּ	Ti-ta-nu	We are neglectful.

Havdalah Spice Box and Candle Holder
Eastern Europe
1720

"We have neglected Your commandments..." reflects the view that failure to live by the ritual and ethical obligations of Jewish tradition wastes human potentials and distances one from a life of "benefit," purpose and fulfillment, as Job's friends counsel him *(33:27)*.

SARNU—WE HAVE NEGLECTED YOUR COMMANDMENTS

Reader

סַרְנוּ מִמִּצְוֹתֶיךָ וּמִמִּשְׁפָּטֶיךָ הַטּוֹבִים וְלֹא שָׁוָה לָנוּ.
וְאַתָּה צַדִּיק עַל כָּל־הַבָּא עָלֵינוּ, כִּי אֱמֶת עָשִׂיתָ
וַאֲנַחְנוּ הִרְשָׁעְנוּ.

We have neglected Your commandments, Your summons for goodness, and it has brought us no benefit. You call us to righteous deeds, to acts of kindness, but we have spurned You, O God of truth.

Congregation

Pardon our transgressions. Grant us atonement for all the sins we have sinned against You.

Reader

We repeat them now....

Responsively, Reader, then Congregation

עַל חֵטְא שֶׁחָטָאנוּ לְפָנֶיךָ בְּכַפַּת שְׁחַד.

Al cheit she-cha-ta-nu...For **Concealing** the truth from ourselves, forgive us.

עַל חֵטְא שֶׁחָטָאנוּ לְפָנֶיךָ בְּלָצוֹן.

Al cheit she-cha-ta-nu...For **Laughing** at the good intentions of others, forgive us.

עַל חֵטְא שֶׁחָטָאנוּ לְפָנֶיךָ בְּמַשָּׂא וּבְמַתָּן.

Al cheit she-cha-ta-nu...For **Misleading** others in our business dealings, forgive us.

עַל חֵטְא שֶׁחָטָאנוּ לְפָנֶיךָ בְּנֶשֶׁךְ וּבְמַרְבִּית.

Al cheit she-cha-ta-nu...For **Negotiating** more than our fair share, forgive us.

עַל חֵטְא שֶׁחָטָאנוּ לְפָנֶיךָ בְּשִׂיחַ שִׂפְתוֹתֵינוּ.

Al cheit she-cha-ta-nu...For **Saying** one thing and doing another, forgive us.

עַל חֵטְא שֶׁחָטָאנוּ לְפָנֶיךָ בְּעַזּוּת מֶצַח.

Al cheit she-cha-ta-nu...For **Acting** with scornful defiance, forgive us.

עַל חֵטְא שֶׁחָטָאנוּ לְפָנֶיךָ בִּפְרִיקַת עֹל.

Al cheit she-cha-ta-nu...For **Pivoting** away from our responsibilities, forgive us.

עַל חֵטְא שֶׁחָטָאנוּ לְפָנֶיךָ בְּצָרוּת עָיִן.

Al cheit she-cha-ta-nu...For **Tormenting** ourselves with envy and jealousy, forgive us.

עַל חֵטְא שֶׁחָטָאנוּ לְפָנֶיךָ בְּקַשְׁיוּת עֹרֶף.

Al cheit she-cha-ta-nu...For **Keeping** stubbornly our own narrow opinions, forgive us.

עַל חֵטְא שֶׁחָטָאנוּ לְפָנֶיךָ בִּרְכִילוּת.

Al cheit she-cha-ta-nu...For **Repeating** slander about others, forgive us.

עַל חֵטְא שֶׁחָטָאנוּ לְפָנֶיךָ בְּשִׂנְאַת חִנָּם.

Al cheit she-cha-ta-nu...For **Sharing** and promoting prejudice, forgive us.

עַל חֵטְא שֶׁחָטָאנוּ לְפָנֶיךָ בִּתְשׂוּמֶת יָד.

Al cheit she-cha-ta-nu...For **Tarnishing** our promises with breaches of trust, forgive us.

All sing

Ve-al ku-lam, E-lo-ah se-li-chot,
se-lach la-nu, me-chal la-nu
ka-per la-nu.

וְעַל כֻּלָּם, אֱלוֹהַּ סְלִיחוֹת,
סְלַח־לָנוּ, מְחַל־לָנוּ,
כַּפֶּר־לָנוּ.

For all our failings, O God of forgiveness, pardon us, help us, grant us atonement.

(For comment, see p. 19)

Havdalah Spice Box
Russian
Mid-19th c.

"Lord, we are not so arrogant..." is by Rabbi Norman Hirsh (1930-).

Lord, we are not so arrogant as to pretend
that the trial of our lives
does not reveal our flaws.
We know ourselves,
in this moment of prayer,
to have failed ourselves and others,
the ones we love and the stranger,
again and again.
We know how often
we did not bring to the surface of our lives
the hidden goodness within.
Where we have achieved, O Lord,
we are proud of ourselves
and grateful to You;
where we have failed,
we ask forgiveness.
Remember how exposed we are
to the chances and terrors of life.
We were afraid.
We sometimes chose to fail.
And we ask:
Turn our thoughts from the hurt to its remedy.
Free us of the torments of guilt.

God, known to our people
As Merciful One, Gracious One, Just One,
Loving One,
Hear my confession. Forgive my sins.

You have given me a treasure of years
Crammed with chambers of pleasure,
And whispered in command:
"Embrace them all for blessing."
Yet, I squander them away.

I build high walls around me
Closing others out.
At times I stumble.
I am harsh not gentle,
Stingy not generous,
Thoughtless not attentive,
Jealous not trusting,
Fickle not faithful,
Impatient not tolerant,
Apathetic not passionate,
Conniving not cooperative,
Obstinate not flexible,
Rash not wise.

Topple the walls about me.
Bring them down.
Repair my broken promises,
Restore me to Your treasure,
Welcome me back to Your chambers,
Reclaim me as I reclaim You.

Reader

אֱלֹהֵֽינוּ וֵאלֹהֵי אֲבוֹתֵֽינוּ, אַל תַּעַזְבֵֽנוּ וְאַל תִּטְּשֵֽׁנוּ
וְאַל תַּכְלִימֵֽנוּ, וְאַל תָּפֵר בְּרִיתְךָ אִתָּֽנוּ. קָרְבֵֽנוּ
לְתוֹרָתֶֽךָ, לַמְּדֵֽנוּ מִצְוֹתֶֽיךָ, הוֹרֵֽנוּ דְרָכֶֽיךָ, הַט לִבֵּֽנוּ
לְיִרְאָה אֶת־שְׁמֶֽךָ, וּמוֹל אֶת־לְבָבֵֽנוּ לְאַהֲבָתֶֽךָ, וְנָשׁוּב
אֵלֶֽיךָ בֶּאֱמֶת וּבְלֵב שָׁלֵם.

Our God and God of our people, do not abandon us or allow us to shame ourselves through neglect of Your sacred covenant. Draw us to the study of Torah.
Engage us in fulfilling Your commandments. Teach us Your ways that we
may prosper in kindness, grow rich in wisdom, and lavish honor upon our
faith and people with deeds of reverence and righteousness, mercy and truth.

Congregation

Turn us to You in sincerity and love. For Your sake and ours, hear our prayers
and forgive our failings.

Reader

כִּי עַל רַחֲמֶֽיךָ הָרַבִּים אָֽנוּ בְטוּחִים, וְעַל צִדְקוֹתֶֽיךָ
אָֽנוּ נִשְׁעָנִים,

We trust in Your compassion and rely upon Your support. For we are Your
people and, joyfully, You are our God.

All sing

Ki anu a-me-cha, ve-a-tah Mal-kei-nu.
A-nu va-ne-cha, ve-a-tah A-vi-nu.
A-nu na-cha-la-te-cha, ve-a-tah
    Go-ra-lei-nu.
A-nu tso-ne-cha, ve-a-tah Ro-ei-nu
A-nu kar-me-cha, ve-a-tah Not-rei-nu.
A-nu ra-ya-te-cha, ve-a-tah Do-dei-nu.

כִּי אָנוּ עַמֶּךָ, וְאַתָּה מַלְכֵּנוּ.
אָנוּ בָנֶיךָ, וְאַתָּה אָבִינוּ.
אָנוּ נַחֲלָתֶךָ, וְאַתָּה גוֹרָלֵנוּ.
אָנוּ צֹאנֶךָ, וְאַתָּה רוֹעֵנוּ.
אָנוּ כַרְמֶךָ, וְאַתָּה נוֹטְרֵנוּ.
אָנוּ רַעְיָתֶךָ, וְאַתָּה דוֹדֵנוּ.

We are Your people, You are our
    Sovereign.
We are Your children, You are our Source.
We are Your possession, You are our
    Portion.
We are Your flock, You are our Guardian.
We are Your vineyard, You are our Keeper.
We are Your beloved, You are our Friend.

Congregation rises as ark is opened

Ki a-nu a-me-cha, "We are Your people," is of medieval origin and is based upon an ancient rabbinic comment found in *Song of Songs, Rabbah, 2:16.* The poem celebrates the intimacy between the people of Israel and God. It is a love that is restored through confession and repentance.

EIN KA-MO-CHA—NONE COMPARES TO YOU

Reader

אֵין כָּמְוֹךָ בָאֱלֹהִים, יְיָ, וְאֵין כְּמַעֲשֶׂיךָ. מַלְכוּתְךָ
מַלְכוּת כָּל־עוֹלָמִים וּמֶמְשַׁלְתְּךָ בְּכָל־דּוֹר וָדֹר.

None compares to You, O God, and nothing equals the mystery and majesty of Your works.

Congregation

Before You we stand in awe.

Reader

Turn toward us, O God, as we turn toward You.

Cantor and Choir

יְיָ, יְיָ אֵל רַחוּם וְחַנּוּן, אֶרֶךְ אַפַּיִם וְרַב־חֶסֶד וֶאֱמֶת,
נֹצֵר חֶסֶד לָאֲלָפִים, נֹשֵׂא עָוֹן וָפֶשַׁע וְחַטָּאָה וְנַקֵּה.

The Lord, the Lord God, is merciful and gracious, endlessly patient, loving, and true, showing mercy to thousands, forgiving iniquity, transgression and sin, and granting pardon.

Some scholars date the public reading of Torah as early as Ezra, 420 B.C.E. *(Nehemiah 8)*. Others believe that the practice originated in the early synagogue, 320 B.C.E. Reading Torah is the heart of Jewish worship. "None compares..." is from *Psalms 86:8.* "The Lord, the Lord..." is from *Exodus 34:6-7.*

Congregation

אָבִינוּ מַלְכֵּנוּ, שְׁמַע קוֹלֵנוּ.

Avinu Malkeinu, she-ma ko-lei-nu.
Avinu Malkeinu, hear our prayer.

אָבִינוּ מַלְכֵּנוּ, חָטָאנוּ לְפָנֶיךָ.

Avinu Malkeinu, cha-ta-nu le-fa-ne-cha.
Avinu Malkeinu, we have sinned against You.

אָבִינוּ מַלְכֵּנוּ, חֲמוֹל עָלֵינוּ וְעַל עוֹלָלֵינוּ וְטַפֵּנוּ.

Avinu Malkeinu, cha-mol a-lei-nu ve-al o-la-lei-nu ve-ta-pei-nu.
Avinu Malkeinu, have mercy upon us and upon our children.

אָבִינוּ מַלְכֵּנוּ, כַּלֵּה דֶּבֶר וְחֶרֶב וְרָעָב מֵעָלֵינוּ.

Avinu Malkeinu, ka-lei de-ver, ve-che-rev, ve-ra-av mei-a-lei-nu.
Avinu Malkeinu, rid us of pestilence, war and famine.

אָבִינוּ מַלְכֵּנוּ, כַּלֵּה כָּל־צַר וּמַשְׂטִין מֵעָלֵינוּ.

Avinu Malkeinu, ka-lei kol tsar u-mas-tin mei-a-lei-nu.
Avinu Malkeinu, rid us of all hatred and oppression.

אָבִינוּ מַלְכֵּנוּ, כָּתְבֵנוּ בְּסֵפֶר חַיִּים טוֹבִים.

Avinu Malkeinu, kot-vei-nu be-sei-fer cha-yim to-vim.
Avinu Malkeinu, inscribe us for blessing in the Book of Life.

אָבִינוּ מַלְכֵּנוּ, מַלֵּא יָדֵינוּ מִבִּרְכוֹתֶיךָ.

Avinu Malkeinu, ma-lei ya-dei-nu mi-bir-cho-te-cha.
Avinu Malkeinu, fill our hands with generous deeds.

אָבִינוּ מַלְכֵּנוּ, כָּתְבֵנוּ בְּסֵפֶר סְלִיחָה וּמְחִילָה.

Avinu Malkeinu, kot-vei-nu be-sei-fer se-li-cha u-me-chi-lah.
Avinu Malkeinu, inscribe us for blessing in the Book of Forgiveness.

אָבִינוּ מַלְכֵּנוּ, חָנֵּנוּ וַעֲנֵנוּ, כִּי אֵין בָּנוּ מַעֲשִׂים,
עֲשֵׂה עִמָּנוּ צְדָקָה וָחֶסֶד וְהוֹשִׁיעֵנוּ.

Avinu Malkeinu, cho-nei-nu va-a-nei-nu, ki ein ba-nu
ma-a-sim, a-sei i-ma-nu tse-da-kah va-che-sed, ve-ho-shi-ei-nu.
Avinu Malkeinu, be gracious and answer us. Treat us generously and with
kindness, and help us.

All sing

Avinu Malkeinu,
Cho-nei-nu va-a-nei-nu (2)
ki ein ba-nu ma-a-sim.

A-sei i-ma-nu tse-da-kah va-che-sed (2)
ve-ho-shi-ei-nu.

Avinu Malkeinu,
cho-nei-nu va-a-nei-nu (2)
ki-ein ba-nu ma-a-sim.

אָבִינוּ מַלְכֵּנוּ, חָנֵּנוּ וַעֲנֵנוּ,
כִּי אֵין בָּנוּ מַעֲשִׂים, עֲשֵׂה
עִמָּנוּ צְדָקָה וָחֶסֶד וְהוֹשִׁיעֵנוּ.

(For comment, see p. 66)

Torah is taken from ark

Reader

הָבוּ גֹדֶל לַאלֹהֵינוּ וּתְנוּ כָבוֹד לַתּוֹרָה.

Let us declare the greatness of our God and give honor to the Torah.

All sing

כִּי מִצִּיּוֹן תֵּצֵא תוֹרָה, וּדְבַר־יְיָ מִירוּשָׁלָיִם.

Ki mi-tsi-yon tei-tsei Torah (2)
u-de-var A-do-nai mi-ru-sha-la-yim.

Torah will come from Zion, the word of God from Jerusalem.

בָּרוּךְ שֶׁנָּתַן תּוֹרָה לְעַמּוֹ יִשְׂרָאֵל בִּקְדֻשָּׁתוֹ.

Ba-ruch she-na-tan To-rah, To-rah (2)
Le-a-mo Yis-ra-eil bi-ke-du-sha-to.

Praised be the One, who has given the Torah to Israel.

שְׁמַע יִשְׂרָאֵל: יְיָ אֱלֹהֵינוּ, יְיָ אֶחָד!

She-ma Yis-ra-eil: A-do-nai E-lo-hei-nu
A-do-nai E-chad!

Hear, O Israel: The Lord is our God, the Lord is One!

The *hakafah,* or "processional with the Torah," dates to the early synagogue and dramatizes that the Torah is not the exclusive possession of a special "priest" class of the Jewish people but belongs to the entire Jewish community. *Le-cha*...is from *I Chronicles 29:11. Ro-me-mu*...is from *Psalms 99:5, 9.*

Cantor

אֶחָד אֱלֹהֵינוּ, גָּדוֹל אֲדוֹנֵינוּ, קָדוֹשׁ וְנוֹרָא שְׁמוֹ.

Our God is One: Our God is great beyond compare. Holy and awesome is
the Lord our God.

Reader

בֵּית יַעֲקֹב: לְכוּ, וְנֵלְכָה בְּאוֹר יְיָ.

O house of Jacob, let us walk in the light of our God.

HAKAFAH

All sing as Torah is carried through the congregation

Le-cha A-do-nai, ha-ge-du-la   לְךָ, יְיָ, הַגְּדֻלָּה וְהַגְּבוּרָה
ve-ha-ge-vu-ra ve-ha-tif-e-ret,   וְהַתִּפְאֶרֶת וְהַנֵּצַח וְהַהוֹד, כִּי כֹל
ve-ha-nei-tsach, ve-ha-hod,   בַּשָּׁמַיִם וּבָאָרֶץ, לְךָ יְיָ הַמַּמְלָכָה
ki chol ba-sha-ma-yim u-va-a-retz, (2)   וְהַמִּתְנַשֵּׂא לְכֹל לְרֹאשׁ.
le-cha, A-do-nai, ha-mam-la-cha
ve-ha-mit-na-sei le-chol le-rosh

Yours, Lord, is the greatness, the power, the glory, the victory, and the majesty;
for all that is in heaven and earth is Yours. Yours is the dominion, O Lord; You
are supreme over all.

Ro-me-mu A-do-nai, ro-me-mu (2)   רוֹמְמוּ יְיָ אֱלֹהֵינוּ,
Ro-me-mu A-do-nai, Elo-hei-nu   וְהִשְׁתַּחֲווּ לְהַר קָדְשׁוֹ,
A-do-nai Elo-hei-nu, ro-me-mu.   יְיָ אֱלֹהֵינוּ.
(Repeat)

Ve-hish-ta-cha-vu, le-har kod-sho, (4)

A-do-nai Elo-hei-nu, ro-me-ru.

Exalt and worship our God; bow down at God's holy mountain.

235

Torah Crowns
United States
20th c.

Israel was elected *for the purpose of* receiving the Torah. Israel was chosen *for the purpose of* entering into a covenant relationship with the God of the whole world, *in order to be* God's "kingdom of priests." Without the Torah, and without the commandments, the "chosen people" ceases to be a meaningful concept and is liable to degenerate into pagan notions of chauvinism and racism. But, by the same token, if Torah is to mean more to us than the "national literature of the ancient Hebrews" which has curiously survived, it has to be read and understood in terms of the election and of the covenant (Jacob J. Petuchowski (1925-), *Ever Since Sinai, p. 64)*.

Ark is closed; all are seated as the Torah is prepared for reading.

READING OF TORAH

Reader

The Torah portion we read on this Yom Kippur morning recalls the covenant made between our people and God at Mount Sinai. They stood together, young and old, rich and poor, leaders and strangers, pledging their loyalty and that of all future generations of Jews, to live by the values and traditions of Torah. They understood that God had set before them a choice—life or death, prosperity or adversity, blessing or curse. Fidelity to their faith meant fulfilling the mitzvah-command to "choose life." The ancient challenge remains ours to this day.

Blessings before the reading

Ba-re-chu et A-do-nai ha-me-vo-rach!
Ba-ruch A-do-nai ha-me-vo-rach
le-o-lam va-ed.

בָּרְכוּ אֶת יְיָ הַמְבֹרָךְ!
בָּרוּךְ יְיָ הַמְבֹרָךְ לְעוֹלָם וָעֶד!

Ba-ruch a-ta, A-do-nai E-lo-hei-nu, me-lech
ha-o-lam, a-sher ba-char ba-nu mi-kol
ha-a-mim, ve-na-tan la-nu et To-ra-to.
Ba-ruch a-ta A-do-nai, no-tein ha-To-rah.

בָּרוּךְ אַתָּה, יְיָ אֱלֹהֵינוּ, מֶלֶךְ
הָעוֹלָם, אֲשֶׁר בָּחַר־בָּנוּ מִכָּל־
הָעַמִּים וְנָתַן־לָנוּ אֶת־תּוֹרָתוֹ.
בָּרוּךְ אַתָּה, יְיָ, נוֹתֵן הַתּוֹרָה.

Praise the Lord, to whom our praise is due! Praised be the Lord, to whom our praise is due, now and forever! Blessed is the Lord our God, Ruler of the universe, who has chosen us from all peoples by giving us the Torah. Be praised, O God, Giver of the Torah.

237

Torah Pointer (yad) and Spice Box
Europe
19th c.

The traditionally assigned Torah portion for reading on Yom Kippur morning is taken from *Leviticus 16,* and from *Numbers 29:7-11,* and describes the ceremony of the scapegoat and the sacrifices offered at the Jerusalem Temple on Yom Kippur. Reform Jews substitute selections from *Deuteronomy 29:9-14; 30:11-30* for the traditional Torah reading. These selections recall the moment when the Torah was given to the people of Israel at Mt. Sinai, and emphasize the lesson that the *mitzvot* "command-ments" were not given to "angels" but are possible for every human being to fulfill.

Deuteronomy 29:9-14, 30:11-16, 19-20

אַתֶּם נִצָּבִים הַיּוֹם כֻּלְּכֶם לִפְנֵי יְהוָה אֱלֹהֵיכֶם רָאשֵׁיכֶם שִׁבְטֵיכֶם
זִקְנֵיכֶם וְשֹׁטְרֵיכֶם כֹּל אִישׁ יִשְׂרָאֵל: טַפְּכֶם נְשֵׁיכֶם וְגֵרְךָ אֲשֶׁר
בְּקֶרֶב מַחֲנֶיךָ מֵחֹטֵב עֵצֶיךָ עַד שֹׁאֵב מֵימֶיךָ: לְעָבְרְךָ בִּבְרִית
יְהוָה אֱלֹהֶיךָ וּבְאָלָתוֹ אֲשֶׁר יְהוָה אֱלֹהֶיךָ כֹּרֵת עִמְּךָ הַיּוֹם:
לְמַעַן הָקִים־אֹתְךָ הַיּוֹם ו׀ לוֹ לְעָם וְהוּא יִהְיֶה־לְּךָ לֵאלֹהִים כַּאֲשֶׁר
דִּבֶּר־לָךְ וְכַאֲשֶׁר נִשְׁבַּע לַאֲבֹתֶיךָ לְאַבְרָהָם לְיִצְחָק וּלְיַעֲקֹב:
וְלֹא אִתְּכֶם לְבַדְּכֶם אָנֹכִי כֹּרֵת אֶת־הַבְּרִית הַזֹּאת וְאֶת־הָאָלָה
הַזֹּאת: כִּי אֶת־אֲשֶׁר יֶשְׁנוֹ פֹּה עִמָּנוּ עֹמֵד הַיּוֹם לִפְנֵי יְהוָה אֱלֹהֵינוּ
וְאֵת אֲשֶׁר אֵינֶנּוּ פֹּה עִמָּנוּ הַיּוֹם:

You stand this day, all of you, before the Lord your God—your tribal heads, your
elders and your officials, all the people of Israel, your children, your wives,
even the stranger within your camp, from woodchopper to waterdrawer—
to enter into the covenant of the Lord your God, which the Lord your God
is concluding with you this day, with its sanctions; to the end that God may
establish you this day as a chosen people and be your God, as was promised you
and sworn to your ancients, Abraham, Isaac, and Jacob. I make this covenant,
with its sanctions, not with you alone, but both with those who are standing
here with us this day before the Lord our God and with those who are not
with us here this day.

כִּי הַמִּצְוָה הַזֹּאת אֲשֶׁר אָנֹכִי מְצַוְּךָ הַיּוֹם לֹא־נִפְלֵאת הִוא
מִמְּךָ וְלֹא־רְחֹקָה הִוא: לֹא בַשָּׁמַיִם הִוא לֵאמֹר מִי
יַעֲלֶה־לָּנוּ הַשָּׁמַיְמָה וְיִקָּחֶהָ לָּנוּ וְיַשְׁמִעֵנוּ אֹתָהּ וְנַעֲשֶׂנָּה:
וְלֹא־מֵעֵבֶר לַיָּם הִוא לֵאמֹר מִי יַעֲבָר־לָנוּ אֶל־עֵבֶר הַיָּם
וְיִקָּחֶהָ לָּנוּ וְיַשְׁמִעֵנוּ אֹתָהּ וְנַעֲשֶׂנָּה: כִּי־קָרוֹב אֵלֶיךָ הַדָּבָר
מְאֹד בְּפִיךָ וּבִלְבָבְךָ לַעֲשֹׂתוֹ:

Surely, this mitzvah which I command you this day is not too baffling for you, nor is it beyond reach. It is not in the heavens, that you should say, "Who among us can go up to the heavens and get it for us and impart it to us, that we may observe it?" Neither is it beyond the sea, that you should say, "Who among us can cross to the other side of the sea and get it for us and impart it to us, that we may observe it?" No, it is very close to you, in your mouth and in your heart, to observe it.

רְאֵה נָתַתִּי לְפָנֶיךָ הַיּוֹם אֶת־הַחַיִּים וְאֶת־הַטּוֹב וְאֶת־הַמָּוֶת וְאֶת־הָרָע:
אֲשֶׁר אָנֹכִי מְצַוְּךָ הַיּוֹם לְאַהֲבָה אֶת־יהוה אֱלֹהֶיךָ לָלֶכֶת בִּדְרָכָיו וְלִשְׁמֹר
מִצְוֺתָיו וְחֻקֹּתָיו וּמִשְׁפָּטָיו וְחָיִיתָ וְרָבִיתָ וּבֵרַכְךָ יהוה אֱלֹהֶיךָ בָּאָרֶץ
אֲשֶׁר־אַתָּה בָא־שָׁמָּה לְרִשְׁתָּהּ: וְאִם־יִפְנֶה לְבָבְךָ וְלֹא תִשְׁמָע
וְנִדַּחְתָּ וְהִשְׁתַּחֲוִיתָ לֵאלֹהִים אֲחֵרִים וַעֲבַדְתָּם: הִגַּדְתִּי לָכֶם הַיּוֹם כִּי
אָבֹד תֹּאבֵדוּן לֹא־תַאֲרִיכֻן יָמִים עַל־הָאֲדָמָה אֲשֶׁר אַתָּה עֹבֵר
אֶת־הַיַּרְדֵּן לָבוֹא שָׁמָּה לְרִשְׁתָּהּ: הַעִדֹתִי בָכֶם הַיּוֹם אֶת־הַשָּׁמַיִם
וְאֶת־הָאָרֶץ הַחַיִּים וְהַמָּוֶת נָתַתִּי לְפָנֶיךָ הַבְּרָכָה וְהַקְּלָלָה וּבָחַרְתָּ בַּחַיִּים
לְמַעַן תִּחְיֶה אַתָּה וְזַרְעֶךָ: לְאַהֲבָה אֶת־יהוה אֱלֹהֶיךָ לִשְׁמֹעַ
בְּקֹלוֹ וּלְדָבְקָה־בוֹ כִּי הוּא חַיֶּיךָ וְאֹרֶךְ יָמֶיךָ לָשֶׁבֶת עַל־הָאֲדָמָה אֲשֶׁר
נִשְׁבַּע יהוה לַאֲבֹתֶיךָ לְאַבְרָהָם לְיִצְחָק וּלְיַעֲקֹב לָתֵת לָהֶם:

See, I set before you this day life and prosperity, death and adversity. For I command you this day to love the Lord your God, to walk in God's ways, keep God's commandments, laws and rules, that you may thrive and increase, and that the Lord your God may bless you in the land that you are about to enter and possess.

I call heaven and earth to witness against you this day: I have put before you life and death, blessing and curse. Choose life—if you and your offspring would live—by loving the Lord your God, heeding God's commandments, and remaining faithful. For thereby you shall have life and shall long endure upon the land which the Lord swore to your ancients, Abraham, Isaac and Jacob, to give to them.

Blessings after the reading of Torah

Ba-ruch a-ta, A-do-nai E-lo-hei-nu,
me-lech ha-o-lam, a-sher na-tan la-nu
To-rat e-met, ve-cha-yei o-lam na-ta
be-to-chei-nu. Ba-ruch a-ta, A-do-nai,
no-tein ha-To-rah.

בָּרוּךְ אַתָּה, יְיָ אֱלֹהֵינוּ, מֶלֶךְ
הָעוֹלָם, אֲשֶׁר נָתַן־לָנוּ תּוֹרַת אֱמֶת
וְחַיֵּי עוֹלָם נָטַע בְּתוֹכֵנוּ.
בָּרוּךְ אַתָּה, יְיָ, נוֹתֵן הַתּוֹרָה.

Blessed is the Lord our God, Ruler of the universe, who has given us the
Torah of truth, implanting within us eternal life. Be praised, O Lord, Giver
of the Torah.

HAGBAHAH—LIFTING THE TORAH

All rise and sing as the Torah is held high

Ve-zot ha-To-rah a-sher sam Mo-sheh
li-fe-nei be-nei Yis-ra-eil, al pi A-do-nai
be-yad Mo-sheh.

וְזֹאת הַתּוֹרָה אֲשֶׁר־שָׂם משֶׁה
לִפְנֵי בְּנֵי יִשְׂרָאֵל, עַל־
פִּי יְיָ בְּיַד־משֶׁה.

This is the Torah that Moses placed before the people of Israel to fulfill the
word of God.

All are seated as Torah is rolled and wrapped.

Since the 1st century B.C.E. it has been customary to read a translation of the Torah
within the synagogue. The reader of the translation was called a *meturgeman*, "trans-
lator" and used either an Aramaic or Greek translation. Throughout the centuries
the Torah has been translated into nearly every vernacular spoken by Jews. "This
is the Torah..." is from *Deuteronomy 44:44*, a statement made just before Moses'
retelling of the revelation of Torah at Mt. Sinai. The tradition of *hagbahah*, or
"lifting," the Torah, allows the congregation to share its contents just as the people
of Israel witnessed its revelation at Sinai. The custom of *gelilah*, or "rolling up,"
the scroll is regarded as a special honor.

Reader

The Haftarah for Yom Kippur morning recounts how the prophet Isaiah, speaking at the Jerusalem Temple during the 8th century B.C.E., sets out Jewish tradition's demands for true piety. Fasting and rituals are of no avail if they do not lead to justice for the oppressed, mercy for those in need. The people of Israel are called to seek God in all their ways, in the beauty of the sanctuary, and in the pursuit of righteousness and peace.

Blessings before the reading

בָּרוּךְ אַתָּה, יְיָ אֱלֹהֵינוּ, מֶלֶךְ הָעוֹלָם, אֲשֶׁר בָּחַר
בִּנְבִיאִים טוֹבִים וְרָצָה בְדִבְרֵיהֶם הַנֶּאֱמָרִים בֶּאֱמֶת.
בָּרוּךְ אַתָּה, יְיָ, הַבּוֹחֵר בַּתּוֹרָה וּבְמשֶׁה עַבְדּוֹ
וּבְיִשְׂרָאֵל עַמּוֹ וּבִנְבִיאֵי הָאֱמֶת וָצֶדֶק.

Praised is the Lord our God, Ruler of the universe, who has chosen faithful prophets to speak words of truth. Praised is the Lord, for the revelation of Torah, for God's servant Moses, and for our prophets of truth and righteousness.

Haftarah means "completion" and refers to selected readings drawn from the Prophets and recited after the Torah is read. By the 2nd Century C.E. the rabbis had designated Haftarah readings for each Sabbath and all holy days. The choice of the Haftarah portion was usually made because of its relationship to the theme of the Torah portion.

Isaiah 58:1-10, 12-14

קְרָא בְגָרוֹן אַל־תַּחְשֹׂךְ כַּשּׁוֹפָר הָרֵם קוֹלֶךָ וְהַגֵּד לְעַמִּי פִּשְׁעָם וּלְבֵית
יַעֲקֹב חַטֹּאתָם: וְאוֹתִי יוֹם יוֹם יִדְרֹשׁוּן וְדַעַת דְּרָכַי יֶחְפָּצוּן כְּגוֹי
אֲשֶׁר־צְדָקָה עָשָׂה וּמִשְׁפַּט אֱלֹהָיו לֹא עָזָב יִשְׁאָלוּנִי מִשְׁפְּטֵי־צֶדֶק
קִרְבַת אֱלֹהִים יֶחְפָּצוּן: לָמָּה צַּמְנוּ וְלֹא רָאִיתָ עִנִּינוּ נַפְשֵׁנוּ וְלֹא תֵדָע
הֵן בְּיוֹם צֹמְכֶם תִּמְצְאוּ־חֵפֶץ וְכָל־עַצְּבֵיכֶם תִּנְגֹּשׂוּ: הֵן לְרִיב וּמַצָּה
תָּצוּמוּ וּלְהַכּוֹת בְּאֶגְרֹף רֶשַׁע לֹא־תָצוּמוּ כַיּוֹם לְהַשְׁמִיעַ בַּמָּרוֹם
קוֹלְכֶם: הֲכָזֶה יִהְיֶה צוֹם אֶבְחָרֵהוּ יוֹם עַנּוֹת אָדָם נַפְשׁוֹ הֲלָכֹף כְּאַגְמֹן
רֹאשׁוֹ וְשַׂק וָאֵפֶר יַצִּיעַ הֲלָזֶה תִּקְרָא־צוֹם וְיוֹם רָצוֹן לַיהוָה:

Cry with full throat, without restraint;
Raise your voice like a ram's horn!
Declare to My people their transgression,
To the House of Jacob their sin.
To be sure, they seek Me daily,
Eager to learn My ways,
Like a nation that does what is right,
That has not abandoned the laws of its God,
They ask Me for the right way,
They are eager for the nearness of God:
"Why, when we fasted, did You not see?
When we starved our bodies, did You pay no heed?"
Because on your fast day
You see to your business
And oppress all your laborers!

243

Because you fast in strife and contention,
And you strike with a wicked fist!
Your fasting today is not such
As to make your voice heard on high.
Is such the fast I desire?
A day for people to starve their bodies?
Is it bowing the head like a bulrush
And lying in sackcloth and ashes?
Do you call that a fast,
A day acceptable to the Lord?

הֲלוֹא זֶה צוֹם אֶבְחָרֵהוּ פַּתֵּחַ חַרְצֻבּוֹת רֶשַׁע הַתֵּר אֲגֻדּוֹת מוֹטָה
וְשַׁלַּח רְצוּצִים חָפְשִׁים וְכָל־מוֹטָה תְּנַתֵּקוּ: הֲלוֹא פָרֹס לָרָעֵב לַחְמֶךָ
וַעֲנִיִּים מְרוּדִים תָּבִיא בָיִת כִּי־תִרְאֶה עָרֹם וְכִסִּיתוֹ וּמִבְּשָׂרְךָ לֹא תִתְעַלָּם:
אָז יִבָּקַע כַּשַּׁחַר אוֹרֶךָ וַאֲרֻכָתְךָ מְהֵרָה תִצְמָח וְהָלַךְ לְפָנֶיךָ צִדְקֶךָ
כְּבוֹד יְהוָה יַאַסְפֶךָ: אָז תִּקְרָא וַיהוָה יַעֲנֶה תְּשַׁוַּע וְיֹאמַר הִנֵּנִי.

No, this is the fast I desire:
To unlock fetters of wickedness,
And untie the cords of the yoke
To let the oppressed go free;
To break off every yoke.
It is to share your bread with the hungry,
And to take the wretched poor into your home;
When you see the naked, to clothe them,
And not to ignore your own family.
Then shall your light burst through like the dawn
And your healing spring up quickly;
Your Vindicator shall march before you,
The presence of the Lord shall be your rear guard.
Then, when you call, the Lord will answer;
When you cry, God will say: Here I am.

אִם־תָּסִיר מִתּוֹכְךָ מוֹטָה שְׁלַח אֶצְבַּע וְדַבֶּר־אָוֶן: וְתָפֵק
לְרָעֵב נַפְשֶׁךָ וְנֶפֶשׁ נַעֲנָה תַּשְׂבִּיעַ וְזָרַח בַּחֹשֶׁךְ אוֹרֶךָ
וַאֲפֵלָתְךָ כַּצָּהֳרָיִם: וּבָנוּ מִמְּךָ חָרְבוֹת עוֹלָם מוֹסְדֵי דוֹר־וָדוֹר
תְּקוֹמֵם וְקֹרָא לְךָ גֹּדֵר פֶּרֶץ מְשׁוֹבֵב נְתִיבוֹת לָשָׁבֶת:
אִם־תָּשִׁיב מִשַּׁבָּת רַגְלֶךָ עֲשׂוֹת חֲפָצֶךָ בְּיוֹם קָדְשִׁי
וְקָרָאתָ לַשַּׁבָּת עֹנֶג לִקְדוֹשׁ יהוה מְכֻבָּד וְכִבַּדְתּוֹ מֵעֲשׂוֹת
דְּרָכֶיךָ מִמְּצוֹא חֶפְצְךָ וְדַבֵּר דָּבָר: אָז תִּתְעַנַּג עַל־יהוה
וְהִרְכַּבְתִּיךָ עַל־בָּמוֹתֵי אָרֶץ וְהַאֲכַלְתִּיךָ נַחֲלַת יַעֲקֹב אָבִיךָ
כִּי פִּי יהוה דִּבֵּר:

If you banish the yoke from your midst,
The menacing hand, and evil speech,
And you offer your compassion to the hungry
And satisfy the famished creature—
Then shall your light shine in darkness,
And your gloom shall be like noonday...
And you shall be called
"Repairer of fallen walls,
Restorer of lanes for habitation."
If you refrain from trampling the Sabbath,
From pursuing your affairs on My holy day;
If you call the Sabbath a "delight,"
The Lord's holy day "honored";
And if you honor it and go not your ways
Nor look to your affairs, nor strike bargains—
Then you can seek the favor of the Lord.
I will set you astride the heights of the earth,
And let you enjoy the heritage of your father, Jacob—
For the mouth of the Lord has spoken.

BLESSINGS AFTER THE READING OF HAFTARAH

Reader

בָּרוּךְ אַתָּה, יְיָ אֱלֹהֵינוּ, מֶלֶךְ הָעוֹלָם, צוּר כָּל־
הָעוֹלָמִים, צַדִּיק בְּכָל־הַדּוֹרוֹת, הָאֵל הַנֶּאֱמָן,
הָאוֹמֵר וְעוֹשֶׂה, הַמְדַבֵּר וּמְקַיֵּם, שֶׁכָּל־דְּבָרָיו אֱמֶת
וָצֶדֶק.

בָּרוּךְ אַתָּה, יְיָ, מֶלֶךְ מוֹחֵל וְסוֹלֵחַ לַעֲוֹנוֹתֵינוּ
וְלַעֲוֹנוֹת עַמּוֹ בֵּית יִשְׂרָאֵל, וּמַעֲבִיר אַשְׁמוֹתֵינוּ בְּכָל־
שָׁנָה וְשָׁנָה, מֶלֶךְ עַל כָּל־הָאָרֶץ, מְקַדֵּשׁ (הַשַּׁבָּת וְ)
יִשְׂרָאֵל וְיוֹם הַכִּפּוּרִים.

We give thanks for the Torah, for the privilege of worship, for the prophets, and for this (**Shabbat and**) Yom Kippur Day. Be praised, O God, who sanctifies (**Shabbat**), Israel and Yom Kippur Day.

(For comment, see p. 114)

Reader

אֱלֹהֵֽינוּ וֵאלֹהֵי אֲבוֹתֵֽינוּ, קַבֶּל־נָא בְּרַחֲמִים אֶת־תְּפִלָּתֵֽנוּ בְּעַד
אַרְצֵֽנוּ וּמֶמְשַׁלְתָּהּ. שְׁלַח רוּחֲךָ עַל כָּל־תוֹשְׁבֵי אַרְצֵֽנוּ וְטַע בֵּין
בְּנֵי הָאֻמּוֹת וְהָאֱמוּנוֹת הַשּׁוֹנוֹת הַשּׁוֹכְנִים בָּהּ אַהֲבָה וְאַחֲוָה שָׁלוֹם
וְרֵעוּת. וְקַיֵּם בִּמְהֵרָה חֲזוֹן נְבִיאֶֽיךָ: לֹא יִשָּׂא גוֹי אֶל גּוֹי חֶֽרֶב
וְלֹא יִלְמְדוּ עוֹד מִלְחָמָה.

Our God, and God of all people, on this Yom Kippur Day accept our prayers on behalf of our nation and troubled world. Banish all hatred and bigotry, injustice and indifference. Bless those who aid the poor, heal the sick, and care for those who have lost their way.

Congregation

May this New Year bring blessings upon our land. Enlighten with wisdom all who have been chosen to serve. Forge bonds of friendship among all peoples. Let the day soon come when "nation shall not lift up sword against nation, nor learn war any more."

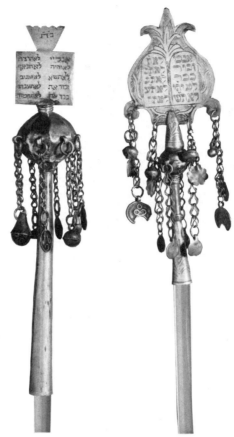

Rimonim 47. 3-4
North Africa 19th c., Tin; Silver
Eric Hockley, Photographer
From the Collection of the Hebrew Union College
Skirball Museum

"This is My covenant...," from *Isaiah 59:21*, was incorporated into the first prayer book by Amram Gaon (9th century C.E.), who headed the academy at Sura in Babylonia. The phrase "words I have put in your mouth" was taken to refer to the Torah. "God's splendor..." is from *Psalms 148:13-14.*

All rise as Torah is lifted; and ark is opened

Reader

וַאֲנִי זֹאת בְּרִיתִי אוֹתָם, אָמַר יְיָ: רוּחִי אֲשֶׁר עָלֶיךָ,
וּדְבָרַי אֲשֶׁר־שַׂמְתִּי בְּפִיךָ, לֹא־יָמוּשׁוּ מִפִּיךָ וּמִפִּי
זַרְעֲךָ וּמִפִּי זֶרַע זַרְעֲךָ, אָמַר יְיָ, מֵעַתָּה וְעַד־עוֹלָם.

"This is My covenant with you," says the Lord. "Let not My spirit, and the words
that I have put in your mouth, depart from you, nor from your children or their
children, from this time forth and forever."

All sing

הוֹדוּ עַל אֶרֶץ וְשָׁמָיִם, וַיָּרֶם קֶרֶן לְעַמּוֹ, תְּהִלָּה לְכָל־
חֲסִידָיו, לִבְנֵי יִשְׂרָאֵל עַם קְרוֹבוֹ. הַלְלוּיָהּ.

Ho-do al e-rets ve-sha-ma-yim
va-ya-rem ke-ren
le-a-mo, te-hi-la le-chol cha-si-dav,
li-ve-nei
Yis-ra-eil, am ke-ro-vo. Ha-le-lu-yah!

God's splendor covers heaven and earth; God is the Source of Israel's strength,
the praise of the faithful, the hope of those who draw near to serve. Halleluyah!

Reader

God's Torah is perfect, renewing life;
God's teachings are enduring,
Making wise the simple.

תּוֹרַת יְיָ תְּמִימָה, מְשִׁיבַת נָפֶשׁ;
עֵדוּת יְיָ נֶאֱמָנָה, מַחְכִּימַת פֶּתִי;

God's precepts are just,
Rejoicing the heart;
God's commandments are lucid,
Giving light to the eyes.

פִּקּוּדֵי יְיָ יְשָׁרִים, מְשַׂמְּחֵי־לֵב;
מִצְוַת יְיָ בָּרָה, מְאִירַת עֵינָיִם;

God's word is pure, enduring forever;
God's judgments are true,
And altogether just.

יִרְאַת יְיָ טְהוֹרָה, עוֹמֶדֶת לָעַד;
מִשְׁפְּטֵי יְיָ אֱמֶת, צָדְקוּ יַחְדָּו.

כִּי לֶקַח טוֹב נָתַתִּי לָכֶם,
תּוֹרָתִי אַל־תַּעֲזֹבוּ.

Behold, a good doctrine has been given you, My Torah; do not forsake it. It is a tree of life to those who hold it fast, and all who cling to it find happiness. Its ways are ways of pleasantness, and all its paths are peace. Return us to You, O God, and we shall return. Renew our days as of old.

All sing

Eits cha-yim hi la-ma-cha-zi-kim ba,
ve-to-me-che-ha me-u-shar.
De-ra-che-ha dar-chei no-am,
ve-chol ne-ti-vo-te-ha sha-lom.

עֵץ־חַיִּים הִיא לַמַּחֲזִיקִים בָּהּ,
וְתֹמְכֶיהָ מְאֻשָּׁר: דְּרָכֶיהָ דַרְכֵי־
נֹעַם, וְכָל־נְתִיבֹתֶיהָ שָׁלוֹם.
הֲשִׁיבֵנוּ יְיָ אֵלֶיךָ, וְנָשׁוּבָה.
חַדֵּשׁ יָמֵינוּ כְּקֶדֶם.

Ha-shi-vei-nu A-do-nai ei-le-cha
ve-na-shu-va.
Cha-deish ya-mei-nu ke-ke-dem.

Ark is closed; all are seated

"It is a tree of life..." is a collection of verses on the importance of Torah taken from *Psalms 19:8-10* and *Proverbs 4:2, 3:12, 17.*

YOM KIPPUR AFTERNOON MEDITATIONS

Reader

God of the beginning, God of the end, God of all creatures, Lord of all generations: With love You guide the world, with love You walk hand in hand with all the living.

You created us in Your image, capable of love and justice, that in creation's long unfolding we might be Your partners. You endowed human beings with freedom; we must not enslave them. You gave them judgment; we must not dictate their course.

You set before us many paths that we might search and find the way that is true for us. We thank You for Your gift of choice. Without it, where would our greatness lie? Created in Your image, we are called upon to choose.

Congregation

Let our reflections on this Yom Kippur day help us to bring into our lives the harmony and blessings we seek.

Reader

On this day, we take a look into the Book of our lives. We peer into the days and nights of a year gone by. We examine the kind and decent things we have done against the sins we have committed. We seek to know where we stand with God and ourselves.

"God of the beginning..." is adapted from *Gates of Repentance, p. 366.*

Reader

Repentance and the Day of Atonement suffice for forgiveness of sins against God alone, but sins against human beings, such as violence or cursing or theft, are not forgiven until restitution is made and the injured person satisfied. And restitution by itself is not enough; one must appease the injured person and ask forgiveness. By the same token, an injured person must not be unforgiving. We should be slow to anger and easily appeased. When our forgiveness is requested, we should grant it with a whole heart and a willing spirit; we should not be vengeful or bear grudges even for a grave injury. This is the way of the upright Jew.

OUR RELIGIOUS SEARCH

Reader

A religious search is a lonely labor. It is like a flight over an ocean or a desert. Its main preoccupation is not the collecting of interesting episodes as one floats along, but the keeping of one's wings aloft and the reading of one's course by constant sun and steadfast stars. And, at the end, one's concern is to leave a few words of guidance, if one can, for other voyagers soon to embark upon a like adventure.

"Repentance and..." is adapted from Moses Maimonides' *Hilchot Teshuvah 2:9f.* "A religious search..." adapted from William L. Sullivan, as quoted in *A Modern Treasury of Jewish Thoughts,* edited by Sidney Greenberg, p. 359.

Reader I

Lord, where can I find You?
Your glory fills the world.
Behold, I find You
Where the ploughman breaks the hard soil,
Where the quarrier explodes stone out of the hillside,
Where the miner digs metals out of the reluctant earth,
Where men and women earn their bread by the sweat of their brow,
Among the lonely and poor, the lowly and lost.
In blazing heat and shattering storm, You are with them.
Behold, I find You
In the mind free to sail by its own star,
In words that spring from the depth of truth,
Where endeavor reaches undespairing for perfection,
Where the scientist toils to unravel the secrets of Your world,
Where the poet makes beauty out of words,
Wherever people struggle for freedom,
Wherever noble deeds are done.

Reader II

Behold, I find You
In the shouts of children happy at their play,
In the mother's lullaby, as she rocks her baby in the cradle,
In the sleep falling on his infant eyelids,
And in the smile that dances on his sleeping lips.
Behold, I find You
When dawn comes up bearing golden gifts,
And in the fall of evening peace and rest from the Western sea.

"Lord, where..." is adapted from a poem by Yehudah Halevi (1085-1140) as translated
by Eugene Kohn in *Reconstructionist Sabbath Prayer Book, pp. 342-349.*

Reader

The Lord is a whisper
at midnight,
and in the spontaneity of songs
at dawn.
I have no fear or hesitation.
In after-Shabbat spice
and wine,
I sense God's presence,
and I walk with confidence
through week-long trivialities.
How shall I doubt
or contradict
the sway of reed grass
by the river?
Shall I speculate away my life,
denying the flight of geese
and the swoop of eagles?
How dare I resist God's glance
through the mountain mist?

FULL OF WORDS

Reader

Once the Baal Shem stopped on the threshold of a House of Prayer and refused
to go in. "I cannot enter," he said. "It is crowded with teachings and prayers from
wall to wall and from floor to ceiling. How could there be room for me?"
When he saw that those around him were staring, unable to understand, he
added: "The words of those whose teaching and praying does not come from
hearts lifted to heaven, cannot rise to heaven; instead, their words fill the house
from wall to wall and from floor to ceiling. Those who rise from prayer better
persons, their prayer is answered."

"The Lord is a whisper..." is by Danny Seigel, *Psalms and Prayers, p. 11.*

Responsively

How does one find God?

> By the doing of good deeds,
> by the study of Torah.

And how does the Holy One find us?

> Through our love, friendship, and respect;
> through companionship, truth, and peace;
> through the service of scholars
> through the discussion of students;
> through decency and a good heart;
> through a No that is truly No,
> through a Yes that is really Yes.

Thus says the Holy One to Israel:
"My children, what do I seek of you?
Only love one another,
honor and respect each other.
Let there be found in you
neither transgression nor theft,
nothing that is shameful."

> It has been told what is good,
> and what the Lord demands of you:
> Do justly, love mercy,
> and walk humbly with your God.

"How does one..." is adapted from passages in *Seder Eliyahu Rabbah 23 and 26* by Rabbi Chaim Stern (1930-).

Reader I

Why in our prayers, do we say: "Our God and the God of people?"

Reader II

Because there are two kinds of people who believe in God. One believes because he has taken over the faith of his parents, and his faith is strong. The other has arrived at faith through thinking and studying.

The difference between them is this: The advantage of the first is that, no matter what arguments may be brought against it, the person's faith cannot be shaken. It is firm because it was taken over from parents. But there is one flaw in it. Such faith derives only from the command of a person. It was acquired without study and personal exploration. The advantage of the second kind of faith is that God is discovered through much thinking and is the outcome of one's own exploration. But here, too, there is a flaw: it is easy to shake such faith by refuting it through evidence.

But the person who unites both kinds of faith is invincible. So we say, "Our God" with reference to our studies and personal struggle with belief, and "God of our people" with an eye to tradition.

"Why in our prayers..." is adapted from the writings of Martin Buber (1878-1965).

Reader I

Where does one find God?
In heaven and earth,
In a clap of thunder, in a whisper of the soul,
In a praise on yellowed parchment in an ancient tongue,
In yearnings of the heart, in a child not yet born.

Reader II

Bless the Eternal One, O my soul.
When we see a pleasing sculpture, we say:
"Blessed the One who fashioned it.
The world is pleasing:
Blessed the Presence that shapes it."

Reader I

Taste of tears and wine, sight of starry skies,
Old men's voices warping the chant, children singing,
Scientists asking, artists proclaiming:
"Blessed the One who shapes it."

Reader II

Where does one find God?
In all the web of creation,
In God's bright sunlight,
In the dew that gathers in darkness.
Blessed is the One who shapes it.
Blessed the One who is and will be.

"Where does one…" is adapted from *Gates of Repentance, p. 386.*

Who is honored in Your Presence more,
One who accepts, or questions?
Are my doubts anathema?
Am I wrong to see a new wilderness
    In this land of unbearable riches?

Lord beyond space and time, bring peace
    To the forked creatures of Your earth
    That we may write Your name with our flights
    Into the cold heavens we know and study
    As airy fire and artless flow.

Who can blame our longing for a sign?
Would one more proof
    For the blind and foolish
    Beast struggling below
    Separated by so many generations
    From Your cleansing fire —
    Shame Your greatness?

Yet my heart echoes still within
For I know that just as my soul
Is suffused throughout my flesh,
    You are here about me, everywhere,
    In all things, in me, in my questions,
    Even in my doubts.

"Who is honored..." is by William Wallis (1946-).

Reader

O God, You are near as the very air we breathe and the light around us, yet our thought's farthest reach falls short of You.

We yearn to reach You. We seek the light and warmth of Your Presence, for we are lost without You.

Let our desire for Your Presence be so strong that it will tear the veil that keeps You from our sight! Let Your light penetrate our darkness, revealing to us the joy of Your nearness.

As the fish gives itself to the sea, and the bird to the air, as all life gives itself to life, so may we give ourselves to You, O God.

SILENT PRAYER

The words of prayer are hopes.
The hopes of prayer are wishes.
The wishes of prayer are dreams,
and the dreams of prayer are made real
by the will of those who pray.

What is prayer, but God speaking to us
through our own voices.

And the words of God can be heard
through the tongues of all human beings.
For the ways of God are deep as love.

"O God..." is adapted from *Gates of Prayer, p. 665.*

Responsively

Create in me a clean heart, O God, and renew a willing spirit within me.

> You who know the thoughts of human beings and understand the minds of mortals, know my longing to do Your will.

Give me a clear mind purged of thoughtless wishes. Save me from every kind of trouble which makes me a stranger to You and keeps me from serving You. Make light the weight of other burdens which hinder me from bearing Yours.

> Body and heart may fail, but the Lord, our God, is forever.

Return us to You, O God, in perfect repentance. Uplift our hearts that we may do Your will.

Reader

This day, O God, sound within us the prophet's voice calling us to judgment. Let Your questions force truth from its deep concealment within us.

Lead us to examine our ways. Open us to hear the children weeping, parents sighing; the lonely words of old people to whom few care to listen; the silent sound when people close their eyes to their sisters and brothers. And let us also hear the laughter of children, the songs of mothers, and the voices of those who give their lives to the search for truth.

This day, O God, open our hearts to the emptiness of those who cannot find You. And, when adrift we wonder where we are, make us to see that our turning to You is Your turning to us.

This day, Lord, help us to make Your will our own. Make firm our trust, that in place of bondage, all will be free; where error reigns, truth shall take hold; where hatred rages, love will prevail.

TRUE PRAYER

Reader

The Baal Shem Tov taught his students that when wood burns, it is the smoke alone that rises upward, leaving the grosser elements below. And so it is with prayer. The sincere intention of our hearts ascends to God, and the test of our prayers is in our fulfillment of them.

Responsively

We pray not only for ourselves, but for the Jewish people, whose destiny is our own, and whose hopes we share. Alas, how much there is in the life of our people that is unworthy of its noble past and its high calling!

> Some have strayed from their ancestral faith and broken the chain of tradition.

Some have despised their birthright and treated their heritage with contempt.

> Some have dishonored the Sabbath and desecrated holy days.

Some are deaf to the music of mitzvot, and they shut their eyes to the beauty of holiness.

> Some have made idols of professional advancement, social status, and material reward.

Some, while pretending to love humanity, have withheld from their own people the love they deserve.

> Some have forgotten that Judaism calls us to love and to serve others.

Some through their apathy and indifference, have failed to pass on to their loved ones a commitment to our people and faith.

> Some, by their wrong actions, or by their failure to act, have brought dishonor upon our people.

Some have promoted needless conflict and groundless hatred, destroying the unity of Israel.

> May this day renew in us a love for our people and the quest to guide our lives by our Torah tradition.

"We pray..." is adapted from *Gates of Repentance, pp. 424-425.*

Reader

What can we do? What difference can we make?

We can talk out when others are silent.
We can persist when others give up.
We can keep on working when others have lost hope.
We can give life large meanings when others give life little meanings.
We can say love when others say hate.
We can try events by a hard test when others try them by an easy test.

What can we do?

We can give ourselves to life when others refuse themselves to life.

GIVING IS NOT
LOSING

Responsively

No person is ever impoverished through giving *tzedakah*—charity, nor is evil or harm ever caused by it; As it is written, "The work of righteousness shall be peace."

God has compassion on those who show mercy to the poor.

Let those seeking sustenance at the hand of God provide sustenance to the poor. Let them realize that the world is a revolving sphere and that eventually they, too, will rely on charity.

Everyone is obliged to contribute to charity. Even those who are maintained by charity should give a portion of what they receive.

EIGHT DEGREES OF CHARITY

Reader

There are eight degrees in the giving of *tzedakah,* each one higher than the next:

To give grudgingly, reluctantly, or with regret;
To give less than one should, but with grace;
To give what one should, but only after being asked;
To give before one is asked;
To give without knowing who will receive it, although the recipient knows
    the identity of the giver;
To give without making known one's identity;
To give so that neither giver nor receiver knows the identity of the other;
To help another to become self-supporting by means of a gift or loan or by
    finding employment for the one in need.

END OUR DARKNESS

Reader

Eternal God, what can we say in Your presence? How account for our sins? We speak of repentance, and yet are slow to change. But now we turn to You with the prayer that Your love may abide with us always, turning our hearts to Your ways, our feet to Your paths. Hope sustains us. Do not turn us away empty-handed from Your presence. End our darkness with Your light and turn our passions to Your purpose. Help us, Lord, in this hour of turning, to make real in our lives the words of our mouths and the meditations of our hearts.

MUSICAL INTERLUDE
AND
MEDITATION

"There are eight..." is by Moses Maimonides, *Code,* "Laws Concerning the Poor," Chapter 10: 7-14. "Eternal God..." is adapted from *Gates of Repentance, p. 374.*

Reader

A young man came to the Riziner and asked to be ordained as a rabbi. The Riziner inquired regarding his daily conduct, and the candidate replied, "I always dress in white; I drink only water; I place tacks in my shoes for self-mortification; I roll naked in the snow; and I order the synagogue caretaker to give me forty lashes daily on my bare back."

Just then a white horse entered the courtyard, drank water, and began rolling in the snow.

"Observe," said the Riziner. "This creature is white, it drinks only water, it has nails in its shoes, it rolls in the snow, and it receives more than forty lashes a day. Still it is nothing but a horse."

THE TALES II

Reader

Rabban Simeon ben Gamaliel said to his servant Tabbai, "Go to the market and buy me some good food."

The servant went and brought back a tongue. He told him, "Go out and bring me some bad food from the market."

The servant went and brought back a tongue. The rabbi said to him, "Why is it that when I said 'good food' you brought me a tongue, and when I said 'bad food' you also brought me a tongue?"

He replied, "The tongue is the source of good and evil. When it is good, there is nothing better; when it is evil, there is nothing worse."

Reader

The rabbi of Berdichev saw a man hurrying along the street, looking neither right nor left. "Why are you rushing so much?" he asked the man.

"I'm rushing after my livelihood," the man answered.

"And how do you know," said the rabbi, "that your livelihood is running on before you so that you have to rush after it? Perhaps it's behind you, and all you need to do is stand still."

THE TALES IV

Reader

Once Emperor Hadrian was walking along the road near Tiberias in Galilee, and he saw an old man working the soil to plant some fig trees.

"If you had worked in your early years, old man," he said, "you would not have to work now so late in your life."

"I have worked both early and late," the man answered, "and God has blessed me with a long life."

"How old are you?" asked Hadrian.

"A hundred years old," the man answered.

"A hundred years old, and you still stand there breaking up the soil to plant trees!" said Hadrian. "Do you expect to eat the fruit of those trees?"

"If I am worthy, I will eat," said the old man. "But if not, as my father worked for me, I work for my children."

Reader

Whoever tells tales about another person violates a prohibition, as it is said; "Do not go about as a talebearer among your fellows."

Who is a talebearer? One who carries reports and goes about from one person to another and says, "So-and-so said this"; "I have heard such-and-such about so-and-so." Even if what he says or repeats may be true, the talebearer ruins the world.

There is a still graver offense that comes within this prohibition, namely, the evil tongue. This means talking disparagingly of anyone, even though what one says is true; but he who utters a falsehood is called a slanderer.

A person with an evil tongue is one who, sitting in company, says, "That person did such a thing"; "So-and-so's ancestors were so-and-so"; "I have heard this about him"; and proceeds to speak scandal and falsehood.

There are modes of speech that may be styled "dust of the evil tongue." Such remarks as "Who would have thought that so-and-so would be as he is now"; or, "Be silent about so-and-so. I don't want to tell what happened."

Equally reprehensible is the person who indulges in evil speech, passing on lies as though innocently, unaware that what he says is an evil utterance.

"Whoever tells tales..." is from Moses Maimonides, *Code,* "Laws Concerning Moral Dispositions and Ethical Conduct," Chapter 7, 1-4. "Do not go about..." is from *Leviticus 19:16.*

Reader

Mark well these three things, and you will not fall into the clutches of sin: Know where you came from, where you are going, and to whom you are destined to give an account and reckoning.

"Where you came from?" A drop of fluid.
"Where you are going?" To a place of dust and worms.
"And before whom are you destined to give an account and reckoning?" Before the Lord of all.

OUR TEACHINGS III

Reader

Our rabbis taught; "Six hundred and thirteen commandments were given to Moses." The prophet Micah reduced them to three; "Do justly, love mercy, and walk humbly with your God."

The prophet Isaiah reduced them to two; "Keep justice and righteousness."

The prophet Amos saw one guiding principle upon which all the mitzvot are founded; "Seek Me and live."

Akiba taught that the great principle of the Torah is expressed in the mitzvah; "You shall love your neighbor as yourself." But Ben Azzai found a principle even more fundamental in the words; "This is the story of humanity. When God created us, we were made in the Divine likeness."

Hillel summed up the Torah with his teaching; "What is hateful to you, do not do to others. The rest is commentary. Go and study it."

"Mark well..." is by Rabbi Akavyah ben Mahalel, 1st century C.E., *Avot 3:1*. "Our rabbis..." is based on *Shabbat 31a* and *Makkot 23b,* with references from *Micah 6:8, Isaiah 56:1, Amos 5:4, Leviticus 19:19.*

271

Reader

Antigonos, one of the ancient rabbis, said, "Be not like servants who serve their master for the sake of receiving a reward, but rather like servants who serve their master without thinking of a reward."

What the sage meant was that we should serve God in a spirit of absolute sincerity.

OUR TEACHINGS V

Reader

Religion to be effective must be real. It should emanate from the heart. We should "Love the Lord our God with all our heart, with all our soul and with all our might" and "our neighbors as ourselves."

The rabbis said, "Build a fence around the Torah, for a vineyard with a fence is safer than one without a fence."

Words of Torah are like golden vessels: the more you scour and polish them, the more they glisten and reflect the face of those who look at them. So with the words of Torah, whenever you repeat them, they glisten and illumine your face. They lead you to deeds of kindness, justice and peace.

OUR TEACHINGS VI

Reader

A favorite saying of the rabbis of Yavneh was, "I am a creature of God and my neighbor is also a creature of God. I work in the city and he works in the country. I rise early for my work and he rises early for his work. Just as he cannot excel in my work, I cannot excel in his work. Will you say that I do great things and he does small things?"

We have learned that it does not matter whether a person does much or little, as long as he directs his heart to heaven.

Reader

And on this day, between teachings and wisdom, we speak a blessing for our children, and for ourselves.

Congregation

May your eyes sparkle with the light of Torah, and your ears hear the music of its words. May the space between each letter of the scrolls bring warmth and comfort to your soul. May the syllables draw holiness from your heart, and may this holiness be gentle and soothing to the world. May your study be passionate, and meanings bear more meanings until Life itself arrays itself to you as a dazzling wedding feast.

And may your conversation, even of the commonplace, be a blessing to all who listen to your words and see the Torah glowing on your face.

MUSICAL INTERLUDE
AND MEDITATION

"Antigonos..." from *Avot 1:3.* "Religion to be..." based on *Deuteronomy 6:3; Leviticus 19:19; Niddah 3b.* "May your eyes..." by Danny Siegel, *Psalms and Prayers, p. 39.*

Reader

The sage was asked, "Why do we never perceive in you a trace of anxiety?" He replied, "Because I never possessed a thing over which I would grieve had I lost it."

He also said, "Everything requires a fence." He was asked, "What is the fence?" He answered, "Trust." "What is the fence of trust?" he was asked. He replied, "Faith." And when he was asked, "What is the fence of faith?" he answered, "To fear nothing."

MORE TALES OF WISDOM II

Reader

Once a disciple of Rabbi Akiba became ill and no one visited him. Rabbi Akiba, however, entered the sick man's room, arranged that it be swept and cleaned, and placed his pillow in order. All this assisted the recovery of the disciple, and he said to Akiba, "O Master, you have revived me."

Later, after Rabbi Akiba died, the disciple told his students: "Whoever neglects to visit a lonely, sick person is as if he shed his blood."

Rabbi Akiba, born in 50 B.C.E., was one of the greatest scholars of his time, and a leader of the revolt against Roman oppression. He was tortured and executed by Roman authorities in 135 C.E.

Reader I

Why were human beings created on the sixth day? To teach that if they are ever swollen with pride, it can be said to them, "A flea came ahead of you in creation."

Reader II

Rabbi Haninah bar Idi said, "Why are words of Torah likened to water?" The answer is, "Just as water flows from a high place and travels to a low one, so do the words of Torah find a resting place only in a person of humble spirit."

Reader I

Rabbi Oshaya said, "Why are the words of the Torah likened to water, wine, and milk?" The answer is, "Just as these liquids are kept only in the simplest of vessels, so the holy words are preserved only in the person of humble spirit."

Reader II

Why are we told to be supple as the reed and not rigid as the cedar?

A reed, when all the winds come and blow upon it, bends with them, and when the winds are still, it is again upright in its place. And what is the end of the reed? Its good fortune is to be used as a pen that writes the Torah scroll.

The cedar, however, does not remain standing in its place. As soon as the south wind blows, it uproots it and tears it down. And what is the end of the cedar? Loggers come upon it and chop it up and use it to cover housetops, and what remains, they cast to the flames.

"Why…" based on comments taken from: *Sanhedrin 37a; Taanit 7a;* and *Avot de'Rabbi Natan, 41.*

Reader I

Those whose wisdom exceeds their deeds, to what are they likened? To a tree whose branches are numerous but whose roots are few. The wind comes along and uproots it and sweeps it down.

But those whose deeds exceed their wisdom, to what can they be likened? To a tree whose branches are few but whose roots are numerous and deep. Then, even if all the winds of the world come along and blow against it, they cannot stir it from its place.

As it is said: "They shall be like trees planted by waters, sending forth their roots by a stream; they do not sense the coming of heat; their leaves are ever fresh; they have no care in a year of drought; they do not cease to yield fruit."

Reader II

We are also taught that wars arise because justice is either delayed or perverted ...also because judges render the wrong decisions.

Reader I

There are four kinds of human beings. One says, "What belongs to me is mine and what belongs to you is yours." Another says, "What is mine is yours and what is yours is mine." A third says, "What is mine is yours and what is yours is yours." Such a person is saintly. The fourth person says, "What is yours is mine and what is mine is mine." This person is evil.

"Those whose wisdom..." based upon *Avot 3:22,* and *5:13.*

276

Reader

My father bequeathed me no wide estates;
No keys and ledgers were my heritage;
Only some holy books with yahrzeit dates
Writ mournfully upon a blank page—

Books of the Baal Shem Tov, and of his wonders;
Pamphlets upon the devil and his crew;
Prayers against road demons, witches, thunders;
And sundry other tomes for a good Jew.

Beautiful: though no pictures on them, save
The scorpion crawling on a printed track;
The Virgin floating on a scriptural wave,
Square letters twinkling in the Zodiac.

The snuff left on this page, now brown and old,
The tallow stains of midnight liturgy —
These are my coat of arms, and these unfold
My noble lineage, my proud ancestry!
And my tears, too, have stained their heirloomed ground,
When reading in these treatises some weird
Miracle, I turned a leaf and found
A white hair fallen from my father's beard.

MUSICAL INTERLUDE
AND
MEDITATION

"My father..." is by A.M. Klein (1909-1972).

Reader

It is an easy thing to triumph in the summer's sun
And in the vintage and to sing on the wagon loaded with corn.
It is an easy thing to talk of patience to the afflicted,
To speak the laws of prudence to the homeless wanderer,
To listen to the hungry raven's cry in wintry season
When the red blood is filled with wine and with the marrow of lambs.

It is an easy thing to laugh at wrathful elements,
To hear the dog howl at the wintry door, the ox in the slaughter house moan;
To see God on every wind and a blessing on every blast;
To hear sounds of love in the thunder storm that destroys our enemies' house;
To rejoice in the blight that covers his field, and the sickness that cuts off his
     children,
While our olive and vine sing and laugh round our door, and our children
     bring fruits and flowers.
It is an easy thing to rejoice in the tents of prosperity.

"It is an easy thing..." is by William Blake (1757-1827).

Reader I

We do not have to discover the world of faith; we only have to recover it... There is no one who has no faith. Every one of us stood at the foot of Sinai and beheld the voice that proclaimed, "I am the Lord your God."

Reader II

There is no faith at first sight. A faith that comes into being like a butterfly is ephemeral... Faith is preceded by awe, by acts of amazement at things that we apprehend but cannot comprehend... We must learn how to see "the miracles which are daily with us"; we must learn how to live in awe, in order to attain the insights of faith.

Reader I

It is not easy to attain faith... Callousness to the mystery is our greatest obstacle. In the artificial light of pride and self-contentment, we shall never see the splendor.

Reader II

Sensitivity to God is given to a broken heart, to a mind that rises above its own wisdom. It is a sensitivity that bursts all abstractions... There is no affirmation without self-engagement... God is a challenge rather than a notion.

"We do not have..." is adapted from Rabbi Abraham J. Heschel (1907-1972), *God In Search of Man, pp. 141, 152-154, 159-160.*

Reader

O God, who can understand the mystery of Your acts?
For You have given our bodies the means to do Your work.
You gave us eyes to see Your signs,
Ears to hear Your wonders,
A mind to comprehend some part of Your secrets,
A mouth to speak Your praises,
A tongue to tell everyone of Your mighty acts.
Today, I sing Your greatness,
Knowing that I am a part of You.

Reader

O Lord—
Number my days this way:

Days of strength to lie,
if the truth brings torment.
Days of weakness,
if strength gives rise to suffering.
Days of noise,
if silence is the cause of loneliness.
And nights of disconcerting dreams
if I turn smug to the taste of hunger.

Pursue me,
Discomfort me,
Destroy my own complacency
with paradox and contradiction.

Remind me I am Yours.

"O God..." is from *The Kingly Crown* by Solomon Gabriol (1021-1056 C.E.).
"O Lord..." is by Danny Siegel, *Psalms and Prayers, p. 26.*

Reader I

A Jew is asked to take a leap of action rather than a leap of thought.

Reader II

It is in deeds that we become aware of what life really is, of our powers to harm and to hurt, to wreck and to ruin; of our ability to derive joy and to bestow it upon others; to relieve and to increase our own and other people's tensions. The heart is revealed in deeds.

Reader I

The mitzvah-deed is the test, the trial, and the risk. We are taught by our tradition that "we should always regard ourselves as though we were half guilty and half meritorious; if we perform one good deed, we are blessed for we move the scale of judgment toward merit; if we commit one transgression, we move it toward evil. One mitzvah-deed may decide the fate of the world; it may save a life."

Reader II

We stand on a razor's edge...With a sacred deed goes more than a stir of the heart. In a sacred deed we echo God's suppressed chant; in loving we intone God's unfinished song...We are not only in need of God but also in need of serving God's ends, and these ends are in need of us.

"A Jew is asked..." is by Rabbi Abraham J. Heschel (1907-1972), *God In Search of Man*, *pp. 283-291.*

Reader

Strange is our situation here upon earth. Each of us comes for a short visit, not knowing why, yet sometimes seeming to divine a purpose. From the stand-point of daily life, however, there is one thing we do know: That we are here for the sake of others... Above all, for those upon whose smile and well-being our own happiness depends, and also for the countless unknown souls with whose fate we are connected by a bond of sympathy. Many times a day I realize how much my own outer and inner life is built upon the labors of others, both living and dead, and how earnestly I must exert myself in order to give in return as much as I have received and am still receiving.

Reader

Unless we believe in ourselves and our tasks, our faith in God as well as our faith in atonement is empty. The moral personality is revealed in its activity upon earth. We bring God into the world. We sanctify the world by sanctifying God in it. We are given the choice to bring into existence that which should be.

MUSICAL INTERLUDE
AND
MEDITATION

"Strange is our..." is by Albert Einstein (1879-1955). "Unless man..." is by Rabbi Leo Baeck (1873–1956), *The Essence of Judaism, pp. 187-188.*

Responsively

At this Yom Kippur hour we, the people of Israel, stand before God. In our prayers, in our hopes, we are one with all Jews on earth.

> This people You have formed still lives to tell Your praise.

Today we say to our children: See this sublime design, which was revealed at the very beginning and which from age to age is realized. See this people, few in number, to the world unknown, choosing the mission which chooses it in the way it was foretold.

> This people You have formed still lives to tell Your praise.

To our friends we say: See this people, exiled twice and twice surviving, teaching in its first exile the unity of God and, in its second, the oneness of humankind.

> This people Israel lives to tell God's praise, and to bear witness to human hopes and dreams.

At this hour our people stands before God. In our prayers, in our hope, we are one with all Jews on earth. We look into each other's faces, and we know who we are.

> We look to our God and know eternity is in us.

"At this Yom Kippur..." is adapted from *Gates of Repentance, pp. 394-395.*

Reader I

You are My witnesses, says the Lord, and My servants whom I have chosen, that you may know Me, and trust Me, and understand that I am the One. Before Me no God was formed, nor shall there be any after Me. I alone am the Lord, and besides Me there is no savior.

Reader II

Behold My servants whom I uphold, My chosen ones, in whom My soul delights; I have put My spirit upon them, that they may bring justice to the nations. They shall not cry out nor shout aloud, nor make themselves heard in the street. Though bent like a reed, they shall not be broken; though their flame burns low, they shall not be snuffed out: faithfully shall they bring forth justice.

Reader I

They shall not weaken, they shall not be broken: at last to establish justice in the earth, as the most distant lands respond to their teaching.

Reader II

God chose us. We chose God. There is a mystery here that reason cannot solve nor cynicism dismiss. We can deny that mystery, or we can humbly recognize it, be a part of it, accept it and say to God: "Here I am; send me."

"You are My witnesses…" is based upon selections from *Isaiah 40-45,* which speak of God's summons to the Jewish people to be "a light to the nations."

Reader

To be a Jew in this century
Is to be offered a gift. If you refuse,
Wishing to be invisible, you choose
Death of the spirit, the stone insanity.
Accepting, take full life. Full agonies:
Your evening deep in labyrinthine blood
Of those who resist, fall, and resist; and God
Reduced to a hostage among hostages.

The gift is torment. Not alone the still
Torture, isolation; or torture of the flesh.
That may come also. But the accepting wish,
The whole and fertile spirit as guarantee
For every human freedom, suffering to be free,
Daring to live for the impossible.

"To be a Jew..." is by Muriel Rukeyser (1913-).

Reader

I am a Jew because the faith of Israel demands of me no abdication of the mind.

I am a Jew because the faith of Israel requires of me all the devotion of my heart.

I am a Jew because in every place where suffering weeps, the Jew weeps.

I am a Jew because at every time when despair cries out, the Jew hopes.

I am a Jew because the word of Israel is the oldest and the newest.

I am a Jew because the promise of Israel is the universal promise.

I am a Jew because, for Israel, the world is not completed; we are completing it.

I am a Jew because, for Israel, humanity is not created; we are creating it.

I am a Jew because Israel places humanity and its unity above the nations and above Israel itself.

I am a Jew because, above humanity, image of the divine Unity, Israel places the unity which is Divine.

"I am a Jew..." is by Edmond Fleg, French-Jewish poet (1874-1963).

Reader

God of Israel, teach us to be worthy of our heritage. May we do nothing to disgrace it. May our every act bring honor to our faith and glory to You. May we understand our responsibility as Jews to continue the task begun by earlier generations of our people who achieved greatness by their faith in the mission to which You had called them: To bring light and blessing to all the families of the earth.

YOU ARE NEAR

Congregation

You have called us into life and set us in the midst of purposes we cannot measure or understand. Yet we thank You for the good we know, for the life we have, and for the gifts that are our daily portion:

Reader

For health and healing, for labor and repose, for the ever-renewed beauty of earth and sky, for thoughts of truth and justice which stir us from our ease and move us to acts of goodness, and for the contemplation of Your eternal presence, which fills us with hope that what is good and lovely cannot perish.

"God, You have..." is adapted from *Gates of Prayer, pp. 673, 675.*

Responsively

When evil darkens our world, give us light.

> When despair numbs our souls, give us hope.

When we stumble and fall, lift us up.

> When doubts assail us, give us faith.

When nothing seems sure, give us trust.

> When ideals fade, give us vision.

When we lose our way, be our guide!

> That we may find serenity in Your Presence, and purpose in doing Your will.

THE MEANING OF PRAYER

Reader

To pray is to take notice of the wonder, to regain a sense of the mystery that animates all beings, the divine margin in all attainments. Prayer is our answer to the inconceivable surprise of living.

"To pray…" is by Abraham J. Heschel (1907-1972), *Man's Quest For God, p. 5.*

Reader

O Lord our God, in our great need for light we look to You. The quick flight of our days impels us to look back with regret or ahead with misgiving. There are times when we are baffled by disorder, and times when we come to doubt life's value and meaning. When suffering and death strike at those we love, our pain and anger embitter us. Our faith fails us; we find it hard to trust in You.

Congregation

Eternal Spirit, make Your Presence felt among us. Help us to find the courage to affirm You and to do Your will. When our own weakness and the storms of life hide You from our sight, teach us that You are near. Urge us in our striving to live truer, gentler, nobler lives. Give us trust. Give us peace. Give us light. O God, let our hearts find their rest in You.

"O Lord..." is adapted from *Gates of Prayer, p. 674.*

Reader

All things pray, and all things pour forth their souls. The heavens pray, the earth prays, every creature and every living thing.

In all life, there is longing. Creation is itself but a longing, a prayer to God.

What are the clouds, the rising and the setting of the sun, the soft radiance of the moon and the gentleness of the night?

Congregation

What are the flashes of the human mind and the storms of the human heart? They are all prayers. They are all outpourings of boundless longing for God.

MUSICAL INTERLUDE
AND
MEDITATION

Reader

Lord, we are not so arrogant as to pretend
that the trial of our lives does not reveal our flaws.
We know ourselves, in this moment of prayer,
to have failed the ones we love and the stranger,
again and again.
We know how often we did not bring to the surface of our lives
the hidden goodness within.
Where we have achieved, O Lord, we are grateful;
where we have failed, we ask forgiveness.
Remember how exposed we are
to the chances and terrors of life.
We were afraid.
We sometimes chose to fail.
And we ask:
Turn our thoughts from the hurt to its remedy.
Free us of the torments of guilt.

ON REPENTANCE

Reader

Rabbi Hama bar Haninah said, "Great is repentance, for it brings healing to the world."

Rabbi Jonathan said, "Great is repentance, for it brings near the time of redemption."

Rabbi Jacob said, "Better one hour of repentance and good works in this world than all the life of the world-to-come."

"Lord, we are not..." is by Rabbi Norman Hirsh. "Rabbi Hama ban Haninah..." is based on Talmudic statements from *Yoma 86 a-b; Avot 4:17,* and *Berachot 34b.*

Reader

The focus of prayer is not the self. Prayer comes to pass in the turning of the heart toward God.

Prayer is an invitation to God to intervene in our lives, to let the divine will prevail in our affairs.

Prayer does not change God but is meant to change the person who prays.

Prayer cannot mend a broken bridge, rebuild a ruined city, or bring water to parched fields.

Prayer can mend a broken heart, lift up a discouraged soul, and strengthen a weakened will.

Our prayers are answered not when we are given what we ask, but when we are challenged to be what we can be.

Congregation

Prayer reveals truths about ourselves and the world that neither scalpel nor microscope can uncover. Prayer is the search for silence amidst the noise of life. Prayer is not escape from duty; it challenges us to do wisely and to act generously.

"Prayer reveals..." is adapted from Rabbi Morris Adler (1906-1966).

I asked God for strength, that I might achieve—
I was made weak, that I might learn humbly to obey.

I asked for health, that I might do greater things—
I was given infirmity, that I might do better things.

I asked for riches, that I might be happy—
I was given poverty, that I might be wise.

I asked for power, that I might have the praise of people—
I was given life, that I might enjoy all things.

I got nothing that I asked for—but everything I had hoped for.

Almost despite myself, my unspoken prayers were answered.
I am, among all, most richly blessed!

Responsively

Come, let us consider and examine our sins and vanities,
And start anew our struggle to master history.

>For the kingdom of God is to be our doing,
>The work of our hands.

In the recesses of our souls,
Knowing full well the vast measure of the unknown,
The treachery of the human heart, even ours,
On this Yom Kippur,
This time of penitence and remembrance,
We urgently pray for the gifts of God:

>For courage and love,
>Order in the world,
>Grace in ourselves,
>And wisdom to worship the Holy One in all our deeds.

THERE ARE MOMENTS

Reader

There are moments when we hear the call of our higher selves, the call that links us to the Divine. Then we know how blessed we are with life and love. May this be such a moment, a time of deeper attachments to the Godlike in us and in our world, for which we shall give thanks and praise!

"There are..." is from *Gates of Repentance, p. 363.*

Reader I

To everything there is a season,
And there is an appointed time for every purpose under heaven.
Now is the time for turning.
The leaves are beginning to turn from green to red and orange.
The birds are beginning to turn and are heading once more toward the south.
The animals are beginning to turn to storing their food for the winter.
For leaves, birds, and animals, turning comes instinctively.
But for us, turning does not come so easily.

Reader II

It takes an act of will for us to make a turn.
It means breaking with old habits.
It means admitting that we have been wrong;
And this is never easy.
It means losing face;
It means starting all over again;
And this is always painful.
It means saying: "I am sorry."
It means admitting that we have the ability to change;
And this is always embarrassing.
These things are terribly hard to do.
But unless we turn, we will be trapped forever in yesterday's ways.

"To everything…" is adapted from a prayer by Rabbi Jack Riemer.

Congregation

Lord, help us to turn—

From callousness to sensitivity,
From hostility to love,

From pettiness to purpose,
From envy to contentment,

From carelessness to discipline,
From fear to faith.

Turn us around, O Lord, and bring us back toward You.
Revive our lives, as at the beginning.

And turn us toward each other, Lord,
For in isolation there is no life.

WE CONFESS OUR SINS

Reader

Lord, today we turn to You, uncertainly proclaiming Your glory with scarce remembered words of a half-forgotten faith. We confess our sins and promise to forsake them. O find us as we grope for You in our darkness. Lord, pardon us as we knock upon Your door, for it has been said: "The gates of repentance are never barred." And it has been taught: "We know our sin is pardoned when we no longer commit it."

Congregation

Lord, make us whole. Make us one with our own hearts: make us one with each other, at last to find ourselves at one with You.

Reader

For the sin of silence,
For the sin of indifference,
For the secret complicity of the neutral,
For the closing of borders,
For the washing of hands,
For the crime of indifference,
For the sin of silence,
For the closing of borders,
For all that was done,
Let there be no forgetfulness before the Throne of Glory;
Let there be remembrance within the human heart.

Congregation

And let there at last be forgiveness
When Your children, O God,
Are free and at peace.

"For the sin of..." is from *Gates of Repentance p. 439.*

Reader I

Let us ask ourselves hard questions, for this is the time for truth. How much time did we waste in the year that is now gone?

Congregation

Did we fill our days with life or were they dull and empty? Was there love inside our home or was the affectionate word left unsaid?

Reader II

Was there a real companionship with our families or was there a living together and growing apart? Were we there when our friends needed us or not?

Congregation

Did we perform the kind deed or postpone it? Did we say the unnecessary remark or hold it back?

Reader I

Did we live by false values? Did we deceive ourselves?

Congregation

Were we sensitive to the rights and feelings of those who worked with us? Did we acquire only possessions or did we acquire new insights as well?

Reader II

Did we fear what the crowd would say and keep quiet when we should have spoken out? Did we mind only our own business or did we feel the heartbreak of others?

Congregation

Did we live right, and if not, then have we learned and will we change?

Reader

Praised be the One whose word made this world to be,
This world so small and strange,
Where all things begin
In the middle of their growth,
And end there;
Where all things hide
From the One who longs to understand them.
Here in space and time they hide
From their beginning in time
To their eternal end.

And praised be the One who keeps a covenant
With this world,
So strange and small,
Where God's good is sown to the winds,
So that hope exalts even the least of us,
So that even I find my spirit rising to redeem me.
And in my heart wells up this word:
Praised be the One whose word made this world to be.

"Praised be..." is by Avraham Eliyahu Kaplan (1890-1924) as translated by Rabbi Chaim Stern.

Reader

O Lord,
You are a consolation to Your creatures,
for in moments of forgetting,
we but call to mind Your care,
and we are comforted.
When we hope no more,
a pattern in the snow
reminds us of Your loving kindness.
Your dawns give us confidence,
and sleep is a friend.
Our sorrows dissipate
in the presence of an infant's smile,
and old men's words revive our will-to-wish.
Your hints are everywhere,
Your signals in the most remote of places.
You are here, and we fail words to say,
"Mah Tov!"
How good our breath, our rushing energies,
our silences of love.

Reader

Though our mouths should overflow with song as the sea, our tongues with melody as the roaring waves, our lips with praise as the heavens' wide expanse—still we could not fully thank You, Lord our God and God of all ages, or bless Your name enough, for even one of Your infinite kindnesses to our ancestors and to us.

"O Lord..." is by Danny Siegel, *Psalms and Prayers, p. 20.* "Though our..." is adapted from the traditional prayer known as *Nishmat Kol Chai,* meaning, "The breath of all life...."

Reader I

You,

> Who give work to the laborer
> and food to the soil,
>> praised be You.

You,

> Who set the ocean waves in motion
> and balance the sunlight,
>> be praised.

You,

> Who show Your eyes in the face
> of the children and the blind,
>> blessed be Your name.

Reader II

And
You,

> Who spray the storm and sleet
> on midnight city streets,
>> be thanked today
>> and every season.

Your variety be sung;
> Your shades be imitated.

Your infinitum-Presence be sensed
> now and forever.
> Blessed be Your name.

"You..." is by Danny Siegel, *Psalms and Prayers, p. 10.*

Responsively

How wonderful, O Lord, are the works of Your hands!
The heavens declare Your glory, the arch of sky displays Your handiwork.

> The heavens declare the glory of God.

In Your love You have given us the power to behold the beauty of Your world, robed in all its splendor. The sun and the stars, the valleys and hills, the rivers and lakes—all disclose Your Presence.

> The earth reveals God's eternal Presence.

The roaring breakers of the sea tell of Your awesome might; the beasts of the field and the birds of the air bespeak Your wondrous will.

> Life comes forth by God's creative will.

In Your goodness You have made us able to hear the music of the world. The raging of the winds, the whispering of trees in the wood, and the precious voices of loved ones reveal to us that You are in our midst.

> Your voice sings through all creation.

"O God, how majestic..." is by William Wallis (1946–).

O God, how majestic is Your evening sky,
    The gold and crimson weave of Your aery mantle
    Above the cloud-brushed western expanse.
The dome of darkening blue is awash
    With purple fleece and thunder song.
The wind's great wing sweeps eastward toward morning.
Beneath this star-pierced map of an exploding,
    Collapsing universe,
Under this great layered growth of time and matter
    Only sketched for the earthbound
    In the cold words of science,
    But veiled in the shroud of cosmic distance—

I seek you everywhere,
Architect of eternity's arch.

Far beneath You I dream,
My eyes strain to fix in the vast swirl,
    The numberless movements
    Above the clouds
    As stars emerge—
    The flickering signature of Your first fire.

Cool wind sweeps down now
    From the mountains to the north,
    And from Your interstellar castle
    Of pure line and point.

Lord of river slide and sea shift
And the earth's ride about the darkening sun,
Accept my restless soul
    Into the vast ocean of your burning night.
    This eternal distance hovering
    Between thought and action.

Reader

O incognito God, anonymous Lord,
with what name shall I call You? Where shall I
discover the syllable, the mystic word
that shall invoke You from eternity?
Is that sweet sound the heart makes,
clocking life, Your appellation?
Is the noise of thunder, it?
Is it the hush of peace, the sound of strife?

I have no title for Your glorious throne,
and for Your presence not a golden word—
only that wanting You, by that alone
I do invoke You, knowing I am heard.

Congregation

You hear us
In words of support we send to those in pain.

You hear us
When we stir against injustice.

You hear us
When, standing proud, we speak the truth.

You hear us
In our silent awe before the splendor of Your stars.

You hear us
When we hear You.

"O incognito God..." is by A.M. Klein (1909-1972).

Reader

You gave us
The power of speech, that magic gift
By which each soul, unique and separate,
Shares its life with others.
Though each individual,
Unaided and alone, is weak and helpless,
Your gift of love brings us strength:
Not by might nor by power,
But by Your spirit arises
The thirst for knowledge,
The urge to create,
The passion for justice,
The will to give love and loyalty.

Congregation

Sometimes we have lived at peace with one another,
But all too often we are deaf
To the divine wisdom within us,
Preferring the law of the jungle,
Preferring war to peace,
Preferring evil to good.

SAVING THE WORLD

Reader

Our tradition says that God created us through Adam, a single being, to teach us that whoever destroys a single human soul has destroyed an entire world; and whoever sustains a single human soul has sustained an entire world.

"Our tradition..." from *J. Sanhedrin 4:5.*

Responsively

Lord, many are tired and lonely;

    Teach us to be their friends.

Many are anxious and afraid;

    Help us to calm their fears.

Some are tortured in body and mind;

    Imbue them with courage and strength.

Others in their emptiness seek only wealth, fame or power;

    Teach them to value other gifts than these.

Some are drained of faith: They are cynical, bored or despairing;

    Let our faith shine forth for them to see, that through us they may come to know Your love.

Some live with death in their souls: They are stunned, violent, and filled with hate.

    Give us wisdom to save them from the wastelands of the spirit.

Teach us to show our love. Let compassion and knowledge combine for the welfare of all Your children that all may know they are not alone.

Responsively

Our tradition teaches, "Let justice roll down like waters and righteousness like a mighty stream."

> "You shall not steal, and you shall not deceive or lie to one another. You shall not oppress or rob your neighbor."

"You shall not hold the wage of a laborer beyond its due time. You shall not insult the deaf, or place a stumbling-block before the blind."

> "You shall do no injustice in judgment. You shall not be partial to the poor or defer to the powerful. You shall judge your neighbor with fairness."

"You shall not oppress a stranger, for you know the heart of a stranger, for you were strangers in the land of Egypt."

> "The strangers in your midst shall be to you as the native-born, and you shall love them as yourself."

"You shall not harden your heart, or shut your hand against the poor, your kin, but you shall love them as yourself."

> "Cease to do evil; learn to do good, seek justice, correct oppression, defend the orphan, plead for the widow."

"The Lord of Hosts is exalted by justice; the holy God is sanctified by righteousness."

––––––––––––––––––––––––

"Our tradition…" is adapted from *Amos 5:24; Leviticus 19:11-19, and Isaiah 1:17.*

Responsively

There is holiness when we strive to be true to the best we know.

> There is holiness when we are kind to someone
> Who cannot possibly be of service to us.

There is holiness when we promote family harmony.

> There is holiness when we forget what divided us and remember what unites us.

There is holiness when we are willing to be laughed at for what we believe.

> There is holiness when we love—truly, honestly and unselfishly.

There is holiness when we remember the lonely and bring cheer into a dark corner.

> There is holiness when we share our bread, our ideas, our enthusiasm.

There is holiness when we gather to pray to God, who gave us the power to declare:

> Holy, holy, holy is the Lord of hosts;
> All of life can be filled with God's glory.

Reader I

We cannot merely pray to You, O God, to end war;
For we know that You have made the world in such a way that we must find the path to peace.

Reader II

We cannot merely pray to You, O God, to end starvation;
For You have already given us the resources with which to feed the entire world, if we would only use them wisely.

Reader I

We cannot merely pray to You, O God, to root out prejudice;
For You have already given us eyes with which to see the good in all, if we would only use them rightly.

Reader II

We cannot merely pray to You, O God, to end despair;
For you have already given us the power to clear away slums and to give hope, if we would only use our power justly.

Reader I

We cannot merely pray to You, O God, to end disease;
For You have already given us great minds with which to search out cures and healing, if we would only use them constructively.

Reader II

Therefore, we pray to You instead, O God, for strength, determination, and will power to do instead of just to pray, to become, instead of merely to wish.

Reader I

Lord of all, let there be no good hope that is not a command. Let there be no prayer that does not ask to become a deed. Let there be no promise unless it be kept.

WE HAVE COME INTO THIS WORLD

Reader

May it be Your will to cause war and bloodshed to vanish from the earth, to let a great and wondrous peace prevail in all the world.

Let all who dwell on earth clearly see the truth that we have come into this world not for strife and discord, not for hatred and envy, and not for rivalry and bloodshed. Rather, we have come into this world to know and understand You and to do Your will.

Congregation

Lord, teach us to use the opportunities for good that dawn with each day. May we look back at each sunset and know that we have sought to serve You.

LET US REMEMBER

Reader

On this Yom Kippur day, let us remember the earth's oppressed, the weak and the weary, all who are imprisoned without cause. Let us seek to bring hope to every home and comfort to every heart.

Congregation

In a world cold with fear and rage, let us never fall victim to despair.

Reader

Let us stand fast against uncertainty and prove capable of unlimited faith.

"On this Yom Kippur..." is adapted from *Gates of Repentance, p. 445.*

We refuse to believe that cruelty will prevail
Because we have felt the strength of kindness.

We refuse to award the ultimate victory to evil
Because we believe in You too much.

So help us, O God, to live by our faith.

Where there is hatred, may we bring love.
Where there is pain, may we bring healing.
Where there is darkness, may we bring light.
Where there is despair, may we bring hope.
Where there is discord, may we bring peace.
Make this a better world and begin with us.

YOM KIPPUR
AFTERNOON SERVICE

Havdalah Spice Box
Austrian
19th c.

The ritual of Yom Kippur has evolved through the centuries. From the time of the Jerusalem Temple, Yom Kippur afternoon was commemorated with special pageantry. The High Priest, dressed in white robes, was escorted to the Temple by the Levites. Once there, he entered the Holy of Holies, confessed his sins, and asked God's forgiveness for all the failings of the people of Israel. All alone inside the Holy of Holies, he pronounced, three times, the ineffable, mysterious name of God, a name forbidden to be uttered at any other time or place by anyone. When the people outside heard the name pronounced, they responded, "Blessed is God's glorious name forever and ever." Known as the *Avodah,* or "Sacrificial Service," these moments of confession, repentance and renewal constituted the spiritual high point of the ancient Yom Kippur observance. After the destruction of the Temple and the institution of the High Priesthood in 70 C.E., the sages introduced a Yom Kippur afternoon service of recollections dramatizing the historic Temple observance. Opportunities for confession and repentance were woven into the poetry and prayers of the worship. Our liturgy for Yom Kippur afternoon connects us with themes celebrated at the Jerusalem Temple and retained as sacred elements throughout the centuries. *Hallelujah,* "Praise God in the sanctuary...," from *Psalms 150,* was sung in the Temple and contains a description of the various musical instruments used by the ancients.

Choir

הַלְלוּיָהּ!
הַלְלוּ־אֵל בְּקָדְשׁוֹ,
הַלְלוּהוּ בִּרְקִיעַ עֻזּוֹ.
הַלְלוּהוּ בִגְבוּרֹתָיו,
הַלְלוּהוּ כְּרֹב גֻּדְלוֹ.
הַלְלוּהוּ בְּתֵקַע שׁוֹפָר,
הַלְלוּהוּ בְּנֵבֶל וְכִנּוֹר.
הַלְלוּהוּ בְתֹף וּמָחוֹל,
הַלְלוּהוּ בְּמִנִּים וְעֻגָב.
הַלְלוּהוּ בְצִלְצְלֵי־שָׁמַע,
הַלְלוּהוּ בְּצִלְצְלֵי תְרוּעָה.
כֹּל הַנְּשָׁמָה תְּהַלֵּל יָהּ.
הַלְלוּיָהּ!

Hallelujah.
Praise God in the sanctuary;
    praise God in the sky, the
    Lord's stronghold.
Praise God for mighty acts;
    praise God for exceeding greatness.
Praise God with blasts of the shofar;
    praise with the harp and lyre,
    with timbrel and dance, with
    lute and pipe.
Praise God with resounding cymbals;
    with loud-clashing cymbals.
Let all that breathes praise the
    Lord.
    Hallelujah.

315

Havdalah Spice Box
Italian Hallmark
19th c.

Human beings need to take constant inventory of their conduct. Unconfessed and unforgiven sins threaten to destroy and obliterate the divine image in each person. "The degenerating effects of pride, greed, and stubbornness, the cleansing power of repentance, and the possibility of returning' to God—whom by sin we banish from our lives—these were the teachings symbolized and enacted in the rites of Yom Kippur" (Max Arzt, *Justice and Mercy: Commentary on the Liturgy of the New Year and the Day of Atonement, p. 250). Ha-shi-vei-nu is from Lamentations 5:21.*

Reader

In a distant time when the holy Temple stood in Jerusalem, our people gathered at this hour on this sacred day to ask forgiveness for their sins. In seeking repentance, the High Priest entered the most holy chamber of the sanctuary. There he pleaded to God for himself and for the people of Israel. He pronounced three times the holy name for God, a name never spoken aloud except at this hour on Yom Kippur. With trembling lips he recited prayers for compassion and for help, prayers for security and abundance, prayers for justice and peace.

Congregation

God of the ages, let our prayers also ascend to You. In the recesses of our souls, let us acknowledge our sins. None of us lives without making mistakes, without hurting others, without the embarrassment and pain of our negligence and insensitivity. We have sinned. We have done perversely, and we know that our renewal can come only from You, O God, Source of forgiveness and love.

Reader

With fearful hearts, hearts that know treachery and thoughtlessness, hearts that anguish over selfishness and greed, we turn to You, O God, as did the High Priest and our people in ages past. We, too, hear the echo of Your voice in the command, "Return, O Israel, to the Lord your God...Take words with you and return to the Lord."

All rise as ark is opened

All sing

Ha-shi-vei-nu A-do-nai ei-le-cha, ve-na-shu-va. Cha-deish ya-mei-nu ke-ke-dem.	הֲשִׁיבֵנוּ יְיָ אֵלֶיךָ, וְנָשׁוּבָה. חַדֵּשׁ יָמֵינוּ כְּקֶדֶם.

Help us return to You, O Lord; then truly shall we return.
Renew our days as of old.

317

Havdalah Spice Box
Italy
Late 18th c.

When the High Priest entered the Holy of Holies, he divided his confession into three sections. In the first he voiced his own sinfulness, in the second he confessed the sins of his fellow priests and, finally, he set forth all the sins of his people. In each confession, he pronounced God's mysterious name, a name whose sound was only allowed to pass his lips at this sacred moment of the year. To this day, Jews do not pronounce the "name" of God, but use *Adonai,* meaning "Lord" as a substitute. When the people heard the High Priest pronounce God's ineffable name, they responded with the Temple choir, *Ba-ruch sheim ke-vod mal-chu-to le-o-lam va-ed,* "Blessed is God's glorious name forever and ever."

Reader

הִנְנִי הֶעָנִי מִמַּעַשׂ, בָּאתִי לַעֲמֹד וּלְחַנֵּן לְפָנֶיךָ עַל
עַמְּךָ יִשְׂרָאֵל אֲשֶׁר שְׁלָחְוּנִי, וְעַל כָּל־פְּשָׁעִים
תְּכַסֶּה בְּאַהֲבָה. וְכָל־צָרוֹת וְרָעוֹת הֲפָךְ־לָנוּ,
וּלְכָל־יִשְׂרָאֵל לְשָׂשׂוֹן וּלְשִׂמְחָה לְחַיִּים וּלְשָׁלוֹם.

Behold, I come to plead before You, O Lord our God, on behalf of Your people
Israel who have sent me. I have sinned. We have sinned. As of old, when the
Temple stood in its splendor, and the High Priest entered the Holy of Holies,
there to repeat Your sublime name three times, we appear before You. We, too,
are filled with awe. We fail to fathom Your glory or the mystery of Your nurturing presence. Nonetheless, we seek You with our prayer. Bonding ourselves to
generations of our people who peer through our eyes, we call out Your ineffable
name. O inexplicable God, defiant of comprehension, shatter our resistance to
Your will by repairing our insensitive hearts with compassion and love. We call
upon Your name: Eternal One, *Adonai,* O Source of forgiveness.

All sing

בָּרוּךְ שֵׁם כְּבוֹד מַלְכוּתוֹ לְעוֹלָם וָעֶד!

Ba-ruch sheim ke-vod mal-chu-to le-o-lam va-ed.

Blessed is God's glorious name forever and ever.

Congregation

We admit our shortcomings. We have failed others when they needed our love.
We have been unfaithful to You when we defied Your laws of compassion
and charity. We have not always spoken with the truth of Torah on our tongues,
nor fulfilled the commandment to teach Torah diligently to our children.

Reader

With all our sins we call upon Your name: Eternal One, *Adonai,* O Source
of forgiveness.

All sing

בָּרוּךְ שֵׁם כְּבוֹד מַלְכוּתוֹ לְעוֹלָם וָעֶד!

Ba-ruch sheim ke-vod mal-chu-to le-o-lam va-ed.

Blessed is God's glorious name forever and ever.

Reader

In Your love, forgive us, O God. Pardon us. Help us. Transform our failings into deeds of caring. Lead us to promote kindness and to enlarge joyfulness in every heart.

Congregation

Count us among those who banish hunger, tears and shame, among those who bring the blessings of peace to Israel and all peoples.

Reader

We call upon Your name: Eternal One, *Adonai,* O Source of forgiveness.

All sing

בָּרוּךְ שֵׁם כְּבוֹד מַלְכוּתוֹ לְעוֹלָם וָעֶד!

Ba-ruch sheim ke-vod mal-chu-to le-o-lam va-ed.

Blessed is God's glorious name forever and ever.

Reader

בָּרוּךְ אַתָּה, שׁוֹמֵעַ תְּפִלָּה.

We praise the One who hears prayer.

Cantor and Choir

Yit-ga-dal ve-yit-ka-dash she-mei ra-ba
be-al-ma di-ve-ra chi-re-u-tei, ve-yam-lich
mal-chu-tei be-cha-yei-chon
u-ve-yo-mei-chon u-ve-cha-yei de-chol beit
Yis-ra-eil, ba-a-ga-la u-vi-ze-man ka-riv,
ve-i-me-ru: a-mein.

יִתְגַּדַּל וְיִתְקַדַּשׁ שְׁמֵהּ רַבָּא
בְּעָלְמָא דִּי־בְרָא כִרְעוּתֵהּ,
וְיַמְלִיךְ מַלְכוּתֵהּ בְּחַיֵּיכוֹן
וּבְיוֹמֵיכוֹן וּבְחַיֵּי דְכָל־בֵּית
יִשְׂרָאֵל, בַּעֲגָלָא וּבִזְמַן קָרִיב,
וְאִמְרוּ: אָמֵן.

Ye-hei she-mei ra-ba me-va-rach le-a-lam
u-le-al-mei al-ma-ya.

יְהֵא שְׁמֵהּ רַבָּא מְבָרַךְ לְעָלַם
וּלְעָלְמֵי עָלְמַיָּא.

Yit-ba-rach ve-yish-ta-bach, ve-yit-pa-ar
ve-yit-ro-mam ve-yit-na-sei, ve-yit-ha-dar
ve-yit-a-leh ve-yit-ha-lal she-mei
de-ku-de-sha, be-rich hu, le-ei-la min kol
bi-re-cha-ta ve-shi-ra-ta, tush-be-cha-ta
ve-ne-che-ma-ta da-a-min-ran be-al-ma,
ve-i-me-ru: a-mein.

יִתְבָּרַךְ וְיִשְׁתַּבַּח, וְיִתְפָּאַר
וְיִתְרוֹמַם וְיִתְנַשֵּׂא, וְיִתְהַדָּר
וְיִתְעַלֶּה וְיִתְהַלָּל שְׁמֵהּ
דְּקוּדְשָׁא, בְּרִיךְ הוּא, לְעֵלָּא
מִן־כָּל־בִּרְכָתָא וְשִׁירָתָא,
תֻּשְׁבְּחָתָא וְנֶחֱמָתָא דַּאֲמִירָן
בְּעָלְמָא, וְאִמְרוּ: אָמֵן.

May God's great name be magnified and made holy in the world created
according to Divine will. May God soon establish a reign of justice and peace
during our life and days, and during the lifetime of the whole house of Israel.
And let us say, Amen.

May God's great name be blessed now and forever.

May the name of the Holy One be blessed, praised, glorified, exalted, extolled,
honored, magnified, and celebrated, even though God is above and beyond
all the blessings, songs, praises, and consolations that are spoken in the world.
And let us say, Amen.

All are seated as ark is closed.

Reader

God, who binds our present to a glorious past of patriarchs and matriarchs, of prophets and psalmists, of saints and sages...

Congregation

We acknowledge You.

Reader

God, who bestows upon history a shadow of the shadows of Your radiance...

Congregation

We praise You.

Reader

God, who with a single word has made the world, hanging before us the heavens like an unrolled scroll, and the earth as an undeciphered manuscript...

Congregation

We seek You.

It is in moments of our being faced with the mystery of living and dying, of knowing and not-knowing, of love and the inability of love—that we pray, that we address ourselves to God who is beyond the mystery (Abraham Joshua Heschel, *Man's Quest For God, p. 63)*. "God, who binds our present..." is based on "Stance of the Amidah" by A.M. Klein, 1909-1972, *Collected Poems, pp. 345-346.*

Reader

All-alluring God, whom we conjecture and surmise and almost know, the Mystery beyond the mysterious, the Holy One be praised.

Congregation

We sing Your glory.

Cantor and Choir

קָדוֹשׁ אַתָּה וְנוֹרָא שְׁמֶךָ, וְאֵין אֱלוֹהַּ מִבַּלְעָדֶיךָ, כַּכָּתוּב:

וַיִּגְבַּהּ יְיָ צְבָאוֹת בַּמִּשְׁפָּט, וְהָאֵל הַקָּדוֹשׁ נִקְדַּשׁ בִּצְדָקָה.

בָּרוּךְ אַתָּה, יְיָ, הַמֶּלֶךְ הַקָּדוֹשׁ.

You are holy; awe inspiring is Your name. There is no God but You, as is written: The Lord is exalted by justice and sanctified by righteousness. Be praised, O God, who rules in holiness.

Kadosh a-ta, "You are holy...," was composed by the rabbis of the Mishnah *(Rosh Hashanah 2:1)* for High Holy Day and Festival worship. It echoes the highest aspiration of Jewish ethics, which is the imitation of God's holiness through acts of justice, compassion and love. This theme, known as *kiddush ha-Shem,* "the sanctification of God's name," also forms the central core of the Yom Kippur afternoon Torah portion, which begins with the commandment, "You shall be holy, for I, the Lord your God, am holy" *(Leviticus 19: 2).* "The Lord of Hosts..." is from *Isaiah 5:16.*

Havdalah Spice Box
Eastern Europe-Polish
Mid-19th c.

The theme of the *U-vechein* prayers is "reverence for God." They were composed by Rabbi Johanan ben Nuri, who lived during the Hadrianic persecutions after the destruction by Rome of the Jerusalem Temple in 76 C.E. Despair for the survival of the Jewish tradition and people was prevalent. Despite the oppression, however, one finds in these prayers, written for the High Holy Days, the hope that reverence for God would prevail over fear of human beings, that a time would dawn when all would realize that "You have made us as one human family meant to do Your will with loving hearts."

Reader

וּבְכֵן תֵּן פַּחְדְּךָ, יְיָ אֱלֹהֵינוּ, עַל כָּל־מַעֲשֶׂיךָ, וְאֵימָתְךָ
עַל כָּל־מַה־שֶּׁבָּרָאתָ.

Now, O God, imbue us with wonder before the grandeur of Your creation;
skies of endless space, the fragile balance of all elements, all the rainbow colors
which adorn the universe You have made.

Congregation

Open our eyes, for carelessly we miss the majesty about us.

Reader

וְיֵעָשׂוּ כֻלָּם אֲגֻדָּה אַחַת לַעֲשׂוֹת רְצוֹנְךָ בְּלֵבָב שָׁלֵם,
כְּמוֹ שֶׁיָּדַעְנוּ, יְיָ אֱלֹהֵינוּ, שֶׁהַשִּׁלְטוֹן לְפָנֶיךָ, עֹז בְּיָדְךָ
וּגְבוּרָה בִּימִינֶךָ, וְשִׁמְךָ נוֹרָא עַל כָּל־מַה־שֶּׁבָּרָאתָ.

Grant us, O God, the healing realization that You have made us as one human
family meant to do Your will with loving hearts.

Congregation

For we live in a world of broken dreams, broken hopes, broken promises, and
broken hearts.

Reader

וּבְכֵן תֵּן כָּבוֹד, יְיָ, לְעַמֶּךָ, תְּהִלָּה לִירֵאֶיךָ וְתִקְנָה לְדוֹרְשֶׁיךָ,

Now, O God, let us merit Your honor by supporting every worthy hope of those who seek You, and by uplifting the fallen with gentle hands of generosity.

Congregation

For we walk among many who seek nothing but self-indulgence and self-gain.

Reader

וּבְכֵן צַדִּיקִים יִרְאוּ וְיִשְׂמָחוּ וִישָׁרִים יַעֲלֹזוּ וַחֲסִידִים בְּרִנָּה יָגִילוּ, וְעוֹלָתָה תִּקְפָּץ־פִּיהָ וְכָל־הָרִשְׁעָה כֻּלָּה כְּעָשָׁן תִּכְלֶה, כִּי תַעֲבִיר מֶמְשֶׁלֶת זָדוֹן מִן הָאָרֶץ.

Now, O God, let healing words instead of excuses flow from our lips. Season our tongues with nurturing praise instead of shattering derision.

Congregation

For on this day You promise to turn our callous hearts back to You.

וּבְכֵן יְהִי רָצוֹן מִלְּפָנֶיךָ, יְיָ אֱלֹהֵינוּ וֵאלֹהֵי אֲבוֹתֵינוּ,
שֶׁתִּסְלַח לָנוּ עַל כָּל־חַטֹּאתֵינוּ וְתִמְחַל לָנוּ עַל כָּל־
עֲונוֹתֵינוּ וּתְכַפֶּר־לָנוּ עַל כָּל־פְּשָׁעֵינוּ.

Now, O God, as the sun begins its arc toward evening, spread forth forgiveness, pardon us, help us.

All sing

Ve-al ku-lam, E-lo-ah se-li-chot,	וְעַל כֻּלָּם, אֱלוֹהַּ סְלִיחוֹת,
se-lach la-nu, me-chal la-nu,	סְלַח־לָנוּ, מְחַל־לָנוּ,
ka-per la-nu!	כַּפֶּר־לָנוּ.

For all our failings, O God of forgiveness, pardon us, help us, grant us atonement!

If you have done even a slight wrong to another person, let it be a great wrong in your eyes, and go and rectify it. If you have done much good for others, let it be accounted little in your eyes. If another has done a small favor for you, let it seem great in your eyes. If another has wronged you greatly, let it be small in your eyes, and be ready to forgive *(Avot de Rabbi Nathan, 41)*. *Ve-al ku-lam*, "For all our failings..." is likely derived from the Jerusalem Talmud, *Yoma 45c,* and was used as a refrain in the *Al cheit* confession; see p. 328.

Havdalah Spice Box
Central Europe
Mid-19th c.

"You, O God, know all the chambers of our mind..." is attributed to Rav (280 C.E.- 352 C.E.), head of the Academy at Pumbedita in Babylonia. It forms one of the central prayers of the Yom Kippur confession. *Al Cheit,* "For the sin...," is an alphabetical acrostic in which our sins are enumerated and expressed. The use of the alphabet is not meant as a clever literary device. Instead, it conveys the message that no person lives without sinning and that the wrongs we commit extend to every possible expression of our lives. The list is not one of generalities. It deals in specifics, detailing our repeated moral failures. The first version of the *Al Cheit* may have been written by Saadyah Gaon, who included six verses. His text was doubled to twelve verses by Amram Gaon. Maimonides was the first to expand the prayer to twenty-two verses, one for every letter of the Hebrew alphabet. In traditional prayer books, the number of verses is fifty-four, double the number of letters in the alphabet. The *Al Cheit,* like the *A-sham-nu,* "We are sinful," prayer on page 337, is repeated by the congregation ten times throughout Yom Kippur.

Reader

You, O God, know all the chambers of our minds. There are no secrets from You. Nothing is hidden from You. We stand before You as an open book. All our faults are known; all our selfish ways are revealed. We are an alphabet of sins seeking, now, Your mercy in our confession.

Congregation

From the beginning of the year to its end, we have missed fulfilling our best intentions. Now, from the beginning of our ancient alphabet to its end, we confess our failings.

Reader

From **Aleph** to **Taf** we name them. Forgive us for them.

WE ARE AN ALPHABET OF SINS

Reader

Aleph: א

עַל חֵטְא שֶׁחָטָאנוּ לְפָנֶיךָ בְּאִמּוּץ הַלֵּב.

Congregation

Al cheit she-cha-ta-nu... For **Acting** callously against others, forgive us.

Reader

Bet: בּ

עַל חֵטְא שֶׁחָטָאנוּ לְפָנֶיךָ בְּבִטּוּי שְׂפָתָֽיִם.

Congregation

Al cheit she-cha-ta-nu... For **Belittling** others with slander and sarcasm, forgive us.

Reader

Gimmel: ג

עַל חֵטְא שֶׁחָטָאנוּ לְפָנֶיךָ בַּגָּלוּי וּבַסָּֽתֶר.

Congregation

Al cheit she-cha-ta-nu... For **Generating** harm against others either secretly or publicly, forgive us.

Reader

Dalet: ד

עַל חֵטְא שֶׁחָטָאנוּ לְפָנֶיךָ בְּדִבּוּר פֶּה.

Congregation

Al cheit she-cha-ta-nu... For **Deceiving** others with clever phrases, forgive us.

Reader

Hei: ה

עַל חֵטְא שֶׁחָטָאנוּ לְפָנֶיךָ בְּהוֹנָאַת רֵעַ.

Congregation

*Al cheit she-cha-ta-nu...*For **Hardening** our hearts against our loved ones, friends and colleagues, forgive us.

Reader

Vav: ו

עַל חֵטְא שֶׁחָטָאנוּ לְפָנֶיךָ בְּוִדוּי פֶּה.

Congregation

Al cheit she-cha-ta-nu...For **Vacillating** between confessing or avoiding the truth about our faults, forgive us.

Reader

Zayin: ז

עַל חֵטְא שֶׁחָטָאנוּ לְפָנֶיךָ בְּזִלְזוּל הוֹרִים וּמוֹרִים.

Congregation

Al cheit she-cha-ta-nu... For **Zigzagging** between contempt and respect for our parents and teachers, forgive us.

Reader

Chet: ח

עַל חֵטְא שֶׁחָטָאנוּ לְפָנֶיךָ בְּחֹזֶק יָד.

Congregation

Al cheit she-cha-ta-nu...For **Charming** others by our use of power, forgive us.

Reader

Tet: ט

עַל חֵטְא שֶׁחָטָאנוּ לְפָנֶיךָ בְּטִפְשׁוּת פֶּה,

Congregation

Al cheit she-cha-ta-nu...For **Talking** foolishly instead of remaining silent, forgive us.

Reader

Yud: י

עַל חֵטְא שֶׁחָטָאנוּ לְפָנֶיךָ בְּיֵצֶר הָרָע.

Congregation

Al cheit she-cha-ta-nu...For **Yielding** to harmful temptations, forgive us.

All sing

Ve-al ku-lam, E-lo-ah se-li-chot,
se-lach la-nu, me-chal la-nu,
ka-per la-nu!

וְעַל כֻּלָּם, אֱלוֹהַּ סְלִיחוֹת,
סְלַח־לָנוּ, מְחַל־לָנוּ,
כַּפֶּר־לָנוּ.

For all of our failings, O God of forgiveness, pardon us, help us, grant us atonement!

Reader

Chaf: כ

עַל חֵטְא שֶׁחָטָאנוּ לְפָנֶיךָ בְּכַחַשׁ וּבְכָזָב.

Congregation

Al cheit she-cha-ta-nu...For **Cheapening** our reputation by trafficking in lies, forgive us.

Reader

Lamed: ל

עַל חֵטְא שֶׁחָטָאנוּ לְפָנֶיךָ בִּלְשׁוֹן הָרָע.

Congregation

Al cheit she-cha-ta-nu...For **Libeling** others with our gossip, forgive us.

Reader

Mem: מ

עַל חֵטְא שֶׁחָטָאנוּ לְפָנֶיךָ בְּמַאֲכָל וּבְמִשְׁתֶּה.

Congregation

Al cheit she-cha-ta-nu...For **Menacing** ourselves with too much food and drink, forgive us.

Reader

Nun: נ

עַל חֵטְא שֶׁחָטָאנוּ לְפָנֶיךָ בִּנְטִיַּת גָּרוֹן.

Congregation

Al cheit she-cha-ta-nu...For **Neglecting** others because of our arrogance, forgive us.

Reader

Sin: שׂ

עַל חֵטְא שֶׁחָטָאנוּ לְפָנֶיךָ בְּשִׂקּוּר עָיִן.

Congregation

Al cheit she-cha-ta-nu...For **Seeing** others as objects for our own satisfaction, forgive us.

Reader

Ayin: ע

עַל חֵטְא שֶׁחָטָאנוּ לְפָנֶיךָ בְּעֵינַיִם רָמוֹת.

Congregation

Al cheit she-cha-ta-nu...For **Acting** boastfully, forgive us.

All sing

Ve-al ku-lam, E-lo-ah se-li-chot,
se-lach la-nu, me-chal la-nu,
ka-per la-nu!

וְעַל כֻּלָּם, אֱלוֹהַּ סְלִיחוֹת,
סְלַח־לָנוּ, מְחַל־לָנוּ,
כַּפֶּר־לָנוּ.

For all our failings, O God of forgiveness, pardon us, help us, grant us atonement!

Reader

Pei: פ

עַל חֵטְא שֶׁחָטָאנוּ לְפָנֶיךָ בִּפְלִילוּת.

Congregation

Al cheit she-cha-ta-nu...For **Peddling** harmful judgments about others, forgive us.

Reader

Tzadi: צ

עַל חֵטְא שֶׁחָטָאנוּ לְפָנֶיךָ בִּצְדִיַּת רָע.

Congregation

Al cheit she-cha-ta-nu...For **Tainting** our success with harmful schemes against others, forgive us.

Reader

Kuf: ק

עַל חֵטְא שֶׁחָטָאנוּ לְפָנֶיךָ בְּקַלּוּת רֹאשׁ.

Congregation

Al cheit she-cha-ta-nu...For **Keeping** company with those who ridicule the good intentions of others, forgive us.

Reader

Reish: ר

עַל חֵטְא שֶׁחָטָאנוּ לְפָנֶיךָ בִּרְצַת רַגְלַיִם לְהָרַע.

Congregation

Al cheit she-cha-ta-nu... For **Rushing** to take advantage of others, forgive us.

Reader

Shin: שׁ

עַל חֵטְא שֶׁחָטָאנוּ לְפָנֶיךָ בִּשְׁבוּעַת שָׁוְא.

Congregation

Al cheit she-cha-ta-nu... For **Shaming** ourselves with acts of pettiness and hatred, forgive us.

Reader

Taf: ת

עַל חֵטְא שֶׁחָטָאנוּ לְפָנֶיךָ בְּתִמְהוֹן לֵבָב.

Congregation

Al cheit she-cha-ta-nu... For **Trading** trust for instant gratification, forgive us.

All sing

Ve-al ku-lam, E-lo-ah se-li-chot,
se-lach la-nu, me-chal la-nu,
ka-per la-nu!

וְעַל כֻּלָּם, אֱלוֹהַּ סְלִיחוֹת,
סְלַח־לָנוּ, מְחַל־לָנוּ,
כַּפֶּר־לָנוּ.

For all our failings, O God of forgiveness, pardon us, help us, grant us atonement!

Reader

This day we face the truth about ourselves. None of us lives without mistakes, without deliberately or inadvertently hurting others. Vows we made last Yom Kippur did not change us. From the mountain peak we fell to common ways. In our hearts we confess that we are **A**rrogant, **B**rutal, **C**areless, **D**estructive, **E**gocentric, **F**alse, **G**reedy, **H**eartless, **I**nsolent, **J**oyless…

In the accents of our tradition, we hear and then pronounce the alphabet of our sins.

Congregation

We listen to the declaration of each failing and then repeat it in reverent confession.

The *A-sham-nu* was composed during the 9th century C.E. in Babylonia and, like the *Al cheit,* is an alphabetical confession of our sins. The recitation incorporates repetition so that each failure can be heard and expressed. It is a custom to tap one's chest with a loosely made fist as a sign of regret as each sin is recited. Isaac Luria (1534-1572), a teacher of Jewish mysticism in Safed, once asked, "Why is it that our confession is arranged in the plural and not singular form? We say, 'We are sinful,' instead of 'I am sinful.' Because the people of Israel are as one body. When one sins, it hurts us all. We are responsible for one another" (Joseph H. Hertz, *Daily Prayer Book, p. 906).*

Cantor pronounces each sin. Congregation then repeats in Hebrew while meditating on the meaning of each human failing.

Cantor	Congregation	Meditation
אָשַׁמְנוּ	A-sham-nu	We are sinful.
בָּגַדְנוּ	Ba-gad-nu	We are faithless.
גָּזַלְנוּ	Ga-zal-nu	We are cruel.
דִּבַּרְנוּ דֹפִי	Di-bar-nu do-fi	We are sarcastic.
הֶעֱוִינוּ	He-e-vi-nu	We are arrogant.
וְהִרְשַׁעְנוּ	Ve-hir-sha-nu	We are vicious.
זַדְנוּ	Zad-nu	We are fraudulent.
חָמַסְנוּ	Cha-mas-nu	We are vulgar.
טָפַלְנוּ שֶׁקֶר	Ta-fal-nu she-ker	We are dishonest.
יָעַצְנוּ רַע	Ya-atz-nu ra	We are deceptive.
כִּזַּבְנוּ	Ki-zav-nu	We are liars.
לַצְנוּ	Latz-nu	We are frivolous.
מָרַדְנוּ	Ma-rad-nu	We are rebellious.
נִאַצְנוּ	Ni-atz-nu	We are insulting.
סָרַרְנוּ	Sa-rar-nu	We are obstinate.
עָוִינוּ	A-vi-nu	We are subverters.
פָּשַׁעְנוּ	Pa-sha-nu	We are offensive.
צָרַרְנוּ	Tza-rar-nu	We are hurtful.
קִשִּׁינוּ עֹרֶף	Ki-shi-nu o-ref	We are stubborn.
רָשַׁעְנוּ	Ra-sha-nu	We are unjust.
שִׁחַתְנוּ	Shi-chat-nu	We are corrupt.
תִּעַבְנוּ	Ti-av-nu	We are pernicious.
תָּעִינוּ	Ta-i-nu	We are erratic.
תִּעְתָּעְנוּ	Ti-ta-nu	We are neglectful.

Havdalah Spice Box
Dutch
1890

The origins of the *U-ne-ta-ne to-kef* prayer are unknown. It is ascribed to Kalonymos ben Meshullam of Mayence (1100 C.E., Germany). It is also attached to the legendary martyrdom of Rabbi Amnon of Mayence who, after being tortured for refusing to renounce his faith, was brought to the synagogue, where he died after reciting this prayer. *U-ne-ta-ne to-kef* grows out of the ancient rabbinic theological conviction that "All is foreshadowed, yet free will is given to each person." *(Avot 3:15)* Against the notion that "fate" rules all life, the rabbis declared that each human destiny is shaped by the free choices each person makes. We are not helpless victims of circumstance. We give life meaning, quality and ethical direction through the *mitzvot,* the deeds we choose to do. Thus this prayer's dramatic conclusion: "through our deeds of repentance, prayer and charity we can influence the ultimate decree."

Cantor and Choir

וּנְתַנֶּה תֹּקֶף קְדֻשַּׁת הַיּוֹם כִּי הוּא נוֹרָא וְאָים. וּבוֹ
תִּנָּשֵׂא מַלְכוּתֶךָ וְיִכּוֹן בְּחֶסֶד כִּסְאֶךָ וְתֵשֵׁב עָלָיו
בֶּאֱמֶת.

Reader

We proclaim the sacred power of this day, for it is wondrous and full of dread. Today, O God, Your rule is exalted. Your glory is celebrated. You are our Judge, our Conscience. You know our dreams and disappointments. We are an open book before You.

Congregation

You remember all that we have forgotten, and today You measure our deeds as the signature of our lives.

Choir

וּבְשׁוֹפָר גָּדוֹל יִתָּקַע וְקוֹל דְּמָמָה דַקָּה יִשָּׁמַע.
וּמַלְאָכִים יֵחָפֵזוּן וְחִיל וּרְעָדָה יֹאחֵזוּן וְיֹאמְרוּ: הִנֵּה
יוֹם הַדִּין.

Reader

The great Shofar will sound, and a still, small voice will declare: "This is the Day of Judgment."

Congregation

Today we pass before You as the flock passes before the shepherd.

Omer Calendar 40.1
(For counting the fifty days between Pesach and Shavuot.)
France 19th c.
Marvin Rand, Photographer
From the Collection of the Hebrew Union College
Skirball Museum

God says: "My hands reach out to those who repent. I will reject no one." Therefore we read: "Peace, peace, to all, far and near" *(Isaiah 57:19).* God says: "Though you be far from Me, I will draw near and heal you—if you come toward Me!" *(Midrash Tehillim to Psalms 120:7).*

Reader

Judge us with mercy as we come before You.

Cantor and Choir

בְּרֹאשׁ הַשָּׁנָה יִכָּתֵבוּן וּבְיוֹם צוֹם כִּפּוּר יֵחָתֵמוּן.
כַּמָּה יַעַברוּן וְכַמָּה יִבָּרֵאוּן, מִי יִחְיֶה וּמִי יָמוּת,
מִי יָנוּחַ וּמִי יָנוּעַ, מִי יַשְׁקִיט וּמִי יְטֹרַף, מִי יַעֲנִי
וּמִי יַעֲשִׁיר, מִי יִשָּׁפַל וּמִי יָרוּם.
וּתְשׁוּבָה וּתְפִלָּה וּצְדָקָה
מַעֲבִירִין אֶת־רֹעַ הַגְּזֵרָה.

Reader

On Rosh Hashanah our destiny is written; at the end of Yom Kippur it is sealed: How many will be born? How many will pass away? Who will live? Who will die? Who will rest? Who will wander? Who will know peace? Who will be troubled? Who will be needy? Who will be content? Who will be humbled? Who will be exalted?

Congregation

May our repentance, prayer and charity influence the ultimate decree.

Reader

For we are but dust, fragile vessels, easily broken.

Congregation

We are passing shadows, fleeting clouds, vanishing dreams.

Reader

וְאַתָּה הוּא מֶלֶךְ אֵל חַי וְקַיָּם!

But You, O God, are the Eternal One of all time and space.

Ark is opened; all rise

Cantor, then all sing

A-lei-nu le-sha-bei-ach la-a-don
ha-kol,
la-teit ge-du-lah le-yo-tseir
be-rei-sheet,
she-lo a-sa-nu ke-go-yei
ha-a-ra-tsot,
ve-lo sa-ma-nu ke-mish-pe-chot
ha-a-da-mah,
she-lo sam chel-kei-nu ka-hem,
ve-go-ra-lei-nu ke-chol ha-mo-nam.

עָלֵינוּ לְשַׁבֵּחַ לַאֲדוֹן הַכֹּל,
לָתֵת גְּדֻלָּה לְיוֹצֵר בְּרֵאשִׁית,
שֶׁלֹּא עָשָׂנוּ כְּגוֹיֵי הָאֲרָצוֹת,

וְלֹא שָׂמָנוּ כְּמִשְׁפְּחוֹת הָאֲדָמָה;
שֶׁלֹּא שָׂם חֶלְקֵנוּ כָּהֶם,
וְגֹרָלֵנוּ כְּכָל־הֲמוֹנָם.

Let us adore the ever-living God, rendering praise to the Creator of all, who chose us from all peoples, singling us out for sacred service, assigning us to a unique destiny.

Va-a-nach-nu ko-re-im u-mish-ta-cha-vim
u-mo-dim
lif-nei me-lech mal-chei
ha-me-la-chim, ha-ka-dosh ba-ruch Hu.

וַאֲנַחְנוּ כֹּרְעִים וּמִשְׁתַּחֲוִים
וּמוֹדִים לִפְנֵי מֶלֶךְ מַלְכֵי
הַמְּלָכִים, הַקָּדוֹשׁ בָּרוּךְ הוּא.

We bow the head in reverence and worship the God of all, the Holy One whom we praise.

Some scholars believe that the *Aleinu* prayer was composed during Maccabean times as a form of protest against idolatry. It was later placed within the Rosh Hashanah and Yom Kippur liturgies by the Babylonian sage, Rav (d. 247 C.E.), and in the 13th century was made the concluding section of the daily and Sabbath liturgies because it expressed complete loyalty to God along with the fervent hope that the Messianic day of justice and peace would soon dawn for all humanity. On Yom Kippur afternoon, the *Aleinu* was often sung by the cantor, or leader of the worship, who prostrated himself in humility before the open ark.

REMEMBER THE COVENANT OF OUR PEOPLE

Reader

אֱלֹהֵינוּ וֵאלֹהֵי אֲבוֹתֵינוּ, קָרְבֵנוּ

לְתוֹרָתֶךָ, לַמְּדֵנוּ מִצְוֹתֶיךָ, הוֹרֵנוּ דְרָכֶיךָ,

Our God, and God of our people, draw us near to Your Torah; teach us Your commandments; instruct us in Your ways.

Congregation

Refine our hearts to love You.

Reader

וְנָשׁוּב אֵלֶיךָ בֶּאֱמֶת וּבְלֵב שָׁלֵם.

On this day, let us return to You with deeds of devotion and loyalty.

Choir

This day, strengthen us! Amen.	הַיּוֹם תְּאַמְּצֵנוּ! אָמֵן.
This day, bless us! Amen.	הַיּוֹם תְּבָרְכֵנוּ! אָמֵן.
This day, exalt us! Amen.	הַיּוֹם תְּגַדְּלֵנוּ! אָמֵן.
This day, look with favor upon us! Amen.	הַיּוֹם תִּדְרְשֵׁנוּ לְטוֹבָה! אָמֵן.
This day, inscribe us for a good life! Amen.	הַיּוֹם תִּכְתְּבֵנוּ לְחַיִּים טוֹבִים! אָמֵן.
This day, hear our plea! Amen.	הַיּוֹם תִּשְׁמַע שַׁוְעָתֵנוּ! אָמֵן.
This day, uplift us with Your righteousness! Amen.	הַיּוֹם תִּתְמְכֵנוּ בִּימִין צִדְקֶךָ! אָמֵן.

Reader

גַּדְּלוּ לַיְיָ אִתִּי וּנְרוֹמְמָה שְׁמוֹ יַחְדָּו.

Magnify the Lord with me, and let us exalt God's name together.

All sing

כִּי מִצִּיּוֹן תֵּצֵא תוֹרָה, וּדְבַר־יְיָ מִירוּשָׁלָיִם.

Ki mi-tsi-yon tei-tsei To-rah (2)
u-de-var A-do-nai mi-ru-sha-la-yim.

Torah will come from Zion, the word of God from Jerusalem.

בָּרוּךְ שֶׁנָּתַן תּוֹרָה לְעַמּוֹ יִשְׂרָאֵל בִּקְדֻשָׁתוֹ.

Ba-ruch she-na-tan To-rah, To-rah (2)
Le-a-mo Yis-ra-eil bi-ke-du-sha-to.

Praised be the One, who has given the Torah to Israel.

שְׁמַע יִשְׂרָאֵל: יְיָ אֱלֹהֵינוּ, יְיָ אֶחָד!

She-ma Yis-ra-eil: A-do-nai E-lo-hei-nu
A-do-nai E-chad!

Hear, O Israel: the Lord is our God, the Lord is One!

Reader

בֵּית יַעֲקֹב: לְכוּ, וְנֵלְכָה בְּאוֹר יְיָ.

O house of Jacob, let us walk in the light of our God.

The *hakafah* or "processional walk with the Torah" dates to the early synagogue and dramatizes that the Torah is not the exclusive possession of a special class of the Jewish people but belongs to the entire Jewish community.

Le-cha…is from *I Chronicles 29:11. Ro-me-mu*…is from *Psalms 99:5, 9.*

All sing as Torah is carried through the congregation

Le-cha A-do-nai, ha-ge-du-la
ve-ha-ge-vu-ra ve-ha-tif-e-ret,
ve-ha-nei-tsach, ve-ha-hod,
ki chol ba-sha-ma-yim u-va-a-retz, (2)
le-cha, A-do-nai, ha-mam-la-cha
ve-ha-mit-na-sei le-chol le-rosh.

לְךָ, יְיָ, הַגְּדֻלָּה וְהַגְּבוּרָה
וְהַתִּפְאֶרֶת וְהַנֵּצַח וְהַהוֹד,
כִּי כֹל בַּשָּׁמַיִם וּבָאָרֶץ,
לְךָ יְיָ הַמַּמְלָכָה וְהַמִּתְנַשֵּׂא
לְכֹל לְרֹאשׁ.

Yours, Lord, is the greatness, the power, the glory, the victory, and the majesty;
for all that is in heaven and earth is Yours. Yours is the dominion, O Lord; You
are supreme over all.

Ro-me-mu A-do-nai, ro-me-mu (2)
Ro-me-mu A-do-nai Elo-hei-nu
A-do-nai Elo-hei-nu, ro-me-mu.
(repeat)

רוֹמְמוּ יְיָ אֱלֹהֵינוּ,
וְהִשְׁתַּחֲווּ לְהַר קָדְשׁוֹ,
יְיָ אֱלֹהֵינוּ.

Ve-hish-ta-cha-vu, le-har kod-sho, (4)
A-do-nai elo-hei-nu, ro-me-mu.

Exalt and worship our God; bow down at God's holy mountain.

Ark is closed; all are seated as the Torah is prepared for reading.

YOU SHALL BE HOLY…

Reader

In this sacred hour we have confessed our sins. Truly, as we look inward we are ashamed. We have piously proclaimed our commitment to uplift our lives with noble purpose and moral conviction but have failed to keep our promises. Yet we are not lost. Like Jews before us, we turn to the wisdom of Torah and here, in flaming letters, find new direction and new inspiration. Now in ancient accents we are commanded: "Be holy"—be different, be unique. Exalt life with celebration. Sanctify it with deeds of justice and compassion. Crown it with love.

Blessings before the reading

Ba-re-chu et A-donai ha-me-vo-rach!
Ba-ruch A-do-nai ha-me-vo-rach
le-o-lam va-ed.

בָּרְכוּ אֶת יְיָ הַמְבֹרָךְ!
בָּרוּךְ יְיָ הַמְבֹרָךְ לְעוֹלָם וָעֶד!

Ba-ruch a-ta, A-do-nai E-lo-hei-nu, me-lech
ha-o-lam, a-sher ba-char ba-nu mi-kol
ha-a-min, ve-na-tan la-nu et To-ra-to.
Ba-ruch a-ta, A-do-nai, no-tein ha-To-rah.

בָּרוּךְ אַתָּה, יְיָ אֱלֹהֵינוּ, מֶלֶךְ
הָעוֹלָם, אֲשֶׁר בָּחַר־בָּנוּ מִכָּל־
הָעַמִּים וְנָתַן־לָנוּ אֶת־תּוֹרָתוֹ.
בָּרוּךְ אַתָּה, יְיָ, נוֹתֵן הַתּוֹרָה.

Praise the Lord, to whom our praise is due! Praised be the Lord, to whom
our praise is due, now and forever! Blessed is the Lord our God, Ruler of the
universe, who has chosen us from all peoples by giving us the Torah. Be praised,
O God, Giver of the Torah.

The blessings before and after the reading of Torah date from the 1st century B.C.E.
They state the belief that the people of Israel has been "chosen" for the privilege of
receiving the Torah, and that loyalty to its study and values assures the Jewish people's
survival.

Leviticus 19:1-3, 9-18

וַיְדַבֵּ֥ר יְהוָ֖ה אֶל־מֹשֶׁ֥ה לֵּאמֹֽר׃ דַּבֵּ֞ר אֶל־כָּל־עֲדַ֧ת בְּנֵֽי־יִשְׂרָאֵ֛ל וְאָמַרְתָּ֥
אֲלֵהֶ֖ם קְדֹשִׁ֣ים תִּֽהְי֑וּ כִּ֣י קָד֔וֹשׁ אֲנִ֖י יְהוָ֥ה אֱלֹהֵיכֶֽם׃ אִ֣ישׁ אִמּ֤וֹ וְאָבִיו֙
תִּירָ֔אוּ וְאֶת־שַׁבְּתֹתַ֖י תִּשְׁמֹ֑רוּ אֲנִ֖י יְהוָ֥ה אֱלֹהֵיכֶֽם׃

The Lord spoke to Moses, saying: Speak to the whole Israelite community and
say to them: You shall be holy, for I, the Lord your God, am holy. You shall each
revere your mother and father and keep My sabbaths: I the Lord am your God.

וּֽבְקֻצְרְכֶם֙ אֶת־קְצִ֣יר אַרְצְכֶ֔ם לֹ֧א תְכַלֶּ֛ה פְּאַ֥ת שָׂדְךָ֖ לִקְצֹ֑ר וְלֶ֥קֶט קְצִֽירְךָ֖
לֹ֣א תְלַקֵּֽט׃ וְכַרְמְךָ֙ לֹ֣א תְעוֹלֵ֔ל וּפֶ֥רֶט כַּרְמְךָ֖ לֹ֣א תְלַקֵּ֑ט לֶעָנִ֤י וְלַגֵּר֙
תַּעֲזֹ֣ב אֹתָ֔ם אֲנִ֖י יְהוָ֥ה אֱלֹהֵיכֶֽם׃ לֹ֖א תִּגְנֹ֑בוּ וְלֹא־תְכַחֲשׁ֥וּ וְלֹֽא־תְשַׁקְּר֖וּ
אִ֥ישׁ בַּעֲמִיתֽוֹ׃ וְלֹֽא־תִשָּׁבְע֥וּ בִשְׁמִ֖י לַשָּׁ֑קֶר וְחִלַּלְתָּ֛ אֶת־שֵׁ֥ם אֱלֹהֶ֖יךָ
אֲנִ֥י יְהוָֽה׃ לֹֽא־תַעֲשֹׁ֤ק אֶת־רֵֽעֲךָ֙ וְלֹ֣א תִגְזֹ֔ל לֹֽא־תָלִ֞ין פְּעֻלַּ֥ת שָׂכִ֛יר
אִתְּךָ֖ עַד־בֹּֽקֶר׃ לֹא־תְקַלֵּ֣ל חֵרֵ֔שׁ וְלִפְנֵ֣י עִוֵּ֔ר לֹ֥א תִתֵּ֖ן מִכְשֹׁ֑ל וְיָרֵ֥אתָ
מֵּאֱלֹהֶ֖יךָ אֲנִ֥י יְהוָֽה׃ לֹא־תַעֲשׂ֤וּ עָ֨וֶל֙ בַּמִּשְׁפָּ֔ט לֹא־תִשָּׂ֣א פְנֵי־דָ֔ל וְלֹ֥א
תֶהְדַּ֖ר פְּנֵ֣י גָד֑וֹל בְּצֶ֖דֶק תִּשְׁפֹּ֥ט עֲמִיתֶֽךָ׃ לֹא־תֵלֵ֤ךְ רָכִיל֙ בְּעַמֶּ֔יךָ לֹ֥א
תַעֲמֹ֖ד עַל־דַּ֣ם רֵעֶ֑ךָ אֲנִ֖י יְהוָֽה׃

When you reap the harvest of your land, you shall not reap all the way to the
edges of your field or gather the gleanings of your harvest. You shall not pick
your vineyard bare or gather the fallen fruit of your vineyard; you shall leave
them for the poor and the stranger: I the Lord am your God.

You shall not steal; you shall not deal deceitfully or falsely with one another.
You shall not swear falsely by My name, profaning the name of your God:
I am the Lord.

You shall not defraud your fellow. You shall not commit robbery. The wages of a laborer shall not remain with you until morning.

You shall not insult the deaf or place a stumbling block before the blind. You shall fear your God: I am the Lord.

You shall not render an unfair decision: do not favor the poor or show deference to the rich; judge others fairly. Do not deal basely with others. Do not profit by the blood of others: I am the Lord.

לֹא־תִשְׂנָא אֶת־אָחִיךָ בִּלְבָבֶךָ הוֹכֵחַ תּוֹכִיחַ אֶת־עֲמִיתֶךָ וְלֹא־
תִשָּׂא עָלָיו חֵטְא׃ לֹא־תִקֹּם וְלֹא־תִטֹּר אֶת־בְּנֵי עַמֶּךָ וְאָהַבְתָּ
לְרֵעֲךָ כָּמוֹךָ אֲנִי יהוה׃

You shall not hate others in your heart. Reprove others but incur no guilt because of your loved ones. You shall not take vengeance or bear a grudge against others. Love your neighbor as yourself: I am the Lord.

Blessings after the reading of Torah

Ba-ruch a-ta, A-do-nai E-lo-hei-nu,
me-lech ha-o-lam, a-sher na-tan la-nu
To-rat e-met, ve-cha-yei o-lam na-ta
be-to-chei-nu. Ba-ruch a-ta, A-do-nai,
no-tein ha-To-rah.

בָּרוּךְ אַתָּה, יְיָ אֱלֹהֵינוּ, מֶלֶךְ
הָעוֹלָם, אֲשֶׁר נָתַן־לָנוּ תּוֹרַת אֱמֶת
וְחַיֵּי עוֹלָם נָטַע בְּתוֹכֵנוּ.
בָּרוּךְ אַתָּה, יְיָ, נוֹתֵן הַתּוֹרָה.

Blessed is the Lord our God, Ruler of the universe, who has given us the Torah of truth, implanting within us eternal life. Be praised, O Lord, Giver of the Torah.

All rise and sing as the Torah is held high

Ve-zot ha-To-rah a-sher sam Mo-sheh
li-fe-nei be-nei Yis-ra-eil, al pi A-do-nai
be-yad Mo-sheh.

וְזֹאת הַתּוֹרָה אֲשֶׁר־שָׂם משֶׁה
לִפְנֵי בְּנֵי יִשְׂרָאֵל, עַל־
פִּי יְיָ בְּיַד־משֶׁה.

This is the Torah that Moses placed before the people of Israel to fulfill the word of God.

All are seated as Torah is rolled and wrapped.

Haftarah means "completion" and refers to selected readings drawn from the Prophets and recited after the Torah is read. By the 2nd century C.E. the rabbis had designated Haftarah readings for each Sabbath and all holy days. The choice of the Haftarah portion was usually made because of its relationship to the theme of the Torah portion. *Jonah* was chosen by the rabbis for Yom Kippur afternoon because of its theme of repentance. Jonah is "every person" struggling with the urge to flee from following God's commandments, with the embarrassment of mistakes, and with the self-righteous predisposition not to forgive others for their human failings.

Reader

Our Haftarah on Yom Kippur afternoon is the Book of Jonah. It was selected by the ancient rabbis because they saw every person in the prophet Jonah. Each of us hears the voice of conscience and is called upon to forgive and repent. Yet, at times, we flee rather than face up to our failures. So it was with Jonah. First, he tried to escape the call of God to prophesy in Nineveh. Then, he resented the repentance of those who, unlike him, carried out God's will. We read Jonah's story in order to remind us that "repentance, prayer and charity" are what God wants from each of us.

Blessings before the reading

בָּרוּךְ אַתָּה, יְיָ אֱלֹהֵינוּ, מֶלֶךְ הָעוֹלָם, אֲשֶׁר בָּחַר
בִּנְבִיאִים טוֹבִים וְרָצָה בְדִבְרֵיהֶם הַנֶּאֱמָרִים בֶּאֱמֶת.
בָּרוּךְ אַתָּה, יְיָ, הַבּוֹחֵר בַּתּוֹרָה וּבְמֹשֶׁה עַבְדּוֹ
וּבְיִשְׂרָאֵל עַמּוֹ וּבִנְבִיאֵי הָאֱמֶת וָצֶדֶק.

Praised is the Lord our God, Ruler of the universe, who has chosen faithful prophets to speak words of truth. Praised is the Lord, for the revelation of Torah, for God's servant Moses, and for our prophets of truth and righteousness.

From the Book of Jonah

וַיְהִי דְּבַר־יהוה אֶל־יוֹנָה בֶן־אֲמִתַּי לֵאמֹר: קוּם לֵךְ אֶל־נִינְוֵה
הָעִיר הַגְּדוֹלָה וּקְרָא עָלֶיהָ כִּי־עָלְתָה רָעָתָם לְפָנָי: וַיָּקָם יוֹנָה
לִבְרֹחַ תַּרְשִׁישָׁה מִלִּפְנֵי יהוה וַיֵּרֶד יָפוֹ וַיִּמְצָא אֳנִיָּה ׀ בָּאָה
תַרְשִׁישׁ וַיִּתֵּן שְׂכָרָהּ וַיֵּרֶד בָּהּ לָבוֹא עִמָּהֶם תַּרְשִׁישָׁה מִלִּפְנֵי
יהוה:

The word of the Lord came to Jonah, son of Amittai: Go at once to Nineveh, that great city, and proclaim judgment upon it; for their wickedness has come before Me. Jonah, however, started out to flee to Tarshish from the Lord's service. He went down to Jaffa and found a ship going to Tarshish. He paid the fare and went aboard to sail with the others to Tarshish, away from the service of the Lord.

וַיהוָֹה הֵטִיל רֽוּחַ־גְּדוֹלָה אֶל־הַיָּם וַיְהִי סַעַר־גָּדוֹל בַּיָּם
וְהָ֣אֳנִיָּ֔ה חִשְּׁבָ֖ה לְהִשָּׁבֵֽר׃ וַיִּֽירְא֣וּ הַמַּלָּחִ֗ים וַיִּזְעֲקוּ֘ אִ֣ישׁ אֶל־
אֱלֹהָיו֒ וַיָּטִ֣לוּ אֶת־הַכֵּלִ֜ים אֲשֶׁ֤ר בָּֽאֳנִיָּה֙ אֶל־הַיָּ֔ם לְהָקֵ֖ל
מֵֽעֲלֵיהֶ֑ם וְיוֹנָ֗ה יָרַד֙ אֶל־יַרְכְּתֵ֣י הַסְּפִינָ֔ה וַיִּשְׁכַּ֖ב וַיֵּֽרָדַֽם׃

But the Lord cast a mighty wind upon the sea, and such a great tempest came upon the sea that the ship was in danger of breaking up. In their fright, the sailors cried out, each to his own god; and they flung the ship's cargo overboard to make it lighter for them. Jonah, meanwhile, had gone down into the hold of the vessel, where he lay down and fell asleep.

וַיִּקְרַ֤ב אֵלָיו֙ רַ֣ב הַחֹבֵ֔ל וַיֹּ֥אמֶר ל֖וֹ מַה־לְּךָ֣ נִרְדָּ֑ם
מַה־מְּלַאכְתְּךָ֙ וּמֵאַ֣יִן תָּב֔וֹא מָ֥ה אַרְצֶ֖ךָ וְאֵֽי־מִזֶּ֥ה עַ֖ם אָֽתָּה׃
וַיִּשְׂא֣וּ אֶת־יוֹנָ֔ה וַיְטִלֻ֖הוּ אֶל־הַיָּ֑ם

The captain went to him and cried out, "How can you be sleeping so soundly?... Where have you come from? What is your country, and of what people are you? And what have you done?" When they discovered that he was fleeing from the service of God, the captain and his men were terrified. They cried out, "Do not let us perish on account of this person's life." And they heaved Jonah overboard, and the sea stopped raging.

וַיְמַן יהוה דָּג גָּדוֹל לִבְלֹעַ אֶת־ יוֹנָה וַיֹּאמֶר יהוה לַדָּג וַיָּקֵא
אֶת־יוֹנָה אֶל־הַיַּבָּשָׁה:

The Lord provided a huge fish to swallow Jonah; and Jonah remained in the
fish's belly three days and three nights. Jonah prayed and the Lord commanded
the fish to spew Jonah out on dry land.

וַיְהִי דְבַר־יהוה אֶל־יוֹנָה שֵׁנִית לֵאמֹר: קוּם לֵךְ אֶל־נִינְוֵה הָעִיר
הַגְּדוֹלָה וּקְרָא אֵלֶיהָ אֶת־הַקְּרִיאָה אֲשֶׁר אָנֹכִי דֹּבֵר אֵלֶיךָ: וַיָּקָם יוֹנָה
וַיֵּלֶךְ אֶל־נִינְוֵה כִּדְבַר יהוה...וַיַּאֲמִינוּ אַנְשֵׁי נִינְוֵה בֵּאלֹהִים וַיִּקְרְאוּ־צוֹם
וַיִּלְבְּשׁוּ שַׂקִּים מִגְּדוֹלָם וְעַד־קְטַנָּם: וַיִּגַּע הַדָּבָר אֶל־מֶלֶךְ נִינְוֵה
וַיָּקָם מִכִּסְאוֹ וַיַּעֲבֵר אַדַּרְתּוֹ מֵעָלָיו וַיְכַס שַׂק וַיֵּשֶׁב עַל־הָאֵפֶר:
וַיַּזְעֵק וַיֹּאמֶר בְּנִינְוֵה...וְיָשֻׁבוּ אִישׁ מִדַּרְכּוֹ הָרָעָה וּמִן־הֶחָמָס אֲשֶׁר
בְּכַפֵּיהֶם: מִי־יוֹדֵעַ יָשׁוּב וְנִחַם הָאֱלֹהִים וְשָׁב מֵחֲרוֹן אַפּוֹ וְלֹא נֹאבֵד:
וַיַּרְא הָאֱלֹהִים אֶת־מַעֲשֵׂיהֶם כִּי־שָׁבוּ מִדַּרְכָּם הָרָעָה וַיִּנָּחֶם הָאֱלֹהִים
עַל־הָרָעָה אֲשֶׁר־דִּבֶּר לַעֲשׂוֹת־לָהֶם וְלֹא עָשָׂה:

Then the word of the Lord came to Jonah a second time: Go at once to Nineveh,
that great city, and proclaim to it what I tell you. This time Jonah went at once
to Nineveh as God had commanded.

Now the people of Nineveh believed God. They proclaimed a fast, and great and
small alike put on sackcloth. When news reached the king of Nineveh, he rose
from his throne, took off his robe, put on sackcloth, and sat in ashes. And he had
the word cried through Nineveh: "Let every person turn from evil and injustice.
Who knows but that God may turn and forgive...so that we do not perish."

God saw what they did, how they were repenting from their evil ways. And
God renounced the punishment planned for them.

353

וַיֵּ֤רַע אֶל־יוֹנָה֙ רָעָ֣ה גְדוֹלָ֔ה וַיִּ֖חַר ל֑וֹ: וַיִּתְפַּלֵּ֣ל אֶל־יְהוָ֗ה
וַיֹּאמַ֣ר אָנָּ֤ה יְהוָה֙ הֲלוֹא־זֶ֣ה דְבָרִ֗י עַד־הֱיוֹתִי֙ עַל־אַדְמָתִ֔י עַל־כֵּ֥ן
קִדַּ֖מְתִּי לִבְרֹ֣חַ תַּרְשִׁ֑ישָׁה כִּ֣י יָדַ֗עְתִּי כִּ֤י אַתָּה֙ אֵֽל־חַנּ֣וּן וְרַח֔וּם
אֶ֤רֶךְ אַפַּ֙יִם֙ וְרַב־חֶ֔סֶד וְנִחָ֖ם עַל־הָרָעָֽה: וְעַתָּ֣ה יְהוָ֔ה קַח־נָ֥א
אֶת־נַפְשִׁ֖י מִמֶּ֑נִּי כִּ֛י ט֥וֹב מוֹתִ֖י מֵחַיָּֽי: וַיֹּ֣אמֶר יְהוָ֔ה הַהֵיטֵ֖ב חָ֥רָה
לָֽךְ:

This displeased Jonah greatly, and he was grieved. He prayed to the Lord,
saying, "O Lord! Isn't this just what I said when I was still in my own country?
That is why I fled beforehand to Tarshish. For I know that You are a compassionate and gracious God, slow to anger, abounding in kindness, renouncing
punishment. Please, Lord, take my life, for I would rather die than live."
The Lord replied, "Are you that deeply grieved?"

וַיֵּצֵ֤א יוֹנָה֙ מִן־הָעִ֔יר וַיֵּ֖שֶׁב מִקֶּ֣דֶם לָעִ֑יר וַיַּעַשׂ֩ ל֨וֹ שָׁ֜ם סֻכָּ֗ה
וַיֵּ֤שֶׁב תַּחְתֶּ֙יהָ֙ בַּצֵּ֔ל עַ֚ד אֲשֶׁ֣ר יִרְאֶ֔ה מַה־יִּהְיֶ֖ה בָּעִֽיר: וַיְמַ֣ן יְהוָֽה־
אֱלֹהִ֣ים קִיקָי֗וֹן וַיַּ֣עַל ׀ מֵעַ֣ל לְיוֹנָ֗ה לִהְי֥וֹת צֵל֙ עַל־רֹאשׁ֔וֹ לְהַצִּ֥יל
ל֖וֹ מֵרָעָת֑וֹ וַיִּשְׂמַ֤ח יוֹנָה֙ עַל־הַקִּֽיקָי֔וֹן שִׂמְחָ֥ה גְדוֹלָֽה: וַיְמַ֣ן
הָאֱלֹהִ֗ים תּוֹלַ֙עַת֙ בַּעֲל֣וֹת הַשַּׁ֔חַר לַֽמָּחֳרָ֑ת וַתַּ֥ךְ אֶת־הַקִּֽיקָי֖וֹן
וַיִּיבָֽשׁ: וַיְהִ֣י ׀ כִּזְרֹ֣חַ הַשֶּׁ֗מֶשׁ וַיְמַ֤ן אֱלֹהִים֙ ר֣וּחַ קָדִים֙ חֲרִישִׁ֔ית
וַתַּ֥ךְ הַשֶּׁ֛מֶשׁ עַל־רֹ֥אשׁ יוֹנָ֖ה וַיִּתְעַלָּ֑ף וַיִּשְׁאַ֤ל אֶת־נַפְשׁוֹ֙ לָמ֔וּת
וַיֹּ֕אמֶר ט֥וֹב מוֹתִ֖י מֵחַיָּֽי: וַיֹּ֤אמֶר אֱלֹהִים֙ אֶל־יוֹנָ֔ה הַהֵיטֵ֥ב חָרָֽה־
לְךָ֖ עַל־הַקִּֽיקָי֑וֹן וַיֹּ֕אמֶר הֵיטֵ֥ב חָֽרָה־לִ֖י עַד־מָֽוֶת:

Now Jonah had left the city and found a place east of the city. He made a booth there and sat under it in the shade, until he should see what happened to the city. The Lord God provided a gourd, which grew up over Jonah, to provide shade for his head and save him from discomfort. Jonah was very happy about the gourd. But the next day at dawn God provided a worm, which attacked the plant so that it withered. And when the sun rose, God provided a sultry east wind; the sun beat down on Jonah's head, and he became faint.

He begged for death, saying, "I would rather die than live." Then God said to Jonah, "Are you so deeply grieved about the plant?" "Yes," he replied, "so deeply that I want to die."

וַיֹּ֣אמֶר יְהוָ֗ה אַתָּ֤ה חַ֙סְתָּ֙ עַל־הַקִּ֣יקָי֔וֹן אֲשֶׁ֥ר לֹא־עָמַ֖לְתָּ בּ֑וֹ
וְלֹ֣א גִדַּלְתּ֑וֹ שֶׁבִּן־לַ֥יְלָה הָיָ֖ה וּבִן־לַ֥יְלָה אָבָֽד: וַֽאֲנִי֙ לֹ֣א
אָח֔וּס עַל־נִֽינְוֵ֖ה הָעִ֣יר הַגְּדוֹלָ֑ה אֲשֶׁ֣ר יֶשׁ־בָּ֡הּ הַרְבֵּה֩
מִֽשְׁתֵּים־עֶשְׂרֵ֨ה רִבּ֜וֹ אָדָ֗ם אֲשֶׁ֤ר לֹֽא־יָדַע֙ בֵּין־יְמִינ֣וֹ
לִשְׂמֹאל֔וֹ וּבְהֵמָ֖ה רַבָּֽה:

Then the Lord said: "You cared about the plant, which you did not work for and which you did not grow, which appeared overnight and perished overnight. And should not I care about Nineveh, that great city, in which there are more than a hundred and twenty thousand persons who do not yet know their right hand from their left, and many beasts as well?"

Torah Crown 58.10
Russia 19th c.
Marvin Rand, Photographer
From the Collection of the Hebrew Union College
Skirball Museum

Meeting with God does not come to us in order that God may be concerned with us, but in order that God may realize meaning in the world through us....The countenance of God reposes, invisible, in an earthen block; it must be carved out of it. To be engaged in this work means to be religious—nothing else...God does not want to be believed in, to be debated and defended by us, but simply to be realized through us *(Martin Buber, 1878-1965)*.

Reader

בָּרוּךְ אַתָּה, יְיָ אֱלֹהֵינוּ, מֶלֶךְ הָעוֹלָם, צוּר כָּל־
הָעוֹלָמִים, צַדִּיק בְּכָל־הַדּוֹרוֹת, הָאֵל הַנֶּאֱמָן,
הָאוֹמֵר וְעוֹשֶׂה, הַמְדַבֵּר וּמְקַיֵּם, שֶׁכָּל־דְּבָרָיו אֱמֶת
וָצֶדֶק.

עַל הַתּוֹרָה וְעַל הָעֲבוֹדָה וְעַל הַנְּבִיאִים וְעַל (יוֹם
הַשַּׁבָּת הַזֶּה וְעַל) יוֹם הַכִּפּוּרִים הַזֶּה, שֶׁנָּתַתָּ לָּנוּ, יְיָ
אֱלֹהֵינוּ, (לִקְדֻשָּׁה וְלִמְנוּחָה) לִמְחִילָה וְלִסְלִיחָה
וּלְכַפָּרָה, לְכָבוֹד וּלְתִפְאֶרֶת, עַל הַכֹּל, יְיָ אֱלֹהֵינוּ,
אֲנַחְנוּ מוֹדִים לָךְ, וּמְבָרְכִים אוֹתָךְ. יִתְבָּרַךְ שִׁמְךָ בְּפִי
כָּל־חַי תָּמִיד לְעוֹלָם וָעֶד. וּדְבָרְךָ אֱמֶת וְקַיָּם לָעַד.
בָּרוּךְ אַתָּה, יְיָ, מֶלֶךְ מוֹחֵל וְסוֹלֵחַ לַעֲוֹנוֹתֵינוּ
וְלַעֲוֹנוֹת עַמּוֹ בֵּית יִשְׂרָאֵל, וּמַעֲבִיר אַשְׁמוֹתֵינוּ בְּכָל־
שָׁנָה וְשָׁנָה, מֶלֶךְ עַל כָּל־הָאָרֶץ, מְקַדֵּשׁ (הַשַּׁבָּת וְ)
יִשְׂרָאֵל וְיוֹם הַכִּפּוּרִים.

We give thanks for the Torah, for the privilege of worship, for the prophets,
and for this (**Shabbat and this**) Day of Atonement. Be praised, O God, who
lovingly forgives our failings year after year, and who sanctifies (**Shabbat**),
the people of Israel and the Day of Atonement.

Reader

מַלְכִּי מִקֶּדֶם פּוֹעֵל יְשׁוּעוֹת בְּקֶרֶב הֲמוֹנִי, נֹצֵר חֶסֶד
לַאֲלָפִים וְנֹשֵׂא פְּשָׁעַי וַעֲוֹנִי. כַּסֵּה חֲטָאַי וּבְרַחֲמֶיךָ
הָרַבִּים חָנֵּנִי, יְיָ.

Source of salvation, You show mercy to thousands of generations, forgiving transgression and wrongdoing. Forgive our sins, be gracious to us.

Congregation

This whole day, be with us.

Reader

הַיּוֹם רַפֵּא מְשׁוּבוֹתֵינוּ, כִּי אָתָאנוּ לְךָ וְהַגֵּנוּ.

This day we look to You. Be gracious as we strive to abandon our selfish ways.

Congregation

This whole day, be with us.

Reader

הַיּוֹם יִגְדַּל נָא כֹּחַ יְיָ וְכַעֲווֹנוֹתֵינוּ אַל תִּגְמוֹל.

This day, let Your power grow within us, turning us to compassion and love.

Congregation

This whole day, be with us.

"Source of Salvation...," with its emphasis upon the repetition of the word *Hayom*, "This whole day...," was written by Mordechai ben Shabtai, a 13th century Greek or Italian Jewish poet, and placed within the Yom Kippur Additional service. It was also included in the *Union Prayer Book II, pp. 281-284.*

Reader

הַיּוֹם רִשְׁעֵנוּ תָסִיר וּבְסֵפֶר הַחַיִּים אוֹתָנוּ תָחוֹק.

This day blot out our misdeeds. Inscribe us for blessing in the Book of Life.

Congregation

This whole day grant pardon to Your people Israel.

Reader

הַיּוֹם כַּפָּיו יִפְרוֹשׂ אֵלֶיךָ וּגְבוּרוֹתֶיךָ יְמַלֵּל.

This day we lift our hearts to You. We approach You seeking forgiveness.

Congregation

This whole day and all days be with us. May we find You at our side.

Reader

הַיּוֹם סְמוֹךְ עַם אֲשֶׁר דְּלָתֶיךָ דוֹפְקִים; וְתִיקַר נָא
נַפְשָׁם, כִּי עָלֶיךָ מִתְרַפְּקִים.

This day we knock at Your door. Welcome us with Your redeeming grace.

All sing

Ki anu a-me-cha, ve-a-ta Mal-kei-nu.
A-nu va-ne-cha, ve-a-ta Avi-nu.
A-nu na-cha-la-te-cha, ve-a-ta
    Go-ra-lei-nu.
A-nu tso-ne-cha, ve-a-ta Ro-ei-nu
A-nu kar-me-cha, ve-a-ta Not-rei-nu.
A-nu ra-ya-te-cha, ve-a-ta Do-dei-nu.

כִּי אָנוּ עַמֶּךָ, וְאַתָּה מַלְכֵּנוּ.

אָנוּ בָנֶיךָ, וְאַתָּה אָבִינוּ.

אָנוּ נַחֲלָתֶךָ, וְאַתָּה גוֹרָלֵנוּ.

אָנוּ צֹאנֶךָ, וְאַתָּה רוֹעֵנוּ.

אָנוּ כַרְמֶךָ, וְאַתָּה נוֹטְרֵנוּ.

אָנוּ רַעְיָתֶךָ, וְאַתָּה דוֹדֵנוּ.

We are Your people, You are our Sovereign.
We are Your children, You are our Source.
We are Your possession, You are our Portion.
We are Your flock, You are our Guardian.
We are Your vineyard, You are our Keeper.
We are Your beloved, You are our Friend.

All rise as Torah is lifted; and ark is opened.

"We Are Your People..." is of medieval origin and is based upon an ancient rabbinic comment found in *Song of Songs Rabbah, 2:16.* The poem celebrates the intimacy between the people of Israel and God. It is that "love" which has now been restored through confession and repentance. The people of Israel are now challenged to serve their "Friend" by fulfilling the sacred commandments of their tradition.

Reader

שְׁכֹן, יְיָ, בְּתוֹךְ עַמֶּךָ, וְתָנְוּחַ רוּחֲךָ בְּבֵית תְּפִלָּתֶךָ.

Dwell, O Lord, among Your people; let Your spirit abide within Your house of prayer.

Choir

הוֹדוֹ עַל אֶרֶץ וְשָׁמָיִם, וַיָּרֶם קֶרֶן לְעַמּוֹ, תְּהִלָּה לְכָל־
חֲסִידָיו, לִבְנֵי יִשְׂרָאֵל עַם קְרוֹבוֹ. הַלְלוּיָהּ!

God's splendor covers heaven and earth; God is the Source of Israel's strength, the praise of the faithful, the hope of those who draw near to serve. Halleluyah!

"God's splendor..." is from *Psalms 148:13-14.*

Torah Breast Plate
Israel
20th c.

"It is a tree of life..." is a collection of verses on the importance of Torah taken from *Psalms 19:8-10* and *Proverbs 4:2, 3:12, 17.*

Reader

God's Torah is perfect, renewing life;
God's teachings are enduring,
Making wise the simple.

תּוֹרַת יְיָ תְּמִימָה, מְשִׁיבַת נָפֶשׁ;
עֵדוּת יְיָ נֶאֱמָנָה, מַחְכִּימַת פֶּתִי;

God's precepts are just,
Rejoicing the heart;
God's commandments are lucid,
Giving light to the eyes.

פִּקּוּדֵי יְיָ יְשָׁרִים, מְשַׂמְּחֵי־לֵב;
מִצְוַת יְיָ בָּרָה, מְאִירַת עֵינָיִם;

God's word is pure, enduring forever;
God's judgments are true
And altogether just.

יִרְאַת יְיָ טְהוֹרָה, עוֹמֶדֶת לָעַד;
מִשְׁפְּטֵי יְיָ אֱמֶת, צָדְקוּ יַחְדָּו.

כִּי לֶקַח טוֹב נָתַתִּי לָכֶם,
תּוֹרָתִי אַל־תַּעֲזֹבוּ.

Behold, a good doctrine has been given you, My Torah; do not forsake it. It is a tree of life to those who hold it fast, and all who cling to it find happiness. Its ways are ways of pleasantness, and all its paths are peace. Return us to You, O God, and we shall return. Renew our days as of old.

All sing

Eits cha-yim hi la-ma-cha-zi-kim ba,
ve-to-me-che-ha me-u-shar.
De-ra-che-ha da-re-chei no-am,
ve-chol ne-ti-vo-te-ha sha-lom.

עֵץ־חַיִּים הִיא לַמַּחֲזִיקִים בָּהּ,
וְתֹמְכֶיהָ מְאֻשָּׁר: דְּרָכֶיהָ דַּרְכֵי־
נֹעַם, וְכָל־נְתִיבֹתֶיהָ שָׁלוֹם.
הֲשִׁיבֵנוּ יְיָ אֵלֶיךָ, וְנָשׁוּבָה.
חַדֵּשׁ יָמֵינוּ כְּקֶדֶם.

Ha-shi-vei-nu A-do-nai ei-le-cha,
ve-na-shu-va.
Cha-deish ya-mei-nu ke-ke-dem.

Ark is closed; all are seated

YOM KIPPUR
YIZKOR SERVICE

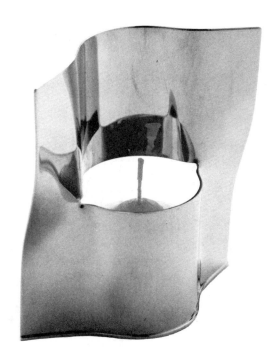

Yizkor Lamp, Brass
United States
20th c.

"Lord, what are we..." is from *Psalms 144:3-4; 90:6,3; Deuteronomy 32:29; Psalms 49:18; 37:37; 34:23.*

Choir

יְיָ, מָה־אָדָם וַתֵּדָעֵהוּ? בֶּן־אֱנוֹשׁ וַתְּחַשְּׁבֵהוּ? אָדָם
לַהֶבֶל דָּמָה; יָמָיו כְּצֵל עוֹבֵר. בַּבְּקֶר יָצִיץ וְחָלָף,
לָעֶרֶב יְמוֹלֵל וְיָבֵשׁ. תָּשֵׁב אֱנוֹשׁ עַד־דַּכָּא, וַתְּאמֶר:
"שׁוּבוּ, בְּנֵי־אָדָם!" לוּ חָכְמוּ יַשְׂכִּילוּ זֹאת, יָבִינוּ
לְאַחֲרִיתָם! כִּי לֹא בְמוֹתוֹ יִקַּח הַכֹּל; לֹא־יֵרֵד אַחֲרָיו
כְּבוֹדוֹ. שְׁמָר־תָּם וּרְאֵה יָשָׁר, כִּי אַחֲרִית לְאִישׁ
שָׁלוֹם. פָּדָה יְיָ נֶפֶשׁ עֲבָדָיו, וְלֹא יֶאְשְׁמוּ כָּל־הַחוֹסִים
בּוֹ.

Lord, what are we, that You are mindful of us? What is our worth, that You take account of us? We are vanity; our days are like a passing shadow. In the morning we flourish; in the evening we are cut down and wither. You turn us to contrition, urging us: "Return, O mortal ones." Would that we were wise and would consider where we are going. For when we die, we will carry nothing away, not even our glory. Mark those whose tastes move to simplicity and those whose deeds are righteous, for their end is peace. You redeem the souls of Your servants, and none who trust in You are forsaken.

Responsively

אֲדֹנָי, מָעוֹן אַתָּה הָיִיתָ לָנוּ בְּדֹר וָדֹר. בְּטֶרֶם הָרִים
יֻלָּדוּ, וַתְּחוֹלֵל אֶרֶץ וְתֵבֵל, וּמֵעוֹלָם עַד־עוֹלָם אַתָּה
אֵל.

Lord, You have been our refuge in all generations—before the mountains were brought forth or You had formed heavens and earth.

From everlasting to everlasting, You are our God.

A thousand years in Your sight are but as yesterday when it is past, and as a watch in the night.

And we are like a dream at daybreak.

In the morning we are like grass growing green and fresh.

In the evening we are cut down and wither.

The days of our years are many or few, but they are speedily gone and we fly away.

So teach us to number our days that we may attain a heart of wisdom.

For You redeem the souls of Your servants, and none who take refuge in You are forsaken.

With You is the fountain of life; in Your light do we see light.

WHAT ARE WE? CHILDREN OF DUST AND DREAMS

Reader

In this Yizkor hour we consider the swift flight of our years. We are feeble and finite. Our best laid plans are subject to frustration and failure. Scarcely are we ushered into life before we begin our pilgrimage to the grave. We are children of dust and dreams. In the marrow of our lives we struggle with success and disappointment, pleasure and pain, temptations and indulgences which dwarf the best impulses of our souls. We battle against forces without and weaknesses within. We prevail, only to succumb; we fail, only to renew the combat the next moment.

Choir

יְיָ, מָה־אָדָם כְּצִיץ הַשָּׂדֶה כֵּן יָצִיץ.

What are we, O Lord? Flowers that fade, children of dust and dreams and dust again.

"Lord, You have been our refuge…" is based upon *Psalms 90:1-17.* "What are we…" is adapted from *Psalms 144:3* and *Psalms 103:15.*

Responsively

The eye is never satisfied with seeing. Endless are the desires of the heart.

We devise new schemes on the grave of a thousand shattered hopes.

Discontent and envy rise up to spoil good intentions.

Like children falling asleep over their toys, we loosen our grasp on our possessions when death spreads its darkness upon us.

Rich and poor, strong and feeble, wise and simple, all are equal in death.

The grave levels all distinctions.

We are flowers that fade, children of dust and dreams and dust again.

Choir

יְיָ, מָה־אָדָם כְּצִיץ הַשָּׂדֶה כֵּן יָצִיץ.

What are we, O Lord? Flowers that fade, children of dust and dreams and dust again.

"The eye is never satisfied..." is adapted from the *Union Prayer Book II, p. 310.*

Reader

You, O God, have infused us with a portion of Your divinity. You have put eternity into our hearts, and implanted within us a vision of enduring righteousness and life. You have blessed us with loved ones who sustained us in moments of weakness, and filled our days with the warmth of their wisdom and embraces of love.

Congregation

We miss them now. Their memories are like glimmering stars overhead, guiding us, drawing us toward brighter visions.

Reader

They dwell in the pupils of our eyes, carrying our sight into the heart of things. When we are lonely they sing gentle songs of affection and encouragement. When we walk through dark trials and sorrow, or journey through the valley of shadows, they fence us about with the faith that You are with us and we need not fear.

"They dwell in the pupil of our eyes..." is based on the poem, "My Song," by Rabindranath Tagore, *Collected Poems and Plays, pp. 67-68.*

Havdalah Spice Box
Italian
19th c.

"The Lord is my shepherd...," *Psalm 23*, is an English rendition of the Hebrew from *The Holy Scriptures*, Jewish Publication Society, 1917. It is retained here because it is considered a classic expression of Elizabethan English.

ADONAI RO-I—THE LORD IS MY SHEPHERD

Cantor and Choir

מִזְמוֹר לְדָוִד. יְיָ רֹעִי, לֹא אֶחְסָר. בִּנְאוֹת דֶּשֶׁא
יַרְבִּיצֵנִי, עַל־מֵי מְנֻחוֹת יְנַהֲלֵנִי. נַפְשִׁי יְשׁוֹבֵב. יַנְחֵנִי
בְמַעְגְּלֵי־צֶדֶק לְמַעַן שְׁמוֹ. גַּם כִּי־אֵלֵךְ בְּגֵיא צַלְמָוֶת
לֹא־אִירָא רָע, כִּי־אַתָּה עִמָּדִי; שִׁבְטְךָ וּמִשְׁעַנְתֶּךָ
הֵמָּה יְנַחֲמֻנִי. תַּעֲרֹךְ לְפָנַי שֻׁלְחָן נֶגֶד צֹרְרָי. דִּשַּׁנְתָּ
בַשֶּׁמֶן רֹאשִׁי, כּוֹסִי רְוָיָה. אַךְ טוֹב וָחֶסֶד יִרְדְּפוּנִי
כָּל־יְמֵי חַיָּי, וְשַׁבְתִּי בְּבֵית־יְיָ לְאֹרֶךְ יָמִים.

The Lord is my shepherd; I shall not want. He maketh me to lie down in green pastures; He leadeth me beside the still waters. He restoreth my soul; He guideth me in straight paths for His name's sake. Yea, though I walk through the valley of the shadow of death, I will fear no evil, for Thou art with me; Thy rod and Thy staff, they comfort me. Thou preparest a table before me in the presence of mine enemies; Thou hast anointed my head with oil; my cup runneth over. Surely goodness and mercy shall follow me all the days of my life; and I shall dwell in the house of the Lord forever.

Responsively

One generation comes into the world to be blessed with years of safety and peace. Another is born to the cruelties of persecution, hunger and war.

Painful and dangerous have been the times assigned to us.

We have endured years of tyranny and destruction, and are well acquainted with grief.

We have seen the just defeated, the innocent driven into the fires of a holocaust as cruel and merciless as any age has ever beheld.

Their very presence on earth was begrudged them, for they brought to mind the recollection of Your covenant of mercy, justice and peace.

They perished because they were a symbol of Your Torah.

Now they lie in nameless graves in far-off forests and lonely fields.

Yet they will not be forsaken or forgotten.

We take them to our hearts and give them place beside the cherished memories of our own loved ones.

They now are ours. Let their unfinished songs sing through us.

Choir

I have set God before me.
God is at my side,
I shall not be moved.
Therefore my heart exults,
My soul rejoices,
For I am secure.
You will not abandon me to death,
Nor let faithful ones be destroyed.
Show me the path of life.
Fill me with joy,
As You favor me with the gift
Of enduring fulfillment.

שִׁוִּיתִי יְיָ לְנֶגְדִּי תָמִיד, כִּי
מִימִינִי בַּל־אֶמּוֹט. לָכֵן שָׂמַח
לִבִּי וַיָּגֶל כְּבוֹדִי, אַף־בְּשָׂרִי
יִשְׁכֹּן לָבֶטַח. כִּי לֹא־תַעֲזֹב
נַפְשִׁי לִשְׁאוֹל, לֹא־תִתֵּן
חֲסִידְךָ לִרְאוֹת שָׁחַת.
תּוֹדִיעֵנִי אֹרַח חַיִּים, שֹׂבַע
שְׂמָחוֹת אֶת־פָּנֶיךָ,
נְעִמוֹת בִּימִינְךָ נֶצַח.

BY LOVE ARE THEY REMEMBERED

Reader

At this sacred moment we turn our thoughts to those we love who have gone from life. We recall the joy of their companionship. We feel the pain of their passing, the echo of that grief when they lay before our stricken eyes. Now we know they will never vanish. So long as heart and thought remain within us, they too will live. By our love they are remembered; in the kindness and generosity of our deeds, they are memorialized. They live through us. We weave garlands of blessing out of their memory.

Meditations for Yizkor are found on p. 377–381.

"One generation…" is adapted from the *Union Prayer Book II, p. 314.* "I have set God…" is traditional to the Yizkor service and is taken from *Psalms 16:8-11.*

Memorial (Yizkor) *Lamp 64.2*
Moshe Zabari, United States, 1974
Marvin Rand, Photographer
From the Collection of the Hebrew Union College
Skirball Museum

"They are not gone from us..." is adapted from a poem by Robert Nichols, from *Ardours and Endurance.*

I

They are not gone from us, O no! they are
The inmost essence of each thing that is
Perfect for us; they flame in every star;
The trees are emerald with their presences.
They are not gone from us; they do not roam
The flaw and turmoil of the lower deep,
But now have made the whole wide world their home,
And in its loveliness themselves they sleep.

II

(For a parent)

My heart fills with tender memories of you in this Yizkor hour. I recall your
care, how you watched over me, goaded and guided me, embraced and
enveloped me with your nurturing love. I miss your concern, your wisdom,
your kind, proud eyes in which I danced. You gave me life and formed my love
for life. You live forever in the goodness I do and in the light I bring into the
lives of others. I give thanks to God for all my precious memories of you.

III

(For a spouse)

We shared the sweet vintage of life together. How fortunate we were, two stars in an infinite sea of space to find each other, and to brighten existence with our embraces of love. We drank from the cup of affection, built our house of dreams, shared sorrows, frustrations and fulfillments. Now I miss you every day, O companion of my life, my closest and best friend. I hear your voice urging me not to dwell in despair, but to grasp life for both of us. I give thanks to God for the gifts of our love and for the inspiration of your memory.

IV

(For a child)

You were a jewel placed in my possession for too little time. I recall your bright, inquisitive eyes, the softness of your touch, all the love that you brought into my life. There is a void I feel that will never be filled. Your loss still assails me with anguish. I cannot allow the gift you were to fade into oblivion. Your life has taught me to cherish life, to reach out with support, generosity and love to others. In all the good I do, you are there. Your memory brings blessings without number.

V

(For a sister or brother)

In this Yizkor moment, I recall you. I remember the days when we shared companionship, laughter and wisdom. You supported me in times of trouble, uplifted my spirits when I was down. You are gone, but your influence continues to echo lovingly inside me. Your thoughts and deeds live on. I cherish your memory. May my life distill its goodness into countless blessings.

VI

Shall I cry out in anger, O God,
Because Your gifts are mine but for a while?
Shall I forget the blessing of health
The moment there is pain?

Shall I be ungrateful for the laughter,
The seasons of joy, the days of gladness…
Shall I blot from mind the love
I have rejoiced in when fate
Leaves me bereft of shining presences
That have lit my way through years
Of companionship and affection?…

Those I have loved, though now beyond my view,
Have given form and quality to my being.
They have led me into the wide universe
I continue to inhabit, and their presence
Is more real to me than their absence.

What You give to me, O Lord,
You never take away.
And bounties granted once
Shed their radiance evermore.

"Shall I cry out…" is adapted from a poem by Rabbi Morris Adler (1906-1966).

VII

What fills the human heart
Is not that life must fade,
But that out of the dark there can
A light like a rose be made,
That seeing in snowflake fall
A heart is lifted up,
That hearing a meadow-lark call
For a moment a person will stop
To rejoice in the musical air
To delight in the fertile earth
And the flourishing everywhere
Of spring and spring's rebirth.
And never a woman or man
Walked through their quickening hours
But found for some brief span
An intervale of flowers,
Where love for a man or a woman
So captured the heart's beat
That they and all things human
Danced on rapturous feet.
And though, for each person, love dies,
The rose to his children's eyes
Will flower again out of shadow
To make the brief heart sing,
And the meadow-lark from the meadow
Will call again in spring.

"What fills the human heart…" is by Theodore Spencer, from "Heritage," in *An Act of Life.*

VIII

Birth is a beginning
And death a destination.
And life is a journey;
From childhood to maturity
And youth to age;
From innocence to knowing;
From foolishness to discretion
  And then, perhaps, to wisdom;
From health to sickness
  And back, we pray, to health again;
From offense to forgiveness,
From loneliness to love,
From joy to gratitude,
From pain to compassion,
And grief to understanding —
  From faith to faith;
From defeat to defeat to defeat —
Until, looking backward or ahead,
We see that victory lies
Not at some high place along the way,
But in having made the journey, stage by stage,
  A sacred pilgrimage.
Birth is a beginning
And death a destination.
And life is a journey,
A sacred pilgrimage —
  To life everlasting.

"Birth is a beginning…" is by Rabbi Alvin Fine (1916-).

Havdalah Spice Box
Eastern Europe
19th c.

"Our God, and God of our people, remember..." is the traditional prayer for *yizkor* and is found in the llth century *Machzor Vitry,* published in France.

Reader

יִזְכּוֹר אֱלֹהִים נִשְׁמוֹת יַקִּירִי....... שֶׁהָלְכוּ לְעוֹלָמָם.
אָנָּא תִּהְיֶינָה נַפְשׁוֹתֵיהֶם צְרוּרוֹת בִּצְרוֹר הַחַיִּים
וּתְהִי מְנוּחָתָם כָּבוֹד. שֹׂבַע שְׂמָחוֹת אֶת־פָּנֶיךָ,
נְעִימוֹת בִּימִינְךָ נֶצַח. אָמֵן.

Our God, and God of our people, remember our loved ones who have gone
to their eternal rest. May they, and all who served our people, all who gave
their lives to sanctify Your name, all whose contributions continue to bless us,
be at one with You. May the beauty of their lives shine brightly in our midst,
and may we always bring honor to their memory.

We name them now in reverence and affection....

All rise

Responsively

In the rising of the sun and in its going down, we remember them.

In the beginning of the year and when it ends, we remember them.

When we are weary and in need of strength, we remember them.

When we are lost and sick at heart, we remember them.

When we have joys we yearn to share, we remember them.

So long as we live, they too shall live, for they are now a part of us, as we remember them.

"In the rising of the sun..." is adapted from a service composed by Rabbi Roland B. Gittelsohn (1910-).

Cantor

אֵל מָלֵא רַחֲמִים, שׁוֹכֵן בַּמְּרוֹמִים, הַמְצֵא מְנוּחָה
נְכוֹנָה תַּחַת כַּנְפֵי הַשְּׁכִינָה עִם קְדוֹשִׁים וּטְהוֹרִים
כְּזֹהַר הָרָקִיעַ מַזְהִירִים לְנִשְׁמוֹת יַקִּירֵינוּ שֶׁהָלְכוּ
לְעוֹלָמָם. בַּעַל הָרַחֲמִים יַסְתִּירֵם בְּסֵתֶר כְּנָפָיו
לְעוֹלָמִים, וְיִצְרוֹר בִּצְרוֹר הַחַיִּים אֶת־נִשְׁמָתָם. יְיָ
הוּא נַחֲלָתָם. וְיָנוּחוּ בְּשָׁלוֹם עַל מִשְׁכָּבָם, וְנֹאמַר:
אָמֵן.

O God, Eternal Spirit of the universe, grant perfect rest unto the souls of our beloved dead. Lord of mercy, may their spirits be bound up in the bond of eternal life. Be their possession, and may their repose be peace. And let us say, Amen.

El molei rachamim...may have been composed during the 17th century, though memorial prayers of its type are found in earlier prayer books.

Yit-ga-dal ve-yit-ka-dash she-mei ra-ba
be-al-ma di-ve-ra chi-re-u-tei, ve-yam-lich
mal-chu-tei
be-cha-yei-chon u-ve-yo-mei-chon
u-ve-cha-yei de-chol beit Yis-ra-eil,
ba-a-ga-la u-vi-ze-man ka-riv, ve-i-me-ru:
a-mein.

יִתְגַּדַּל וְיִתְקַדַּשׁ שְׁמֵהּ רַבָּא
בְּעָלְמָא דִּי־בְרָא כִרְעוּתֵהּ,
וְיַמְלִיךְ מַלְכוּתֵהּ בְּחַיֵּיכוֹן
וּבְיוֹמֵיכוֹן וּבְחַיֵּי דְכָל־בֵּית
יִשְׂרָאֵל, בַּעֲגָלָא וּבִזְמַן קָרִיב,
וְאִמְרוּ: אָמֵן.

Ye-hei she-mei ra-ba me-va-rach le-a-lam
u-le-al-mei al-ma-ya.

יְהֵא שְׁמֵהּ רַבָּא מְבָרַךְ לְעָלַם
וּלְעָלְמֵי עָלְמַיָּא.

Yit-ba-rach ve-yish-ta-bach, ve-yit-pa-ar
ve-yit-ro-mam ve-yit-na-sei,
ve-yit-ha-dar ve-yit-a-leh ve-yit-ha-lal
she-mei de-ku-de-sha, be-rich hu,
le-ei-la min kol bi-re-cha-ta ve-shi-ra-ta
tush-be-cha-ta ve-ne-che-ma-ta,
da-a-mi-ran be-al-ma,
ve-i-me-ru: a-mein.

יִתְבָּרַךְ וְיִשְׁתַּבַּח, וְיִתְפָּאַר
וְיִתְרוֹמַם וְיִתְנַשֵּׂא, וְיִתְהַדָּר
וְיִתְעַלֶּה וְיִתְהַלָּל שְׁמֵהּ
דְּקוּדְשָׁא, בְּרִיךְ הוּא, לְעֵלָּא
מִן־כָּל־בִּרְכָתָא וְשִׁירָתָא,
תֻּשְׁבְּחָתָא וְנֶחֱמָתָא דַּאֲמִירָן
בְּעָלְמָא, וְאִמְרוּ: אָמֵן.

Ye-hei she-la-ma ra-ba
min she-ma-ya ve-cha-yim
a-lei-nu ve-al kol Yis-ra-eil
ve-i-me-ru: a-mein.

יְהֵא שְׁלָמָא רַבָּא מִן־שְׁמַיָּא
וְחַיִּים עָלֵינוּ וְעַל־כָּל־יִשְׂרָאֵל,
וְאִמְרוּ: אָמֵן.

O-seh sha-lom bi-me-ro-mav, hu ya-a-seh
sha-lom a-lei-nu
ve-al kol Yis-ra-eil
ve-i-me-ru: a-mein.

עֹשֶׂה שָׁלוֹם בִּמְרוֹמָיו, הוּא
יַעֲשֶׂה שָׁלוֹם עָלֵינוּ וְעַל־
כָּל־יִשְׂרָאֵל
וְאִמְרוּ: אָמֵן.

May God's great name be magnified and made holy in the world created according to Divine will. May God soon establish a reign of justice and peace during our life and days and during the lifetime of the whole house of Israel. And let us say, Amen.

May God's great name be blessed now and forever.

May the name of the Holy One be blessed, praised, glorified, exalted, extolled, honored, magnified, and celebrated, even though God is above and beyond all the blessings, songs, praises, and consolations that are spoken in the world. And let us say, Amen.

May there be great peace from heaven, and life for us and all Israel. And let us say, Amen.

May the One who makes peace in the heavens make peace for us and for all Israel. And let us say, Amen.

YOM KIPPUR
NEILA SERVICE

Candle Snuffer, Brass
Europe
19th c.

Rabbi Alexander (4th century C.E) observed that "human beings object to using broken vessels, but God loves them" *(Pesikta Shuvah, Buber, 158)*. Yom Kippur is about facing up to our failings, wrongdoings, sins. Through our confession, prayers, and repentance we seek God's forgiveness. Now, as the sun sets on the sacred day, we are given a final opportunity for atonement. At Neila, in the fading hour of the day, the gates are still open; God still seeks "broken vessels" for the repair and redemption of the world.

Reader

The sun is slanting down in western sky,
And in its decline the sacred day is waning;
The gates are closing.

In ten Days of Awe
We sift through the pages of our lives,
All our failures, hopes and hurts,
Repenting sins, shattered noble goals,
Restoring hope with healing faith
And courage to fill the New Year
With generous deeds of justice, mercy and love.

Will you hold open the gates for us,
Gates of righteousness and charity,
Gates of compassion and kindness,
Gates of tranquility and joy,
Gates of integrity and truth,
Gates of pardon and peace?

Congregation

We knock at Your gates, O God.
Hold them open for a moment more.
Hear our sunset prayer,
Seal us in the Book of Life.
Do not turn us away.
Open the gates for us.

Cantor and Choir

פְּתַח לָנוּ וּלְכָל־יִשְׂרָאֵל אַחֵינוּ בְּכָל־מָקוֹם: שַׁעֲרֵי
אוֹרָה, שַׁעֲרֵי בְּרָכָה, שַׁעֲרֵי גִילָה, שַׁעֲרֵי דִיצָה,
שַׁעֲרֵי הוֹד וְהָדָר, שַׁעֲרֵי וַעַד טוֹב, שַׁעֲרֵי זְכִיוֹת,
שַׁעֲרֵי חֶדְוָה, שַׁעֲרֵי טָהֳרָה, שַׁעֲרֵי יְשׁוּעָה, שַׁעֲרֵי
כַפָּרָה, שַׁעֲרֵי לֵב טוֹב, שַׁעֲרֵי מְחִילָה, שַׁעֲרֵי נֶחָמָה,
שַׁעֲרֵי סְלִיחָה, שַׁעֲרֵי עֶזְרָה, שַׁעֲרֵי פַרְנָסָה טוֹבָה,
שַׁעֲרֵי צְדָקָה, שַׁעֲרֵי קוֹמְמִיוּת, שַׁעֲרֵי רְפוּאָה
שְׁלֵמָה, שַׁעֲרֵי שָׁלוֹם, שַׁעֲרֵי תְשׁוּבָה.

Open the gates for us and for our people everywhere. The gates of light, blessing, rejoicing, happiness, splendor, goodness, merit, happiness, purity, salvation, atonement, integrity, forgiveness, compassion, pardon, help, sustenance, charity, independence, complete healing, peace, and repentance.

"Open the gates for us..." centers on the theme of holding open the gates, which is celebrated by many poets who have contributed to the Neila service. This poem, in the Hebrew version, forms an alphabetical acrostic naming all of the gates of our lives. Its author is unknown. *Eil no-rah a-li-lah...* is from the Sephardic liturgy and is attributed to Moses ibn Ezra (1055-1135), who lived in Spain.

EIL NO-RAH A-LI-LAH—GOD OF SPLENDOR

Responsively

אֵל נוֹרָא עֲלִילָה, אֵל נוֹרָא עֲלִילָה, הַמְצֵא לָנוּ
מְחִילָה בִּשְׁעַת הַנְּעִילָה. אֵל נוֹרָא עֲלִילָה.

Eil no-rah a-li-lah, God of splendor, grant us pardon as the gates begin to close.

Eil no-rah a-li-lah, where we have been weak, strengthen us.

Eil no-rah a-li-lah, where we have been wrong, correct us.

Eil no-rah a-li-lah, where we have caused pain, forgive us.

Eil no-rah a-li-lah, where we have fallen into complacency, arouse us.

Eil no-rah a-li-lah, where we have neglected the teachings of our tradition, renew us.

Be-sha-at ne-i-lah, in this hour of the fading day as the gates are closing, embrace us.

Eil no-rah a-li-lah, God of splendor, care for Your people in the New Year. Be at our side.

Be-sha-at ne-i-lah, as the gates close in this descending hour of the day, guard us, protect us, hear our prayer.

Torah Case 57.1
Nablus, Palestine 1756
Marvin Rand, Photographer
From the Collection of the Hebrew Union College
Skirball Museum

At Neila, the phrase, *ve-chot-vei-nu be-sei-fer ha-cha-yim,* "may we merit inscription in Your Book of Life," which has been used throughout the High Holy Days, is now changed to *ve-chot-mei-nu be-sei-fer ha-cha-yim,* "seal us for merit in Your Book of Life." The change reflects the urgency of the worshiper as the gates of prayer close at the end of Yom Kippur day.

Cantor

Ba-ruch a-ta, A-do-nai, E-lo-hei-nu
vei-lo-hei a-vo-tei-nu, E-lo-hei Av-ra-ham,
E-lo-hei Yits-chak, vei-lo-hei Ya-a-kov:
ha-eil ha-ga-dol, ha-gi-bor ve-ha-no-ra, Eil
el-yon, go-meil cha-sa-dim to-vim,
ve-ko-nei ha-kol, ve-zo-cheir cha-se-dei
a-vot, u-mei-vi ge-u-lah li-ve-nei
ve-nei-hem le-ma-an she-mo, be-a-ha-va.

בָּרוּךְ אַתָּה, יְיָ אֱלֹהֵינוּ
וֵאלֹהֵי אֲבוֹתֵינוּ, אֱלֹהֵי
אַבְרָהָם, אֱלֹהֵי יִצְחָק וֵאלֹהֵי
יַעֲקֹב: הָאֵל הַגָּדוֹל, הַגִּבּוֹר
וְהַנּוֹרָא, אֵל עֶלְיוֹן, גּוֹמֵל
חֲסָדִים טוֹבִים וְקוֹנֵה הַכֹּל,
וְזוֹכֵר חַסְדֵי אָבוֹת, וּמֵבִיא
גְאֻלָּה לִבְנֵי בְנֵיהֶם לְמַעַן
שְׁמוֹ בְּאַהֲבָה.

All sing

Zoch-rei-nu le-cha-yim, me-lech
cha-feitz ba-cha-yim, v'chot-mei-nu
be-sei-fer ha-cha-yim, le-ma-an-cha
Elo-him cha-yim.

זָכְרֵנוּ לַחַיִּים, מֶלֶךְ חָפֵץ
בַּחַיִּים; וְחָתְמֵנוּ בְּסֵפֶר הַחַיִּים,
לְמַעַנְךָ אֱלֹהִים חַיִּים.

Cantor

Me-lech o-zeir u-mo-shi-a u-ma-gein.
Ba-ruch a-ta A-do-nai, ma-gein
Av-ra-ham.

מֶלֶךְ עוֹזֵר וּמוֹשִׁיעַ וּמָגֵן.
בָּרוּךְ אַתָּה יְיָ, מָגֵן אַבְרָהָם.

Responsively

We praise You for sustaining our people in every trial and oppression.

Great and awesome God, may we their children remain loyal to Your
Torah and faithful to Your commandments.

In this descending hour of the day, remember us with the blessings of life.

O God of life, seal us for merit in Your Book of Life.

395

Havdalah Spice Box
Germany
cir. 1850

"Hear us…" is a refrain from a poem written for Neila by Rabbi Simeon ben Isaac ben Abun of Mayence, France, 11th century C.E. "Open the gates…" is a poem written for the *kedushah,* or "holiness" section of the Neila service. The author is unknown. "The Lord, the Lord…" is from *Exodus 34:6-7.*

Reader

שְׁמַע נָא, סְלַח נָא הַיוֹם, עֲבוּר כִּי פָנָה יוֹם.

Hear us, forgive us, for the day is ending.

כִּי אַתָּה קָדוֹשׁ וְשִׁמְךָ קָדוֹשׁ וּשְׁעָרֶיךָ בִּקְדֻשָּׁה נִכָּנֵס.

O God, You are holy, Your name is holy, and we enter now Your gates of holiness.

All rise as ark is opened

Choir

פִּתְחוּ־לָנוּ שַׁעֲרֵי־צֶדֶק, נָבוֹא בָם נוֹדֶה יָהּ.
דְּלָתֶיךָ דָּפַקְנוּ רַחוּם וְחַנּוּן
נָא אַל תְּשִׁיבֵנוּ רֵיקָם מִלְּפָנֶיךָ.

Reader

Open the gates, open them wide.

Congregation

We knock at Your gates, O merciful God.

Reader

Do not send us away empty-handed.

Cantor and Choir

יְיָ, יְיָ אֵל רַחוּם וְחַנּוּן, אֶרֶךְ אַפַּיִם וְרַב־חֶסֶד וֶאֱמֶת,
נוֹצֵר חֶסֶד לָאֲלָפִים, נֹשֵׂא עָוֹן וָפֶשַׁע וְחַטָּאָה וְנַקֵּה.

The Lord, the Lord God, is merciful and gracious, endlessly patient, loving,
and true, showing mercy to thousands, forgiving iniquity, transgression and sin,
and granting pardon.

Reader

Your glory streams through all time and space, flows through the eternal
silence of sublime spheres, urges our longings for liberation, love and peace.
Embraced by You, we sing Your praise.

All sing

Ka-dosh, ka-dosh, ka-dosh, A-do-nai	קָדוֹשׁ, קָדוֹשׁ, קָדוֹשׁ
tse-va-ot,	יְיָ צְבָאוֹת,
me-lo chol ha-a-retz ke-vo-do.	מְלֹא כָל־הָאָרֶץ כְּבוֹדוֹ.
Ba-ruch ke-vod A-do-nai mi-me-ko-mo.	בָּרוּךְ כְּבוֹד־יְיָ מִמְּקוֹמוֹ.

Holy, holy, holy is the Lord of hosts; the whole earth is filled with God's
glory. Blessed is the glory of God in heaven and earth.

Reader

מִמְּקוֹמוֹ הוּא יִפֶן בְּרַחֲמִים, וְיָחֹן עַם הַמְיַחֲדִים שְׁמוֹ, בְּאַהֲבָה.

Turn, O Compassionate One, in mercy to Your people. Grant forgiveness for
all the failings of those who lovingly proclaim, as we do now, Your Oneness.

All Sing

She-ma Yis-ra-eil: A-do-nai	שְׁמַע יִשְׂרָאֵל: יְיָ אֱלֹהֵינוּ, יְיָ אֶחָד!
E-lo-hei-nu, A-do-nai E-chad.	

Hear, O Israel: the Lord is our God, the Lord is One!

אֶחָד הוּא אֱלֹהֵינוּ, הוּא אָבִינוּ, הוּא מַלְכֵּנוּ, הוּא
מוֹשִׁיעֵנוּ, וְהוּא יַשְׁמִיעֵנוּ בְּרַחֲמָיו לְעֵינֵי כָּל־חָי.

God alone is our Creator, our Ruler, our Helper; and God is revealed in works of love in the sight of all the living.

All sing

יִמְלֹךְ יְיָ לְעוֹלָם, אֱלֹהַיִךְ צִיּוֹן, לְדֹר וָדֹר. הַלְלוּיָהּ!

Yim-loch A-do-nai le-o-lam, E-lo-ha-yich Tsi-yon, le-dor va-dor. Ha-le-lu-yah!

Reader

לְדוֹר וָדוֹר נַגִּיד גָּדְלֶךָ, וּלְנֵצַח נְצָחִים קְדֻשָּׁתְךָ נַקְדִּישׁ.
וְשִׁבְחֲךָ, אֱלֹהֵינוּ, מִפִּינוּ לֹא יָמוּשׁ לְעוֹלָם וָעֶד.
בָּרוּךְ אַתָּה, יְיָ, הָאֵל הַקָּדוֹשׁ.

To all generations we will make known Your greatness, and to all eternity proclaim Your holiness. Your praise shall never depart from our lips. We praise You, the God of holiness.

Ark is closed; all are seated

Havdalah Spice Box
Palestine
19th c.

"You reach out Your hand..." was included in the early prayer book created by the Babylonian teacher, Rav Amram Gaon, during the 9th century, C.E. It is likely that Rav Amram Gaon based these prayers upon language found in the Talmud *(Yoma 87b)*. Our English version is based upon *Union Prayer Book II, pp. 338-342.*

Reader

אַתָּה נוֹתֵן יָד לְפוֹשְׁעִים, וִימִינְךָ פְּשׁוּטָה לְקַבֵּל
שָׁבִים.

You reach out Your hand to those who go astray. You embrace all who sincerely repent and return to You.

Congregation

O God, pardon our failings, our confusions, our regrets. Judge us with mercy. For what are we, what is our life, what is our goodness, what is our power? What can we say in Your presence? Are not all the mighty as nothing before You, and those of great renown as though they had never been? Before Your judgment, are not the wise as if without knowledge, and those of understanding as if without discernment? So many of our works are vain, and our days pass away like a shadow.

Reader

וַתִּתֶּן־לָנוּ, יְיָ אֱלֹהֵינוּ, בְּאַהֲבָה אֶת־יוֹם הַכִּפּוּרִים
הַזֶּה, קֵץ וּמְחִילָה וּסְלִיחָה עַל כָּל־עֲוֹנוֹתֵינוּ, לְמַעַן
נֶחְדַּל מֵעֹשֶׁק יָדֵינוּ, וְנָשׁוּב אֵלֶיךָ לַעֲשׂוֹת חֻקֵּי רְצוֹנְךָ
בְּלֵבָב שָׁלֵם.

In Your love, O Lord our God, You have given us this Yom Kippur Day, that we might seek forgiveness for all our transgressions and, in turning away from them, rise to do Your will for goodness and truth, for kindness and generosity, for healing and helping, for justice and compassion, for hope and faith, for liberation and love.

Congregation

Hear our prayers. Reach out to us. Accept our sincere repentance. We return to You as the gates close in this descending hour of the day.

Circumcision Bench 15.32
Germany, Westphalia 1803, wood
John R. Forsman, Photographer
From the Collection of the Hebrew Union College
Skirball Museum

"O Lord—show us how to fashion…" is by Danny Siegel, from *Psalms and Prayers*, *p. 28.*

Choir

פְּתַח לָנוּ שַׁעַר בְּעֵת נְעִילַת שַׁעַר, כִּי פָנָה יוֹם.
הַיּוֹם יִפְנֶה, הַשֶּׁמֶשׁ יָבוֹא וְיִפְנֶה, נָבוֹאָה שְׁעָרֶיךָ!

Open the gates for us; open the closing gates in this descending hour of the day.
For the day is fading; the sun is setting. Let us enter Your gates.

A MEDITATION BEFORE THE GATES

O Lord—

Show us how to fashion
holiness from waste,
uncovering sparks in the broken shells
of people beaten down by circumstance
and mired in the boredom of hollowness...

Instruct us in sympathy,
that we may learn to tear away at hopelessness...

Remove shallowness from our lives
and destroy senselessness,
that we may discover Your plan
and fulfill Your purposes...

Show us Life in all its glory,
and we will glorify Your name,
here and now,
everywhere and forever.

Reader

The day is fading; the sun is setting. We turn to You, O God. Be our guiding star on our homeward journey. As long ago You led our people from degradation to freedom, from Egypt to Mount Sinai, set our hopes high for the Promised Land. Enlighten us with Your Torah; guide us to fulfill Your commandments for caring and righteousness, for charity and love, for truth and tranquility. Plant virtue in our hearts and generosity in our deeds that from us may sprout not the barren thistle but a fragrant, flourishing myrtle of blessings in Your honor.

Congregation

In this twilight hour we pray for the people of Israel. We have known storms of evil. Enemies have arisen to annihilate us. Let neither fear nor apathy ever dissolve our faith. May our people everywhere remain loyal to Your covenant to be a light unto the nations. Establish and preserve tranquility and peace for those who inhabit the Land of Israel. Bring the day soon when Your promise of old will be fulfilled: Your word will go forth from Jerusalem, and nation shall not lift up sword against nation, nor learn war anymore.

Reader

You alone know when such reconciliation will be fulfilled, yet allow us no rest until we push the gates of salvation and peace wide open for all humanity. Illumine heavy-laden souls with hope. Rage through us at iniquity; condemn all callous greed, all selfish schemes. Uplift our hands and hearts to work for the day when faith will conquer every fear, when love will heal every hurt, when famine and fighting, calamity and quarrel will no longer afflict us; when every human heart will discover Your image and rise to protect its sanctity in others.

Congregation

Preserve us in the New Year that we might open the gates to such a time.

Reader

Open heaven's gates, Your treasure of wisdom and visions. Save us, O God of salvation.

All rise as ark is opened

Choir

Lift up your heads, O gates!	שְׂאוּ שְׁעָרִים רָאשֵׁיכֶם,
Lift yourselves up, O ancient doors!	וְהִנָּשְׂאוּ פִּתְחֵי עוֹלָם,
Let the Lord of Glory enter.	וְיָבוֹא מֶלֶךְ הַכָּבוֹד!
Who is the Lord of Glory?	מִי הוּא זֶה מֶלֶךְ הַכָּבוֹד?
The Lord of Hosts—	יְיָ צְבָאוֹת—
Is the Lord of Glory!	הוּא מֶלֶךְ הַכָּבוֹד! סֶלָה.

"The day is fading…" is adapted from the *Union Prayer Book II, pp. 344-346.* That version was based upon an original German version written by Rabbi David Einhorn (1809-1879) and published in 1858 in his prayer book known as *Olat Tamid, pp. 367-371.* "Lift up your heads…" is from *Psalms 24:7-10.*

אָבִינוּ מַלְכֵּנוּ, פְּתַח שַׁעֲרֵי שָׁמַיִם לִתְפִלָּתֵנוּ.

Avinu Malkeinu, pe-tach sha-a-rei sha-ma-yim li-te-fi-la-tei-nu.
Avinu Malkeinu, open the gates to our prayer.

אָבִינוּ מַלְכֵּנוּ, נָא אַל תְּשִׁיבֵנוּ רֵיקָם מִלְּפָנֶיךָ.

Avinu Malkeinu, na el te-shi-vei-nu rei-kam mil-fa-ne-cha.
Avinu Malkeinu, do not turn us away from You empty handed.

אָבִינוּ מַלְכֵּנוּ, חַדֵּשׁ עָלֵינוּ שָׁנָה טוֹבָה.

Avinu Malkeinu, cha-deish a-lei-nu sha-nah to-vah.
Avinu Malkeinu, let the New Year be a good year for us.

אָבִינוּ מַלְכֵּנוּ, חֲמוֹל עָלֵינוּ וְעַל עוֹלָלֵינוּ וְטַפֵּנוּ.

Avinu Malkeinu, cha-mol a-lei-nu ve-al o-la-lei-nu ve-ta-pei-nu.
Avinu Malkeinu, have mercy upon us and upon our children.

אָבִינוּ מַלְכֵּנוּ, כַּלֵּה כָּל־צַר וּמַשְׂטִין מֵעָלֵינוּ.

Avinu Malkeinu, ka-lei kol tsar u-mas-tin mei-a-lei-nu.
Avinu Malkeinu, rid us of all hatred and oppression.

אָבִינוּ מַלְכֵּנוּ, חָתְמֵנוּ בְּסֵפֶר חַיִּים טוֹבִים.

Avinu Malkeinu, chot-mei-nu be-sei-fer cha-yim to-vim.
Avinu Malkeinu, seal us for blessing in the Book of Life.

אָבִינוּ מַלְכֵּנוּ, מַלֵּא יָדֵינוּ מִבִּרְכוֹתֶיךָ.

Avinu Malkeinu, ma-lei ya-dei-nu mi-bir-cho-te-cha.
Avinu Malkeinu, fill our hands with generous deeds.

אָבִינוּ מַלְכֵּנוּ, חָנֵּנוּ וַעֲנֵנוּ, כִּי אֵין בָּנוּ מַעֲשִׂים,
עֲשֵׂה עִמָּנוּ צְדָקָה וָחֶסֶד וְהוֹשִׁיעֵנוּ.

Avinu Malkeinu, cho-nei-nu va-a-nei-nu, ki ein ba-nu ma-a-sim, a-sei i-ma-nu
tse-da-kah va-che-sed, ve-ho-shi-ei-nu.
Avinu Malkeinu, be gracious and answer us. Treat us generously and with kindness, and help us.

Congregation and Choir

Avinu Malkeinu,
cho-nei-nu va-a-nei-nu (2)
ki ein ba-nu ma-a-sim.

A-sei i-ma-nu tse-da-kah va-che-sed (2)
ve-ho-shi-ei-nu.

Avinu Malkeinu,
cho-nei-nu va-a-nei-nu (2)
ki ein ba-nu ma-a-sim.

אָבִינוּ מַלְכֵּנוּ, חָנֵּנוּ וַעֲנֵנוּ,
כִּי אֵין בָּנוּ מַעֲשִׂים, עֲשֵׂה
עִמָּנוּ צְדָקָה וָחֶסֶד וְהוֹשִׁיעֵנוּ.

The Neila version of *Avinu Malkeinu*, like that of the *Avot*, changes the word *chot-
vei-nu*, "inscribe us," to *chot-mei-nu*, "seal us," for blessing in the Book of Life.

OPEN THE GATES OF RECONCILIATION AND RENEWAL

Reader

Where shall we go from Your spirit? Where shall we flee from Your presence? It we ascend into heaven, You are there; if we make our bed in the netherworld, behold, You are there. If we take the wings of morning and dwell in the uttermost parts of the sea, even there do you lead us and hold us. If we say: The darkness envelops us, and the light resembles night, even the darkness is not too dark for You, and the night shines as daylight. How wonderful are Your works, O Lord.

When we behold the heavens, the countless stars You have set in the firmament; when we consider the wonders of the universe, and seek to comprehend the excellence of Your majesty, we are overwhelmed by Your power and greatness. The myriad of stars scattered through infinity are but a breath of Your spirit. The luminous orbs are but beams of Your light. What, then, are we—fragile specks of life, perishable earth fused to immortal soul, children of dust and dreams, finite matter fettered to time and space? Yet You have given us dominion over all Your works.

Congregation

As the gates close in this descending hour of the day, we proclaim Your grandeur, O Fountain of Life.

Reader

Your mercy, O God, is without end. You desire not the death of those who sin, but with compassion counsel us that no person lives without failures, regrets, sins. So return to Me, O Israel, and live. Wide open are the gates of Your forgiveness to those who seek reconciliation and renewal.

Congregation

As the gates close in this descending hour of the day, forgive us, pardon us, help us, renew us.

Reader

How beautiful Your sanctuary, O Lord! In this descending hour of the day, light dawns within us. Hope and trust revive. Heavy shadows of regret begin to vanish. Through the passing cloud there breaks, with the last rays of the setting sun, the radiance of Your forgiving love and the promise of peace. With Yom Kippur fasting and prayer we have nurtured our spirits, we have strengthened our will, Your will, to accomplish the triumph of justice and mercy, truth and beauty, love and peace.

O God, what are we that You have planted destiny in our hands? What are we that You are mindful of us, that You summon us to serve You? Where shall we find words to thank You, to praise You, to adore You?

Congregation

All we can offer are our songs of faith and deeds of love.

"Where shall we go..." is from *Psalms 139:7-11.* "When we behold..." is from *Psalms 8:4-7.* "You desire not the death..." is from *Ezekiel 33:11.* This adaptation is based upon *Union Prayer Book II, pp. 346-348,* which was derived from *Olat Tamid* (1856), a German-Reform prayer book written in Baltimore, Maryland, by Rabbi David Einhorn (1809-1879).

Havdalah Spice Box
Italian
Late 18th c.

As Neila concludes, Jews relive the historic moment at Mt. Sinai when they accepted responsibility for carrying out the commandments of Torah. Echoing the words of commitment from that historic moment, the congregation repeats the sacred summons, *She-ma Yis-ra-eil...*, as it appears written in the Torah text *(Deuteronomy 6:4).* The last letter of the first word, *ayin,* and the last letter of the last word, *dalet,* are enlarged. Taken together, the *ayin* and *dalet* spell *eid,* or "witness," carrying the message that the role of Jews is to bear witness to God through their deeds of justice, mercy and love.

Va-a-nach-nu ko-re-im u-mish-ta-cha-vim
u-mo-dim
lif-nei me-lech mal-chei
ha-me-la-chim, ha-ka-dosh ba-ruch Hu.

וַאֲנַחְנוּ כּוֹרְעִים וּמִשְׁתַּחֲוִים וּמוֹדִים
לִפְנֵי מֶלֶךְ מַלְכֵי הַמְּלָכִים,
הַקָּדוֹשׁ בָּרוּךְ הוּא.

We bow the head in reverence and worship the God of all, the Holy One whom we praise.

She-ma Yis-ra-eil: A-do-nai
E-lo-hei-nu, A-do-nai E-chad.

שְׁמַע יִשְׂרָאֵל יְהֹוָה אֱלֹהֵינוּ יְהֹוָה | אֶחָד׃

Hear, O Israel: the Lord is our God, the Lord is One!

Cantor, then Choir, then Congregation

Ba-ruch sheim ke-vod
mal-chu-to
le-o-lam va-ed.
(Repeated three times)

בָּרוּךְ שֵׁם כְּבוֹד
מַלְכוּתוֹ
לְעוֹלָם וָעֶד!

Blessed is God's glorious power forever and ever.

Cantor and Choir

A-do-nai Hu ha-E-lo-him
(Repeated seven times)

יְיָ הוּא הָאֱלֹהִים!

The Lord is God.

Havdalah Spice Box
Eastern Europe
Late 19th c.

"May God bless..." is from *Psalms 121:8.*

Reader

And now, at the close of this Yom Kippur Day, we pray that the New Year upon which we have entered will be for us, for Israel, and all humanity,

A year of blessing and prosperity.

    Choir: Amen.

A year of reconciliation and love.

    Choir: Amen.

A year of justice and generosity.

    Choir: Amen.

A year of spiritual well being and peace.

    Choir: Amen.

יְיָ יִשְׁמָר־צֵאתְךָ וּבוֹאֶךָ מֵעַתָּה וְעַד־עוֹלָם.

At the closing of the gates, may God bless our going out and coming in from this time forth and for ever.

    Choir: Amen.

תקיעה גדולה

Tekiah-Gedolah
The Shofar is sounded, and the ark is closed.

SONGS

Ein kei-lo-hei-nu, Ein ka-do-nei-nu,
Ein ke-mal-kei-nu, Ein ke-mo-shi-ei-nu.

אֵין כֵּאלֹהֵינוּ, אֵין כַּאדוֹנֵינוּ,
אֵין כְּמַלְכֵּנוּ, אֵין כְּמוֹשִׁיעֵנוּ.

Mi chei-lo-hei-nu, mi-cha-do-nei-nu,
mi che-mal-kei-nu, mi che-mo-shi-ei-nu.

מִי כֵאלֹהֵינוּ? מִי כַאדוֹנֵינוּ?
מִי כְמַלְכֵּנוּ? מִי כְמוֹשִׁיעֵנוּ?

No-deh lei-lo-hei-nu, no-deh la-do-nei-nu,
no-deh le-mal-kei-nu, no-deh le-mo-shi-ei-nu.

נוֹדֶה לֵאלֹהֵינוּ, נוֹדֶה לַאדוֹנֵינוּ,
נוֹדֶה לְמַלְכֵּנוּ, נוֹדֶה לְמוֹשִׁיעֵנוּ.

Ba-ruch E-lo-hei-nu, ba-ruch A-do-nei-nu,
ba-ruch Mal-kei-nu, ba-ruch Mo-shi-ei-nu.

בָּרוּךְ אֱלֹהֵינוּ, בָּרוּךְ אֲדוֹנֵינוּ,
בָּרוּךְ מַלְכֵּנוּ, בָּרוּךְ מוֹשִׁיעֵנוּ.

A-ta hu E-lo-hei-nu,
a-ta hu A-do-nei-nu.
A-ta hu Mal-kei-nu,
a-ta hu Mo-shi-ei-nu.

אַתָּה הוּא אֱלֹהֵינוּ,
אַתָּה הוּא אֲדוֹנֵינוּ,
אַתָּה הוּא מַלְכֵּנוּ,
אַתָּה הוּא מוֹשִׁיעֵנוּ.

There is none like our God, none like our Lord, none like our Sovereign, none like our Savior. Who is compared to our God, our Lord, our Sovereign, or our Savior? We give thanks to our God, our Lord, our Sovereign, and our Savior. Blessed is our God, our Lord, our Sovereign, and our Savior. You are our God, our Lord, our Sovereign and our Savior.

Ein Keiloheinu was composed sometime during the 8th century C.E. and has been a popular concluding song ever since. Originally, it began with the second stanza, "Who is compared to our God...." Later, someone reversed the stanzas so that when the first letters of the first three stanzas were combined, they would spell the word, *Amen*.

Yig-dal E-lo-him chai ve-yish-ta-bach,
nim-tsa ve-ein eit el me-tsi-u-to.
E-chad ve-ein ya-chid ke-yi-chu-do,
ne-lam ve-gam ein sof le-ach-du-to.

יִגְדַּל אֱלֹהִים חַי וְיִשְׁתַּבַּח,
נִמְצָא וְאֵין עֵת אֶל־מְצִיאוּתוֹ.
אֶחָד וְאֵין יָחִיד כְּיִחוּדוֹ,
נֶעְלָם וְגַם אֵין סוֹף לְאַחְדוּתוֹ.

Ein lo de-mut ha-guf ve-ei-no guf,
lo na-a-roch ei-lav ke-du-sha-to.
Kad-mon le-chol da-var a-sher niv-ra,
ri-shon ve-ein rei-sheet le-rei-shi-to.

אֵין לוֹ דְמוּת הַגּוּף וְאֵינוֹ גוּף,
לֹא נַעֲרוֹךְ אֵלָיו קְדֻשָּׁתוֹ.
קַדְמוֹן לְכָל־דָּבָר אֲשֶׁר נִבְרָא,
רִאשׁוֹן וְאֵין רֵאשִׁית לְרֵאשִׁיתוֹ.

Cha-yei o-lam na-ta be-to-chei-nu,
ba-ruch a-dei ad sheim te-hi-la-to (2)

חַיֵּי עוֹלָם נָטַע בְּתוֹכֵנוּ,
בָּרוּךְ עֲדֵי עַד שֵׁם תְּהִלָּתוֹ.

May God, whose existence is eternal, be magnified and praised. God is one and unique, unfathomable and infinite.

God is without bodily form, and nothing compares to God's holiness. God existed before creation and is without beginning or end. God placed within us the potential for eternal life. Be praised, O God, whose glorious name is forever.

Yigdal is ascribed to the 14th century poet, Daniel ben Judah of Rome. His poem was based upon the Thirteen Principles of Faith, composed by the philosopher Moses Maimonides (1135-1204).

Havdalah Spice Box and Candle Holder
Hungary
19th c.

Adon Olam is one of the best known of all Jewish songs. Some believe it was written by the Spanish-Jewish poet, Solomon ibn Gabirol (1021-1058); others argue that it may have been composed while Jews lived in Babylonia. It has been included within the prayer book for the past six centuries. Its verses contain a Jewish definition of God as a single, infinite, merciful and caring Power creating cosmic harmony and encountered, personally, in the human mind and heart.

A-don o-lam, a-sher ma-lach be-te-rem kol
ye-tsir niv-ra, le-eit na-a-sa ve-chef-tso kol,
a-zai me-lech she-mo nik-ra

אֲדוֹן עוֹלָם, אֲשֶׁר מָלַךְ
בְּטֶרֶם כָּל־יְצִיר נִבְרָא,
לְעֵת נַעֲשָׂה בְחֶפְצוֹ כֹּל,
אֲזַי מֶלֶךְ שְׁמוֹ נִקְרָא.

Ve-a-cha-rei ki-che-lot ha-kol, le-va-do
yim-loch no-ra, ve-hu ha-ya ve-hu ho-veh,
ve-hu yi-he-yeh be-tif-a-ra.

וְאַחֲרֵי כִּכְלוֹת הַכֹּל,
לְבַדּוֹ יִמְלוֹךְ נוֹרָא,
וְהוּא הָיָה, וְהוּא הֹוֶה,
וְהוּא יִהְיֶה בְּתִפְאָרָה.

Ve-hu e-chad, ve-ein shei-ni le-ham-shil lo,
le-hach-bi-ra, be-li rei-sheet, be-li tach-lit,
ve-lo ha-oz ve-ha-mis-ra.

וְהוּא אֶחָד, וְאֵין שֵׁנִי
לְהַמְשִׁיל לוֹ, לְהַחְבִּירָה,
בְּלִי רֵאשִׁית, בְּלִי תַכְלִית,
וְלוֹ הָעֹז וְהַמִּשְׂרָה.

Ve-hu Ei-li, ve-chai go-a-li, ve-tzur chev-li
be-eit tsa-ra, ve-hu ni-si u-ma-nos li, me-nat
ko-si be-yom ek-ra.

וְהוּא אֵלִי, וְחַי גּוֹאֲלִי,
וְצוּר חֶבְלִי בְּעֵת צָרָה,
וְהוּא נִסִּי וּמָנוֹס לִי,
מְנָת כּוֹסִי בְּיוֹם אֶקְרָא.

Be-ya-do af-kid ru-chi be-eit i-shan ve-a-i-ra,
ve-im ru-chi ge-vi-ya-ti: A-do-nai li, ve-lo i-ra.

בְּיָדוֹ אַפְקִיד רוּחִי
בְּעֵת אִישָׁן וְאָעִירָה,
וְעִם־רוּחִי גְּוִיָּתִי:
יְיָ לִי, וְלֹא אִירָא.

The Eternal reigned before creation; and after all was made, God reigned alone. God was, and is, and will be for infinity. God is one, without beginning or end, an infinite Power. God lives and liberates, is my support in times of trouble; my banner of pride, my source of strength, my cup of hope when I call out. I place my spirit with God's Will; both when I sleep and when I awake, God is with me, I shall not fear.

Havdalah Spice Box
Israel
20th c.

Hatikvah, or "The hope," was composed in 1878 by Naphtali Herz Imber and first published in 1886. Its inspiration seems to have been the founding of Petach Tikvah (Gateway of Hope), one of the first Zionist settlements. The original version was changed after the declaration of the State of Israel in 1948. It read: "Our hope is not yet lost. The age old hope to return to the land of our fathers; to the city where David dwelt." In about 1878, the poem was set to music by Samuel Cohen who based his work on the Moldavian-Rumanian folk song, *Carul cu Boi,* "Cart and Oxen." It was adopted as the national Jewish anthem by the Zionist Congress meeting in Prague in 1933.

Kol od ba-lei-vav pe-ni-ma,
ne-fesh Ye-hu-di ho-mi-ya.
U-le-fa-a-tei miz-rach ka-di-ma,
a-yin le-tsi-yon tso-fi-ya.

Od lo a-ve-da tik-va-tei-nu,
ha-tik-va she-not al-pa-yim,
li-he-yot am chof-shi be-ar-tsei-nu,
be-e-rets tsi-yon vi-ru-sha-la-yim.

כָּל עוֹד בַּלֵּבָב פְּנִימָה,
נֶפֶשׁ יְהוּדִי הוֹמִיָּה,
וּלְפַאֲתֵי מִזְרָח קָדִימָה
עַיִן לְצִיּוֹן צוֹפִיָּה.

עוֹד לֹא אָבְדָה תִקְוָתֵנוּ,
הַתִּקְוָה שְׁנוֹת אַלְפַּיִם,
לִהְיוֹת עַם חָפְשִׁי בְּאַרְצֵנוּ,
בְּאֶרֶץ צִיּוֹן וִירוּשָׁלָיִם.

As long as deep in the heart the soul of a Jew yearns, and toward the East an eye looks to Zion, our hope is not yet lost—the hope of two thousand years to be a free people in our land, the land of Zion and Jerusalem.

ALBUM

From Book for Mohel,
(Person trained to perform circumcision),
Francis Henry Library.
John R. Forsman, Photographer
From the Collection of the Hebrew Union College
Skirball Museum

At the birth of a child it is a *mitzvah* to celebrate a *brit milah*, "a covenant of circumcision," if a boy, and a naming ceremony if a girl. Jewish tradition teaches that "each child brings blessing into the world."

Births

Bar/Bat Mitzvah Celebrations

_____   _____

_____   _____

_____   _____

_____   _____

_____   _____

_____   _____

_____   _____

_____   _____

_____   _____

_____   _____

_____   _____

_____   _____

_____   _____

_____   _____

_____   _____

_____   _____

_____   _____

_____   _____

_____   _____

_____   _____

_____   _____

_____   _____

_____   _____

Confirmation Celebrations

Ketubah 34.73
(A Jewish marriage contract.)
Bucharest, Romania 1831
Marvin Rand, Photographer
From the Collection of the Hebrew Union College
Skirball Museum

Marriages

_____

_____ Date _____

_____

_____ Date _____

_____

_____ Date _____

_____

_____ Date _____

_____

_____ Date _____

_____

_____ Date _____

_____

_____ Date _____

_____

_____ Date _____

_____

_____ Date _____

_____

_____ Date _____

_____

_____ Date _____

_____

_____ Date _____

Special Occasions

Deaths